The Cambridge Introduction to
the Eighteenth-Century Novel

In the eighteenth century, the novel became established as a popular
literary form all over Europe. Britain proved an especially fertile
ground, with Defoe, Fielding, Richardson, and Burney as early
exponents of the novel form. *The Cambridge Introduction to the
Eighteenth-Century Novel* considers the development of the genre in
its formative period in Britain. Rather than present its history as a
linear progression, April London gives an original new structure to the
field, organizing it through three broad thematic clusters – identity,
community, and history. Within each of these themes, she explores
the central tensions of eighteenth-century fiction: between secrecy
and communicativeness, independence and compliance, solitude and
family, cosmopolitanism and nation-building. The reader will gain a
thorough understanding of both prominent and lesser-known novels
and novelists, key social and literary contexts, the tremendous formal
variety of the early novel, and its growth from a marginal to a
culturally central genre.

APRIL LONDON is Professor of English at the University of Ottawa.

The Cambridge Introduction to
the Eighteenth-Century Novel

APRIL LONDON

CAMBRIDGE
UNIVERSITY PRESS

CAMBRIDGE UNIVERSITY PRESS
Cambridge, New York, Melbourne, Madrid, Cape Town,
Singapore, São Paulo, Delhi, Mexico City

Cambridge University Press
The Edinburgh Building, Cambridge CB2 8RU, UK

Published in the United States of America by Cambridge University Press, New York

www.cambridge.org
Information on this title: www.cambridge.org/9780521719674

First published 2012

Printed in the United Kingdom at the University Press, Cambridge

A catalogue record for this publication is available from the British Library

Library of Congress Cataloguing in Publication data
London, April.
    The Cambridge introduction to the eighteenth-century novel / April London.
        pages   cm. – (Cambridge introductions to)
    Includes bibliographical references and index.
    ISBN 978-0-521-89535-4 (hardback) – ISBN 978-0-521-71967-4 (paperback)
    1. English fiction–18th century–History and criticism.   I. Title.
    PR851.L55 2012
    823′.509–dc23
    2011052556

ISBN 978-0-521-89535-4 Hardback
ISBN 978-0-521-71967-4 Paperback

To Tony and Andrea

Contents

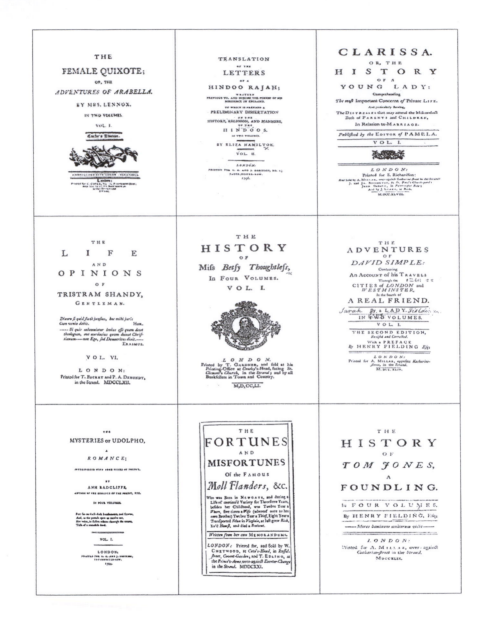

Introduction

The title pages of early to mid-eighteenth-century fictions rarely announce that what follows is a "novel." Instead, they forecast tales, memoirs, travels, fortunes and misfortunes, histories, lives and opinions, sketches, journals, adventures, and expeditions. These tags point to the long gestation of what Samuel Richardson called this "new manner of writing" and its equally protracted struggle to escape its lowly rank in the hierarchy of genres. Only late in the period, in fact, do the novel's contours as a distinct and creditable form become fully visible. Its deferred elevation owes something to the writing of literary critical histories that began with Clara Reeve's 1785 *Progress of Romance* and to such collections as Anna Laetitia Barbauld's 1810 *The British Novelists* in fifty volumes and Walter Scott's 1821–4 *Ballantyne's Novelist's Library* in ten volumes. Even before such efforts to label and sort, however, the vagueness about names was more apparent than real, since actual readers throughout the period clearly grasped the family connection between the diverse titles. But the categorical slippages also, and importantly, reflect the status of the novel as a mode in process, its history one of continuous, if uneven, experimentation. This *Introduction to the Eighteenth-Century Novel* aims to convey a sense of that variety and experimentation by listening to the conversations novelists pursued through the medium of their fictions with their fellow writers, literary forebears, and surrounding culture.

Looking back, we can partially reconstruct the context for some of these experiments and speculate about the reasons for their eclipse or survival. Numbers flourished only briefly and left little trace (including the "it-narratives" written from the perspective of objects that follow Charles Johnstone's *Chrysal: Or, The Adventures of a Guinea* in the 1750s and 1760s). Other subgenres seemed to drop from favor only to be adapted later to a more complex hybrid form (as with Samuel Richardson's modifications of amatory and pious tales). Intrinsic merit in itself rarely accounts for the endurance of certain modes and the disappearance of others. In some instances, the reasons for these contrary courses postdate the original publication by several generations. Many early eighteenth-century writers, for instance, were casualties of early nineteenth-century efforts to enhance the respectability of novels by defining a masculine tradition stretching from Henry Fielding and Tobias Smollett through to Walter Scott. Some fell victim to Romantic-era disciplinary divisions that assigned value to works of a certain kind of imagination, relegating exceptions to the lesser status of the local or ephemeral. Over the very long term, the vagaries of fashion also resulted in particular writers and political stances cycling in and out of critical repute. Many of our shapely, received histories of the early novel, in short, are products of their own critical moments and hence less than true to the disorderliness of the contemporary literary field.

And what of readers? Do their tastes and expectations offer an alternative route to a fuller understanding of the early phases of the novel? In a *Rambler* essay from 1750, Samuel Johnson declares that "the young, the ignorant, and the idle" are the principal consumers of what he refers to at first as the "comedy of romance" and later as "familiar histories."[1] Modern scholars agree that novel readers were likely to be young, but resist the slurs of ignorance and idleness, suggesting that these express Johnson's own prejudices and insecurities: he regarded Greek and Latin as essential components of a good education and was ambivalent about the leveling impulses intrinsic to the eighteenth-century commercialization of leisure. Behind his lamenting of the novel's appeal to "minds unfurnished with ideas, and therefore easily susceptible of impressions; not fixed by principles, and therefore easily following the current of fancy; not informed by experience, and consequently open to every false suggestion and partial account" (21) lies an anxiety about the potentially disruptive effects of the spread of solitary reading across social ranks. Concern was roused not simply by the doubling of literacy over the course of the century, but by the patchiness of an expansion that saw it take hold first within concentrated and volatile populations – urban dwellers were more likely to read than rural ones, and young men, at least initially, more than women. The absence of reliable statistics on the spread of literacy, however, makes it difficult to quantify or categorize reading audiences. The surviving limited sources of quasi-statistics are themselves controversial (hence the ongoing historical debate about what hard information might be extracted from the registry signatures required after the mid-century passing of Lord Hardwicke's Marriage Act). In relation specifically to novels, subscription lists – authors sometimes appealed to friends, family, and patrons to underwrite the costs of their publications and then publicized the names of the contributors – and circulating library records offer glimpses into the network of print exchanges. But neither of these very partial archives captures a social or chronological range sufficient to take us much beyond Johnson's generalizations.

Information about authors and publishers is similarly limited. While an exceptional few had their correspondence preserved or personalities noted in the letters and diaries of their peers, many authors are known only through occasional records and anecdotal scraps, and even more left no trace beyond their surviving texts. The tradition of anonymous and pseudonymous publication (governing over 80 percent of novels in the 1770s and 1780s) further complicates the task of assembling reliable individual or corporate profiles. It is generally accepted that before the 1790s, more men than women wrote novels, and that most came from the ranks of the middling or propertied orders. Throughout the period, the economics of the publishing industry were stacked against authorial self-sufficiency; the combination of cheap copyright, steady demand for new material from circulating libraries, and the high price of books sold to individuals created what amounted to a buyer's market for novels. At the other end of the publication spectrum reaching from composition to distribution, little survives to indicate the identities of those involved in the trade as investors and promoters. We do know that most novels appeared first in London, that some booksellers refused on ethical grounds to deal in them, and that London publishers gradually strengthened ties with their English provincial counterparts in an effort to protect their monopoly and offset the threat of pirated editions from Dublin, Edinburgh, and Glasgow. An important aspect of this slow devolution was the tendency of the London booksellers to found circulating libraries to rent out the fiction they published (which they also continued to sell directly to individual readers and to other commercial libraries). By 1770, there were more than twenty circulating libraries in London and by 1790, in excess of 250 operating in the provinces.

The breaking up of the London publishing cartels after a 1774 legal ruling upheld the limits on copyright established in the 1710 Copyright Act (and more or less continuously since then simply ignored) transformed the industry. The 1774 House of Lords decision on the case of an Edinburgh bookseller, Alexander Donaldson, abruptly ended the long-standing control of the trade by a clutch of copy-owning booksellers. One consequence of the ensuing instability was a sudden flush of early "classics" made available to less affluent readers through the cheap reprints issued after the 1780s by entrepreneurs like John Cooke, John Harrison, and John Bell and through the second-hand market that these in turn created. But this late-century expansion of audiences was principally fed by reissues rather than new works. In the face of modes of publication that favored booksellers – including subscription, outright copyright sale, self-funding, or assumed liability for any losses – most contemporary novelists continued to struggle financially.

Recent scholarly interest in book history has led to significant gains in knowledge about contemporary print culture. But the mass of archival material available for research in the Victorian period simply does not exist for the previous century. The surviving advertising, taxation, and in-house records of eighteenth-century booksellers are as incomplete and erratically preserved as the identities and biographical details of the novelists who supplied them with their fictions. Many literary critics sidestep problems relating to this dearth of information about readers, authors, and publishers by looking to the novels themselves for evidence of the impulses that shaped the genre's emergence and development. Most respond – either through adjustment or active resistance – to the arguments presented in Ian Watt's 1957 study, *The Rise of the Novel*. Watt there identifies Daniel Defoe as the first English novelist on the grounds that he fulfills the "lowest common denominator of the novel genre as a whole, its formal realism" when he purports to offer a "full and authentic record of human experience, and is therefore under an obligation to satisfy its reader with such details of the story as the individuality of the actors concerned, the particulars of the times and places of their actions, details which are presented through a more largely referential use of language than is common in other literary forms."[2] This combination of specificity of time and place, original plot, exploration of a multi-faceted personality, and language unshackled by inherited romance or epic conventions was, again according to Watt's thesis, a product of its historical moment, one that enabled a synchronized "triple rise" of the novel, of the Protestant privileging of individual conscience, and of a coherent bourgeoisie hostile to aristocratic mores.

Aspects of Watt's argument have been questioned, including its reliance on a Whig model of progress that makes the novel's anticipation of nineteenth-century norms a foregone conclusion, its highly selective survey of early eighteenth-century fiction, and its assumption of a coherent middle class already in existence by the 1720s. Numbers of critics contest his claim that the novel emerged first in eighteenth-century England by citing Continental instances of sixteenth- and seventeenth-century romance fictions or reaching further back to the classical period. Some of the evidential limits of his account have been corrected by considering the significant role played by women as both writers and readers of novels. Alternative models for describing the relation between author, text, and culture have also helped to refine Watt's account. These include theories that complicate the straightforward "rise" pattern by invoking ideologically inflected processes of "dialectical engagement," ones that pay close attention to the huge range of texts available to early readers, or

that identify the consolidation of the novel as a distinct genre with the win-
nowing down, repudiation, or willed forgetting of these diverse materials, and
still others that argue that the novel emerges to counteract the unsettling effects
of political crises. Each of these indirectly testifies to the enduring power of
Watt's thesis by making it a touchstone for gauging the role of particular historical and formal elements in the emergence and development of the novel.

Many of the theories alluded to in this very truncated list will be touched on
later in the analysis of individual works. So, too, will paradigms drawn from
political history and philosophy. Among these is Isaac Kramnick's framing
of eighteenth-century political ideology through the contrasting metaphors
of the "chain of being" and "the race." The "chain of being" images the divinely sanctioned, hierarchical order of classical republicanism, addressed at
the beginning of the period through a civic humanist discourse that envisions,
in the words of the poet Alexander Pope, "All [as] but parts of one stupendous
whole."[3] The metaphor of the "race" appealed, in turn, to those who rejected
the defense of the status quo central to the "chain of being" model. In adapting John Locke's ideas, these proto-modernists made marketplace competition (rather than submission to God's order) the governing figure for a view
of life as a "race" in which individuals are pitted against one another. Another
important context is supplied by Charles Taylor's description of a distinctively
eighteenth-century notion of identity, itself the foundation of modernity, that
he argues depends on three key factors: first, a conceptualizing of inwardness
based on the powers of disengaged reason and of self-exploration, second, an
assumption of the uniqueness of individual selves, and third, an affirmation
of ordinary life and of the egalitarianism that promises. The convergence of
these three impulses in the period had wide-ranging effects. One relates to
the eclipse of medieval and early modern temporalities by a new sense of time
that allows identity to be articulated not through reference to archetypes but
through circumstantial details that anchored the self in relation to memory,
unfolding experiences, and, as we will see, new ways of conceptualizing history. More recently, the literary critic Michael McKeon has suggested that this
eighteenth-century turn away from traditional attitudes involved a supersed-
ing of tacit, often unexamined, political, social, and cultural practices by a
distinctively modern self-consciousness, itself discernible in a new sequence
of conceptual divisions in the period, including sex from gender, the private
from the public, inwardness from exteriority, political absolutism from political hegemony.

The history of novel criticism from Ian Watt to the present moment in
many ways recapitulates the formation of the genre he described. When modern literary critics gain a purchase for their narratives by refuting those of

their predecessors, in other words, they rehearse the early novel's own habit of overriding inherited modes. But the process is not straightforwardly react-ive or backward-looking. Nor is it insular. Both eighteenth-century fiction *and* society change over the era charted here and another of the aims of this Introduction is to argue for the novel's alertness to the larger transformations it helped to mediate for an expanding and increasingly knowledgeable audi-ence. The intersections between literary and other developments, however, are too approximate to allow for the designation of a specific "first" novel. Even within the orbits of single careers, the cross-generic reach of individual writ-ers defies neat classification: Daniel Defoe adds to hundreds of previous titles when he publishes *Robinson Crusoe* (1719) in late middle age (and then capi-talizes on its success with the series of fictions discussed in Chapter 1), Henry Fielding was a successful playwright (until the 1737 Stage Licensing Act closed down all but two state-sanctioned theaters in London and required that per-formances be licensed by the Lord Chamberlain) and Tobias Smollett hoped to be one; Eliza Haywood was not only an actress in Fielding's Little Theatre in the Haymarket in the 1730s, but also a drama critic, translator, poet, and peri-odical editor. At century's end, William Godwin was, like Defoe, Haywood, Smollett, and Fielding before him, a journalist, historian, and political com-mentator (and a philosopher, biographer, literary critic, and children's writer as well). The three broad clusters that structure this Introduction – "Secrets and singularity," "Sociability and community," "History and nation" – aim to order this thematic, formal, and contextual diversity without unduly regimenting it. Before describing these rubrics in more detail, it might be helpful to pursue an alternate approach and consider what some more miscellaneous elements – the representation of children, of place, of domestic interiors, and of writing and reading – can tell us about changes in novelistic representation over the course of the period.

In their own right, children play minimal directive roles in contemporary fiction (though the period caters to the emerging modern sense of childhood as distinct and special with the publication of juvenile novels, including Sarah Fielding's *The Governess; Or, Little Female Academy* [1741], the anonym-ous *History of Little Good Two-Shoes* [1765], and Thomas Day's *Sanford and Merton* [1783]). When Samuel Richardson's and Henry Fielding's novels close with references to the birth of a new generation, they are not romanticizing a privileged state of innocence, but marking the adult protagonist's achieve-ment of a coherent social identity and, with it, the ability confidently to look to the future. The ending of Fielding's *Tom Jones* – retirement to the country, marriage, and the birth of a son and daughter – thus folds the hero into a lar-ger narrative of continuity and progress. The legatees, in particular, resolve the novel's inheritance themes (personal and national) by making possible the orderly conveyance of "real" property and power. The historical specificity of these emblematic functions accounts in part for the differences between early and later novelistic representations of children. In Defoe's fiction, the impermanence of familial bonds and raw numbers of children abandoned without harsh moral judgment are consistent with the tendency of his characters to regard others as instrumental to the true business of their lives, the amassing of "mobile" property or money. Even the apparent exceptions, Moll Flanders and Roxana, confirm the pattern since their maternal feelings are depicted as merely situational, a form of emotional interest at best enjoyed in middle age and only after their finances have been secured. Later in the century, in keeping with new views of maternity, the narrative functions of children change again. Many 1790s novels, including those of Mary Hays, Mary Wollstonecraft, and Elizabeth Inchbald, foreground a strong sentimental bond between mother and child, representing it as both innate and mutually authenticating. In doing so, they confirm Dror Wahrman's speculation that after 1770 a growing intolerance of behavioral transgressions goes hand in hand with a naturalizing of gender differences that makes maternity essential to women's identity (and in the process constrains her powers of choice).

Such biological determinism contrasts sharply with the easy assumption and discarding of roles in Defoe. In his fiction, characters often seem impelled less by self-conscious decisions than by random events on which they opportunistically seize. Over the course of the century, the contingent sense of self that such openness to experience makes possible is gradually reined in. Circumstances may drive protagonists to undertake adventures or to experience a dislocating estrangement from the past, but after Defoe, the serial invention (and equally inconsequential shedding) of distinct identities is increasingly unusual. Role-playing now comes to mark individuals of unusual villainy, frequently those who have betrayed their family origins. At one end of the social spectrum, the well-born Lovelace in Samuel Richardson's *Clarissa* willfully confuses class distinctions in his filial relationship with the bawd "Mother" Sinclair, his corruption of servants, and his direction of prostitutes to pose as his aristocratic relations; at the other end, the street urchin Vallaton in Elizabeth Hamilton's *Memoirs of Modern Philosophers* invents a romance narrative to conceal his low birth and uses the cover of revolutionary rhetoric to indulge his desire for wealth, power, and sexual dominance.

The physical backdrop to these dangerously multiple, performative selves, in *Clarissa* and *Memoirs of Modern Philosophers*, as in Defoe's work, is the city. Throughout eighteenth-century fiction, spaces that provide visual evidence of deeper cultural changes – from the generalized emblems of city and country to the specific domestic architectural innovations of corridors, realigned living quarters, and private closets – highlight tensions between customary and vanguard impulses. In particular, novels exploit the relation between literal and figurative mobility, that is, between physical movement and the aspirational desire for social advancement (and its alternatives, the graceful acceptance of one's given position or the much-feared fall into ignominious poverty).

Defoe represents this newly mobilized self as most perfectly and continuously realized in London. Later novels more often make urban experience a testing ground or prelude to rural retreat (the latter confirming the triumph of assigned identity over the assumed or experimental ones associated with the city). The reward of return, as Samuel Richardson's *Clarissa* makes clear, is not limited to the comic marriage endings of Henry Fielding's *Tom Jones* or Frances Burney's *Evelina*. Clarissa's wish that her corpse be brought from London and buried in the family vault denotes the tragic culmination of her unswerving faith in the social hierarchies traditionally identified with the country. When Frances Burney re-writes this plot of female exile and return, she maintains and further specifies the dangers of mobility emblematized in Clarissa's London experiences: Evelina's encounters with those like Sir Clement Willoughby or her grandmother Madame Duval who wish to take advantage of her uncertain standing recurrently involve conflicts in or about carriages, vehicles that carry the heroine beyond the reach of those who would protect her. At the same time, however, the alienating conditions in London push her "not only to *judge*, but to *act*" independently, a forced self-reliance that paradoxically (but typically) is made a condition of the final social integration she achieves as acknowledged daughter and beloved wife.[4]

This development of the ambiguities attaching to mobility – actual, social, and individual – is observable throughout eighteenth-century fiction. It is often manifested in attention to comparably transitional architectural spaces, including closets, the forerunner of the modern bedroom or individual study (Samuel Richardson's *Pamela*), passages and hallways (Laurence Sterne's *Tristram Shandy*), and staircases (William Godwin's *Fleetwood*). Each of these structural features is also implicated in the growing period connection between privacy and privilege, a connection Mark Girouard traces in the evolution of domestic interiors to afford improved access to both seclusion and hospitality for the socially advantaged. Thus back stairs allowing unobtrusive movement through the house and sleeping quarters in distant attic rooms reinforce the lesser status of servants, part of a larger process that sees a narrowing of the definition of "family" from all household members to immediate blood relatives only; the isolation of bedrooms on the second floor formalizes the distinction of private from public space; and, from the 1720s, the reorganization of the ground floor as part of what Girouard calls "the social house" creates dedicated venues for self-display and sociability.

Another important site for negotiating the relation between private and communal domains is print itself, one to which novelists are, hardly surprisingly, particularly attuned. The "instrumental stance" that the modern identity assumes in relation to self and world, Charles Taylor suggests, is bound up with the expressive powers of language.[5] Early in the century, novels underscore their own language–centered status by making articulateness a critical survival mechanism. For Daniel Defoe, Jane Barker, and Delarivier Manley's characters, writing is connected with secrecy, a form of self-mastery through print that often serves as an alternative to intimacy with the family, friends, and business acquaintances from whom knowledge is deliberately withheld. At the same time, in their novels as in Aphra Behn's, internal conversations about reading and writing function obliquely to direct the interpretations of the "real" audience. Later fictions retain this interest in the integrity of individuals while also authenticating various kinds of consensual experience that cast a negative light on those who choose autonomy over community. A favored method of conveying these tensions is scenes of reading. From the 1750s (Henry Fielding's *Amelia*, Charlotte Lennox's *The Female Quixote*) through to the end of the period (Jane Austen's *Sense and Sensibility*, Amelia Opie's *Adeline Mowbray*), authors depict their characters' reading habits as variously leading to redemption and social reconciliation or infamy and exile.

These reflexive representations are both local and global in intent: they express the desire to guide interpretation of particular texts and reflect the increasing awareness of the potential ungovernability of actual readers. In response to the latter anxiety, authors attempt to shape readers into something resembling a community of the like-minded. Many of the novel's formal features contribute to this end, most notably through participation in what the literary critic Carey McIntosh describes as the mid-century shift away from the oral and colloquial and toward a decorous civility identified with print. The normalizing of polite speech in turn allows exemptions from this standard to be exploited to political, ethical, or aesthetic ends. Dialect, idiolect, and vernacular are thus increasingly used to signal exceptionality, sometimes an authentic because untutored sincerity, but more often in the negative terms of Tobias Smollett's *Humphry Clinker* where the characters' speech and writing graduate their class, gender, and intellectual traits on a scale stretching from illiteracy to gentility. When the irredeemably vulgar Mrs. Botherim in Elizabeth Hamilton's *Memoirs of Modern Philosophers* praises Dr. Orwell for his ability to "speak in print", she testifies to the familiarity of 1790s audiences with this marker of difference – and consolidates their corporate identification as a group sympathetic to Hamilton's conservative values. That Mrs. Botherim cannot discriminate between Orwell's unaffectedly polished speech and her own daughter's entirely derivative "talking out of them there books" might well also confirm her readers' doubts about the late-century pressure to extend literacy.[6]

These general comments about family, place, and language will be subject to qualification in the analysis of individual works to follow. The broad themes to which the Introduction's separate parts refer – "Secrets and singularity," "Sociability and community," "History and nation" – are likewise intended to be flexible rather than prescriptive. They are designed to map the contemporary novel in relation to a trio of contexts, each of which undergoes substantial modification over the course of the century. The first part, "Secrets and singularity," focuses on the representation of exceptionality in three distinct registers. Chapter 1, "The power of singularity," traces the depiction of autonomy through *Robinson Crusoe* (1719), *Capt. Singleton* (1720), *Col. Jacque* (1723), *Moll Flanders* (1721), and *Roxana* (1724). Chapter 2, "The virtue of singularity," looks at the rewarding of exemplary goodness in Fielding's *Joseph Andrews* (1742) and *Amelia* (1751) and in Richardson's *Pamela* (1740) and *Clarissa* (1747–8). Chapter 3, "The punishment of singularity," examines sensibility in both female-authored novels – Charlotte Lennox's *The Female Quixote* (1752), Sarah Fielding's *Ophelia* (1760), Frances Sheridan's *Sidney Bidulph* (1761), and Jane Austen's *Sense and Sensibility* (1811) – and male-authored ones – Laurence Sterne's *Tristram Shandy* (1765–7) and *A Sentimental Journey* (1768), Henry Mackenzie's *Man of Feeling* (1771), and William Godwin's *Fleetwood: Or, The New Man of Feeling* (1805). Whether shaped by a proto-modern solipsism or nostalgic views of integrity, these novels imagine an adversarial and alienated relationship between character and world.

The second part, "Sociability and community," explores the complementary spheres of conciliation and connection from three widening and increasingly abstract perspectives. In Chapter 4, "The reformation of family," paired texts from mid-century forward – Samuel Richardson's *Sir Charles Grandison* (1753–4) and Oliver Goldsmith's *The Vicar of Wakefield* (1766); Eliza Haywood's *Betsy Thoughtless* (1751) and Jane Austen's *Emma* (1815); Eliza Fenwick's *Secresy* (1795) and George Walker's *Theodore Cyphon* (1796) – help to elucidate the complexities of the nuclear and extended family. Chapter 5, "Alternative communities," considers novels that describe unfamiliar collectivities either by drawing on established subgenres, such as utopian and travel narratives, or by advancing new conventions, as in Gothic. Among the former are Sarah Scott's *Millenium Hall* (1762) and *Sir George Ellison* (1766), and Clara Reeve's *School for Widows* (1791). The anonymous *Henry Willoughby*

(1798) and *Berkeley Hall* (1796) blend utopian elements with the exoticism also evident in the contrasts between home and alien cultures exploited in Aphra Behn's *Oroonoko* (1688), the anonymous *Female American* (1767), Elizabeth Hamilton's *Hindoo Rajah* (1796), and George Cumberland's *Castle of Sennaar* (1798) and *The Reformed* (c. 1800). This chapter closes with the late-century exploration of institutional excesses in Ann Radcliffe's *Mysteries of Udolpho* (1794) and *The Italian* (1797) and M. G. Lewis's *The Monk* (1796). Chapter 6, "The sociability of books," examines the ways in which eighteenth-century novels mimic familial structures by invoking genealogical affiliations, either directly, through the writing of sequels, as in Jane Barker's *Galesia Trilogy* (1713–26) and Sarah Fielding's *David Simple* (1744) and *Volume the Last* (1753); obliquely, through the re-writing of predecessor texts, as in Frances Burney's *Evelina* (1778), Elizabeth Inchbald's *A Simple Story* (1791), and Amelia Opie's *Adeline Mowbray* (1805); or ironically, through parody, as in William Beckford's *Modern Novel Writing* (1796), Eaton Stannard Barrett's *The Heroine* (1814), and Jane Austen's *Northanger Abbey* (1817).

The last part, "History and nation," addresses the realm of public, historical event. As the first two parts will have made clear, many eighteenth-century fictions engage themes that contemporaries understood to refer at once to personal relationship and public institutions: marriage, family, property. At moments of historical crisis, novelists appear particularly attuned to the inherent instability of these structures and inclined to use the medium of fiction to present arguments for their dismantling, repair, or full renovation. Chapter 7, "History, novel, and polemic," will trace the partisan uses of fiction over the course of the century from Delarivier Manley and Jane Barker, through Daniel Defoe's *Plague Year* (1722), to the revolutionary and the anti-Jacobin novels of the 1790s, William Godwin's *Caleb Williams* (1794), Robert Bage's *Hermsprong* (1796), Mary Hays's *Victim of Prejudice* (1799), Elizabeth Inchbald's *Nature and Art* (1796), Charlotte Smith's *Young Philosopher* (1798), and Elizabeth Hamilton's *Memoirs of Modern Philosophers* (1800). Chapter 8, "Historical fiction and generational distance," counterpoints three representations of the 1745 Jacobite rebellion – Henry Fielding's *Tom Jones* (1749), Tobias Smollett's *Expedition of Humphry Clinker* (1771), and Walter Scott's *Waverley* (1814) – and two oblique depictions of the revolutionary crisis of the 1790s, Charlotte Smith's *The Old Manor House* (1793) and George Walker's *The Vagabond* (1799). In their varied adaptations of the gap between the present moment and recoverable memory, these novels reveal the depletion of certain eighteenth-century modes and the parallel emergence of new nineteenth-century ones.

Part I

Secrets and singularity

Introduction

Questions of identity – its nature, expression, ethical, economic, and political correlatives, as well as its individual and social formations – fascinated eighteenth-century writers. Daniel Defoe approaches the exploration of such questions in his novels by disabling the customary markers of private and public being, among them, names, family status, religious affiliation, and place of birth. In certain novels, including *Capt. Singleton* (1720), *Moll Flanders* (1721) and *Col. Jacque* (1723), our knowledge of these remains almost entirely incomplete; in others, like *Robinson Crusoe* (1719) and *The Fortunate Mistress* or *Roxana* (1724), limited information is advanced in the opening pages, but then just as swiftly undermined or made irrelevant by changing circumstances. In later eighteenth-century fiction, the destabilizing effects of such patterns of concealment and disclosure are often made preliminary to the consolidation of personal and social knowledge. But in Defoe's novels, as Chapter 1 suggests, two narrative elements work to sustain the contingency of identity: first, the focus on secrets, and second, the depiction of the protagonists' singularity, paradoxically defined through their connections to character doubles. Most often developed through plots that set individual freedoms against a secular domain of financial necessity and a spiritual one of providential order, this unstable self characteristically achieves only partial resolution, leaving unsettled the ancillary relation of the private to the social.

Chapter 2, "The virtue of singularity," opens with Mary Davys's 1724 *The Reform'd Coquet*, treating it as a hinge between Defoe's representations of identity and those advanced by his mid-century successors, Samuel Richardson and Henry Fielding. In Richardson's *Pamela* (1740) and *Clarissa* (1747–8), the heroines' singularity takes the form of an exemplary virtue that alienates them from the acquisitiveness of their extended and immediate families. Fielding's *Joseph Andrews* (1742) and *Amelia* (1751), the first in a pattern of near-sequels to be discussed in this study, develop more fully than the Richardson novels to which they respond the capacity of those same family structures – often represented as microcosms of a larger providential order – to counterbalance, correct, supplement, or reward the forced autonomy of the protagonists.

Chapter 3, "The punishment of singularity," turns to mid- to late-century fictions that foreground the imperfect fit between the individual and the social in order to represent personal and institutional failures as mutually constitutive of their protagonists' experiences. In exploring the potential incompatibility of private sentiment and family, these novels provide a platform for the airing of gender differences. They are therefore treated separately by sex with the discussion of Charlotte Lennox's *The Female Quixote* (1752), Sarah Fielding's *Ophelia* (1760), Frances Sheridan's *Sidney Bidulph* (1761), and Jane Austen's *Sense and Sensibility* (1811) followed by discussion of Laurence Sterne's *Tristram Shandy* (1765–7) and *A Sentimental Journey* (1768), Henry Mackenzie's *The Man of Feeling* (1771), and William Godwin's *Fleetwood: Or, The New Man of Feeling* (1805).

Chapter 1

The power of singularity

Family is the ground against which the defining features of Defoe's protagonists come into focus. But it is the *failure* of the domestic realm to offer the requisite intellectual, emotional, or (sometimes) physical nourishment that proves decisive to the autonomous self who emerges either through necessity or an act of will. *Robinson Crusoe* and *Roxana* provide relatively detailed accounts of their protagonists' youthful circumstances, in both instances distinctly comfortable ones. While the intervening *Capt. Singleton, Moll Flanders,* and *Col. Jacque* are as indebted as *Crusoe* and *Roxana* to travel narratives, spiritual autobiography, picaresque, and economic and political treatises for their rendering of adult experience, they withhold the information about family lineages that Defoe's first and last novels provide, information that later eighteenth-century interpretations of character, real or imagined, make crucial. In all three of the middle novels, the few facts that exist are conveyed orally and by hearsay rather than by written report, a significant factor given the first-person narrators' subsequent stress on the importance of recording their adventures: Singleton hears that he was stolen from his nursemaid and bought by the "Woman, whom I was taught to call Mother ... for Twelve Shillings of another Woman";[1] Moll is born in Newgate and thus "had no Parish to have Recourse to for my Nourishment in my Infancy," but "as I have been told, some Relation of my Mothers took me for a while as a Nurse"[2] before selling her (presumably) to the gypsies by whom she is subsequently abandoned; Jack learns from "oral Tradition" that his "Mother was a Gentlewoman, [and] that my Father was a Man of Quality."[3] Untended by birth parents and made articles of trade, these characters are denied the social advantages that Crusoe enjoys and then has the luxury of rejecting when he boards ship "without asking God's Blessing, or my Father's, without any Consideration of Circumstances or Consequences."[4] In thus indulging his "meer wandring Inclination" (58), Crusoe not only chooses to launch himself into the very condition of uncertainty that Defoe makes the birthright of Singleton, Moll, and Jack, he also repudiates his own inheritance, the classically mandated "middle Station of Life" with its promise of unchanging "Temperance, Moderation, Quietness,

Health, Society, all agreeable Diversions, and all desirable Pleasures." To his father, this decision seems entirely eccentric: "He told me it was for Men of desperate Fortunes on one Hand, or of aspiring, superior Fortunes on the other, who went abroad upon Adventures, to rise by Enterprize, and make themselves famous in Undertakings of a Nature out of the common Road; that these things were all either too far above me, or too far below me" (58). What Crusoe's father condemns – the proto-modern, self-constructed, aspirational self – is what all Defoe protagonists in turn cultivate. If they at times experience "desperate Fortunes," all finally acquire wealth and power "superior" to that of their birth status.

Such accomplishments, however, are neither unproblematically achieved nor uniformly celebrated. The generational conflict between father and son and the sinking of the ship on which Crusoe flees his native York for London – the latter event seen as providential by both his father and the captain – hint at the continuing pressure that customary affiliations of belief and action put on self-determination in *Robinson Crusoe* (and all other Defoe novels). One additional detail mentioned in passing also proves pivotal to the exploration of individual volition in subsequent novels: Crusoe leaves his family home with a "Companion, who had indeed entic'd me away" (61). Crusoe depicts himself as compelled by his own nature (curiosity, restlessness, ambition) and by another person who is typically more commanding than even the hero. Later Defoe novels will retain the inward compulsion and the double figure while also introducing as additional justifications for disobedience (in forms that range from paternal defiance to criminal behavior) extreme poverty or physical threat. While the narrative roles of these doubles vary tremendously, they all function as complements to the chosen or imposed singularity of the hero.

Before his shipwreck, Crusoe's connections with others are primarily defined by their situational usefulness, as with Xury, who helps him escape from Moorish slavery (and is later sold by Crusoe for 60 pieces of eight), and the Portuguese Captain who first teaches him mathematics and navigation and then continues to provide assistance after Crusoe begins a new career as Brazilian plantation owner. Once castaway on the island, however, he is deprived even of these nominal forms of companionship, an isolation forecast by the sad detritus of his drowned shipmates – "three of their Hats, one Cap, and two Shoes that were not Fellows" (91). Yet he instinctively continues to act in ways shaped more by the terms of exchange than of solitude, calling "a Council, that is to say, in my Thoughts" (97) when decisions must be made, retrieving and then hoarding gold from the shipwreck, dividing up the day – as will Samuel Richardson's Clarissa – with regular tasks, humanizing and when possible domesticating his animal companions, including a parrot that he comes to see as a "sociable Creature" (162) capable of moving him to tears, despite knowing that the bird merely repeats what it has been taught. In time, and particularly after he gains in physical security, the initial doublings – Crusoe and his own thoughts, Crusoe and his parrot – are transmuted into imagined networks of relationship defined by his position as patriarch:

> It would have made a Stoick smile to have seen, me and my little
> Family sit down to Dinner; there was my Majesty the Prince and Lord
> of the whole Island; I had the Lives of all my Subjects at my absolute
> Command. I could hang, draw, give Liberty, and take it away, and no
> Rebels among all my Subjects.   (166)

Absolute solitude, in short, is unthinkable: the alienated Defoe protagonists habitually find ways to preserve their disengagement and at the same time to cushion themselves from a sense of utter aloneness in the world.

The control over himself and his environment that enables Robinson Crusoe to make parallels between domestic and political orders vanishes abruptly when fifteen years into his exile he comes across the "Print of a Man's naked Foot on the Shore … I stood like one Thunder-struck, or as if I had seen an Apparition" (170). The paralyzing fear that drives Crusoe back into himself is almost immediately – as the externalized image of an apparition suggests – succeeded by a purposive commitment to defending himself against this spectral presence. In the years following the sighting, he undertakes for the first time a comprehensive survey of the island and an intense fortification "to keep my self entirely conceal'd where I was, unless I found a better sort of Creatures than *Canibals* to make my self known to" (179). Nine years later, the "Apparition" materializes in the form of Friday, not a powerful antagonist, but a victim rescued from sacrifice who soon makes "all the Signs to me of Subjection, Servitude, and Submission imaginable, to let me know, how he would serve me as long as he liv'd" (209). Over time, he is remade from cannibal to Crusoe's subordinate double: dressed, schooled, and converted to Protestantism. Three years later, another rescue leaves Crusoe even more "rich in Subjects" (235), and finally, a failed ship mutiny brings further inhabitants to the island and allows Crusoe to return to Europe with Friday. He escapes from his "silent State of Life" to one of immense privilege, and to renewed acquaintance with two former mentors who help him manage his accumulated assets.

Crusoe responds to this apparent good fortune with an anxiety so intense he slips when expressing it into identifying his altered circumstances with his wealth, his person with his property: "I had now a great Charge upon me, and my Business was how to secure it. I had ne'er a Cave now to hide my Money in, or a Place where it might lye without Lock or Key … On the contrary, I knew not where to put it, or who to trust with it" (270). In subsequent Defoe novels, the elaboration of this uncertainty will draw together key elements from *Robinson Crusoe*: the singularity of the hero, the zeal to accumulate, the psychological and material reliance on doubles, and in *Moll Flanders* and *Roxana* in particular, an instinct for secrecy so deeply entrenched as to appear essential to identity itself. With each novel, these various strands become more complexly intertwined. The heroes in both *Capt. Singleton* and *Col. Jacque*, for instance, advance their fortunes by affiliating themselves with mentor figures who help them to protect their riches. In *Singleton*, as in *Robinson Crusoe*, these men have relatively discrete existences, passing out of the narrative when their particular roles are fulfilled. But differences between the first and second of the double figures in *Singleton*, the Gunner and William the Quaker, suggest Defoe's growing interest in exploring the possibilities of reciprocally defining characters, an interest further developed in *Col. Jacque*.

The Gunner who dominates the first half of *Capt. Singleton*, giving direction to the hero's aspirations and helping him accumulate a fortune in gold and ivory, is left behind when Singleton returns to England from Africa. His successor, William, however, is not only assigned a name rather than being identified solely through his profession, but also has distinctive personality traits that prove critical to the novel's conclusion. For instance, as a Quaker, William believes that answering his pirate captors' appeals for direction would offend his religious integrity (though he occasionally volunteers advice). Singleton meets William's request that they give up their roving, repent, and retire home by exacting complementary conditions that allow both men to repress their past lives as pirates, preserve their secret identities along with their accumulated wealth, and "pass for *Grecians* and Foreigners" (225) in England. By these mutually satisfying means, Singleton guards against his earlier experience of finding himself "in such Pain for *William*, that I could not be without him" (143) and even manages, when he subsequently marries William's sister, doubly to legitimate his ties to the family.

Col. Jacque begins to develop the multi-faceted relationship between the singular hero and sets of "good" and "bad" doubles that will be so important to *Moll Flanders* and *Roxana*. Raised by a nurse as part of a trio differentiated by mock rankings – Captain, Colonel, and Major Jack – Col. Jack offers a retrospective account of his life in which he makes the hearsay report of his parents' gentility definitive: even as a child, he claims to have sought out "the better Sort" (38) and as a young man in Edinburgh and later in America, this aspiration leads to alignments with hapless but educated men from whom he acquires literacy in Latin and English and a developed taste for history. His early conviction that he stands apart from "the general Wickedness of the rest of my Companions" (76), not least in escaping the consequences of his thieving, is borne out by his ability to enlist the help of the powerful through his eloquence: with a "plausible Story" (88), he hoodwinks a Custom-house clerk into investing his stolen money and later in America, when an indentured laborer, wins the sympathy first of the manager and then the Master of the Maryland plantation with a touching account of his plight. As in *Moll Flanders*, these embedded narratives alert readers to the artfulness of the hero's own first-person account, particularly when they rework models like the good and bad apprentice that circulated widely throughout the eighteenth century. The twelve linked engravings of William Hogarth's *Industry and Idleness* (1747), contrasting the alternate life courses of Francis Goodchild and Thomas Idle, testify to the power of this narrative, the possibilities for its ironic amendment, and the interpenetration of the visual and the verbal in the culture at large. Thus, while Col. Jack the almost-goodchild prospers, his original companions, the Captain and the Major, thieves to the end, are executed as highwaymen.

Tricked into indentured servitude in America, Col. Jack reveals the characteristic resilience of the Defoe hero by repeating his childhood ascent from extreme poverty. Once he has been promoted from "sold Slave" to overseer, he dedicates himself to reinforcing his connections with the colonial property-owning class, instituting techniques for managing labor that echo the English patrician control of plebeian masses through awe rather than fear. But when he finally achieves security as an estate owner in his own right, his habitual restlessness drives him from America back to England in the hope of achieving through the pseudo-aristocratic channels of marriage and service to the king the fully realized traditional "Life of a Gentleman" (161). Unfortunately, his marriages are disastrous (twice to women who cuckold him, then to a third who descends into alcoholism, and finally to a fourth who dies accidentally) and in serving the Old Pretender, James Francis Edward Stuart (son of the monarch deposed when the 1688 Revolution sought to assure a Protestant ascendancy by installing William and Mary on the throne), he opens himself to prosecution after the abandoned 1708 Jacobite invasion of Scotland. He is horrified to discover on his return to Virginia after a twenty-four-year absence evidence of this incriminating past: among the recently transported felons are not only men who can place him with the banned Jacobites, but also the second of his adulterous wives.

Defoe handles these private and public threats to Col. Jack's autonomy with a sophistication that comes more fully into focus when the conclusion of his novel is compared to that of Aphra Behn's 1688 *Fair Jilt*. In Behn's novel – which like its successor has Jacobite connections and turns obsessively on secrets – the forgiveness of the adulteress Miranda and absence of any form of distributive justice seem jarringly sudden and unsatisfying. After she admits to inveigling her husband Tarquin into murdering her sister and "confess'd" in addition "all the Lewdness of her Practices with several Princes and great men," Miranda and Tarquin, we are told, "retir'd to a Country-house" where she "has been very penitent for her Life past, and gives Heaven the Glory for having given her these Afflictions, that have reclaim'd her, and brought her to as perfect a State of Happiness as this troublesome World can afford."[5] Col. Jack's clemency, by contrast, makes his wife pivotal to the novel's concluding adjustment of emotional, political, and fiscal strands: she is the last of the double figures who help him overcome the threat of poverty, and in making arrangements for his protection from the dangers of arrest and property confiscation (for supporting the Old Pretender and for bigamy), she secures a political pardon for him that corresponds to his domestic or marital pardon of her adultery. Under her aegis, the various projections of his aspirational self – money, real property, secret or disguised identities – are managed in ways that allow the couple to retire to England, having apparently assured a continuing flow of profits from the American plantation.

Col. Jack's concerted efforts to gain and retain wealth are fueled throughout by a single-mindedness that reinforces his solitary condition. Yet, at the same time (as the efforts of his second wife suggest), he aligns himself with a series of doubles – helpmates who variously aid in the pursuit and concealment of property, provide a sounding-board for anxieties, project an image of his desires, and serve when necessary as instruments for reversing the consequences of illegal or immoral acts (as opposed to *Roxana* where Amy's active direction of illicit deeds is emphasized). This paradoxical coupling of separateness with the doubling of the hero through figures both negative and positive is related in turn to a number of narrative strategies that underscore the protagonist's singularity. One of the most important is repetition, with moments of repentance providing the most striking examples: each novel, following the pattern of spiritual autobiographies, touches on the grace made possible by yielding to divine authority. Submission in these terms runs counter to the hero's urge to self-sufficiency, but in Defoe's novels neither providential deference nor economic aggression unequivocally triumphs. The continuing tension between these religious and secular models is sustained by additional forms of repetition that foster ambiguity about the heroes' motivations and highlight their voracious appetites for change. Among these can be included verbal and structural repetition.

Verbal echoing draws together apparently discrete moments in the texts, and in doing so, invites the reader to consider the possibility of their thematic and formal connection. When partway through his travels, Crusoe, for instance, laments that as a Brazilian plantation owner, he has "com[e] into the very Middle Station, or upper Degree of low Life, which my Father advised me to before; and which if I resolved to go on with, I might as well ha' staid at Home, and never have fatigu'd my self in the World as I had done" (82). This second quotation of his father's words, first referred to in the novel's opening pages, conveys Crusoe's awareness of the ironies of his position and, by extension, the potentially insatiable desire that drives him. That desire excludes him from the pleasures of sociability, as suggested by his succeeding comment – here metaphorical, but soon to be literalized – that on the Brazilian plantation "I liv'd just like a Man cast away upon some desolate Island" (83).

The implicit patterns of meaning to which we gain access through repetition and foreshadowing cut across the apparent artlessness of Crusoe's account, conjuring the designing hand of the author and reinforcing our sense of the constructedness of the narrative. Equally elaborate instances of repetition appear in Moll and Roxana's persistent habit of rehearsing their life plots just prior to descriptions of morally questionable acts, a compensatory reflex that often sees them appealing to past hardships to justify present venality. The effects, however, move well beyond the revelation of personality quirks. Interrupting the narrative's forward momentum with such summaries injects an element of self-conscious design that momentarily suspends our engagement with the character and encourages our recognition of larger patterns of meaning. In Moll's case, structural repetition of this kind often coincides with the end of a relationship, as she tallies events to date through a calculated response – both literally and figuratively – that underscores her fierce will to survive. In *Roxana*, Defoe exploits the intricate temporality of the first-person retrospective point of view by having Roxana break with narrative chronology to forecast a later moment that will then be re-described in its proper sequence. Here, for instance, Roxana explains her relationship with the prince:

> Thus, in the Case of this Child of mine, while he [the prince] and I convers'd, there was no need to make any … Maintenance for the Child … for [the prince] supplied me more than sufficiently … but afterward, when Time, and a particular Circumstance, put an End to our conversing together; as such things always meet with a Period, and generally break off abruptly; I say, after that, I found he appointed the Children a settled Allowance … tho' I came to be sunk and forgotten in the Case; nor did the Children ever know anything of their Mother, to this Day, other, than as you may have an Account hereafter.[6]

The labored syntax – typically in Roxana's story-telling the signal of a troubling event – and the gesture toward shaping the reader's response in anticipation of its "Account hereafter" combine to alert us to the importance of children in this novel: as projected others or potential doubles, as repressed aspects of the past, as rivals, as vengeful agents.

In *Roxana* and *Moll Flanders*, children figure more prominently than in Defoe's novels with male protagonists, although not principally, as will be the case in late century, because he sets women within a fully articulated domesticity or represents maternal instinct as definitive. In fact, children here serve almost a reverse function. They not only reveal the incompatibility of self-making with maternal tenderness, but their expendability also highlights Moll and Roxana's willingness to cultivate secrecy in order to avoid being held accountable for their actions. The logic underlying the symbolic importance of children to later eighteenth-century fiction – they affirm generational and hence cultural continuity – is thus directed to a contrary end, since in Defoe's work they threaten to cramp the mobility of the reinvented self. Children, in short, do not point (as in *Tom Jones* or *Evelina* or even *Humphry Clinker*) to the positive consequences for the future of acknowledging past errors and making the hidden visible. Instead, they are links connecting Moll and Roxana to families and marriages that they must slough off to ensure their own survival and possible advancement. The ruthless behavior of the first families into which they marry may invite consideration of how differently the two women's plots might have developed under a kinder regimen, but subsequently, both characters set courses that place a premium on independent action.

Secrecy is crucial to the self-determination Moll and Roxana crave, and separateness within marriage essential to its preservation. Since Moll's relationships involve an escalating series of illicit connections, her progress in fact increasingly hangs on burying the past. Even the initial legitimate marriage is presented as tainted, and from that point forward the need for concealment multiplies alongside her infringements of both law and custom. To her mind, the reluctance with which she contracts to marry Robin, the younger brother of her first lover, means that she "committed Adultery and Incest with him [the lover] every Day in my Desires, which without doubt, was as effectually Criminal in the Nature of the Guilt, as if I had actually done it" (65). After Robin dies and her second husband abandons her, she realizes that "Criminal" status (if not internalizing the "Guilt") when she unwittingly marries her own brother. On the advice of her mother/mother-in-law, she leaves the brother/husband with their children in Virginia, returns to England and is twice abandoned (by the Bath gentleman and Lancashire Jemy) before returning to the London banker whom she had deserted when Jemy momentarily appeared to be a better prospect.

To this point, Moll has been variously duped by her partners, a dilemma she casts as the usual fate of her sex and more specifically of those who lack an "advisor," a

> Body to whom I could in confidence commit the Secret of any
> Circumstances to, and could depend upon for their Secresie and
> Fidelity; and I found by experience, that to be Friendless is the worst
> Condition, next to being in want, that a Woman can be reduc'd to: *I say
> a Woman*, because 'tis evident Men can be their own Advisers, and their
> own Directors.   (116)

But her status as victim changes with the London banker. With the sense of
power over this man whom she "PLAY'D with ... as an Angler does with a
Trout" (126) comes the luxury of choice, and in particular, the possibility of
choosing to repent:

> it occur'd to me what an abominable Creature am I! and how is this
> innocent Gentleman going to be abus'd by me! How little does he
> think, that having Divorc'd a Whore, he is throwing himself into the
> Arms of another! that he is going to Marry one that has lain with two
> Brothers, and has had three Children by her own Brother! One
> that was born in *Newgate*, whose Mother was a Whore, and is now a
> transported Thief; one that has lain with thirteen Men, and has had a
> Child since he saw me!   (157)

Ultimately, of course, she preserves her silence about the past and with it a
separate self oriented toward worldly advancement at the expense of religious submission. Setting aside full disclosure or retreat, she resolves instead
to "make him amends, if possible, by what he shall see, for the Cheats and
Abuses I put upon him, which he does not see" (157). The reversal of her starting premise is complete: surreptitious "Cheats and Abuses" are now certainties
and contrived "amends" are merely optional.

   Moll's synopsis, like the other forms of repetition mentioned above, inter-
rupts her unfolding narrative, signaling to the reader that this moment is of
pivotal importance to her retrospective account. Most obviously, the rehearsal
of her history foregrounds her sense that her control over the banker breaks
with the precedents of very bad luck and dependency on unreliable men. Five
years later, however, this run of good fortune ends with the financial ruin of
the banker, who lacking "Spirit and Courage to have look'd his Misfortunes
in the Face" (162) dies of sorrow. Just as Crusoe's semi-ironic celebration of
his role as "Prince and Lord of the whole Island" (166) is quickly followed
by the catastrophic sighting of the footprint, so too does Moll's security van-
ish, leaving her similarly exposed to danger. In both instances, the reversal
serves as an object lesson to the reader of the uncertainties of circumstance.
But the two cases also differ. While, as Moll comments, "Men can be their own
Advisors, and their own Directors" and, like Crusoe, can set about to fortify

their holdings, her property inheres in her attractiveness. At forty-eight, she has already exceeded average life expectancy for the period and, as she discovers over the next two years, the "kind of Livelihood" that attachment to a "Spark" once made possible was "quite out of the way after 50" (169). The summary account now takes on another meaning. In its enumeration of her "thirteen men," the passage makes the London banker appear the high point of a string of liaisons and marriages; subsequently, we realize that, with the exception of the drunken Baronet she meets at Batholomew Fair who "never came into a settled way of Maintenance" (197), he was also the end point of her sexual career. What follows is a fundamental adjustment in the novel's representation of Moll's relationship to property. No longer able to inveigle men by treating her own person as saleable, she redirects her focus outward and concentrates through her career as petty criminal on amassing mobile forms of real property.

This new phase of Moll's life is also marked by a reconfiguration of geographic place. All of her previous relationships with men had associations with places beyond London (even the banker is married at a rural coaching inn), but as shoplifter and pickpocket her orbit becomes the metropolis and her success there a measure of a spatial awareness that helps her capitalize on the need for anonymity and stealth. Her first theft, like her first sexual encounter, is represented as guided by external agents: Robin's brother seduced her as a young woman by plying her with five guineas that her own "unbounded Stock of Vanity and Pride" (40) made irresistible. Now, in language evocative of Scripture, she again implies that her fall into criminality was directed by another: the "Devil carried me out and laid his Bait for me, so he brought me sure to the place, for I knew not whether I was going or what I did" (163). Her claims to unconscious action are immediately qualified in our minds by the precision with which she renders the interior of the "Apothecary's Shop in *Leadenhall-Street*" and the opportunity presented by the chance distraction of the maid and apprentice. After the Devil tells her – "'twas like a Voice spoken to me over my Shoulder" (164) – to steal the bundle sitting unattended on the counter, she again professes a lack of volition, although her successful negotiation of the welter of streets through which she escapes suggests greater competency than she admits. Moll's wicked other – the "evil Counsellor within" (165) – soon prompts a second, more premeditated theft when she leads a child into an alley and steals her gold bead necklace. Now a woman of some property, Moll finds that these filched objects present her with a dilemma, the converse of Robinson Crusoe's and Col. Jack's, in that she wishes not to secure her treasures, but to convert them into ready cash. New needs generate new affiliations and consequently the Devil – first an externalized voice, then one heard from "within" – fades from view as Moll revives her friendship with the Governess who helped conceal the birth of the child she had with Jemy before she married the London banker.

The multiple transitions – from the disembodied Devil to the real Governess, from male to female, from iconic figure of evil to protector and teacher – underscore the more complex handling of the Governess as double relative to such other examples as Crusoe's Friday, Singleton's two doubles, the Gunner and William the Quaker, or Col. Jack's wife. Unlike these others, the Governess becomes a mentor not simply under the pressure of the moment, but because Moll, with a foresight that speaks to her cunning, has kept her on retainer since her pregnancy with occasional payments of £5. Moll now tests her loyalty: "I told her I had a Secret of the greatest Consequence in the World to commit to her if she had respect enough for me to keep it a Secret: She told me she had kept one of my Secrets faithfully [the birth of Jemy's child]; why should I doubt her keeping another?" (170). Even with this assurance, Moll hedges, offering in return only limited details of what she has done, and questioning, on the grounds that "hitherto I had had no Confederates" (171), her mentor's advice that she take up pilfering as a way of life. As her subsequent adventures suggest (and Roxana's reinforce), the caution is partially warranted. In both novels, the protagonist depends on one double figure at a time to maintain both secrecy and critical support; affiliations beyond this chosen ally invariably prove hazardous. The Governess thus continues as a valued collaborator, but Moll escapes being impeached by a temporary partner only because she has concealed her sex by cross-dressing and no man corresponding to the circulated description can be found. From this near disaster, Moll learns both to work alone and to magnify her singularity by assuming a succession of disguises: "I took up new Figures, and contriv'd to appear in new Shapes every time I went abroad" (216).

When she is finally caught and taken to Newgate prison, Moll once again draws on her powers to persuade by offering a story framed to appeal to her audience. Her narrative of repentance convinces her first auditor, the Minister sent by the Governess, to arrange for her reprieve and transportation to America. Her second auditor, appearing fortuitously just as she is about to lose contact with the Governess, is Jemy, now imprisoned as a highwayman. While he confides fully in her, she conceals much from him in her efforts to convince him that they will be able to "live as new People in a new World, no Body having any thing to say to us, or we to them" (247). Yet once in America, unforeseen financial opportunities nearly break both the Edenic pairing and the compact of mutual silence. When Moll's son/nephew Humphry responds positively to her covert attempts to claim property left to her by her mother,

Jemy begins to look like an encumbrance: "and thus I was as if I had been in a new World, and began secretly now to wish that I had not brought my *Lancashire* Husband from *England* at all" (269). By novel's end, with the "old Wretch" her brother/husband dead and Humphry compliant with her wishes, Moll finally confesses her full history of "little Difficulties" to Jemy, after which, she announces, all secrets apparently past, "we liv'd together with the greatest Kindness and Comfort imaginable" (274).

Like *Moll Flanders*, *Roxana* probes the notion of singularity by interweaving the motifs of secrets and doubles, though the later novel is both darker throughout and more ambivalent in its conclusion than its predecessor. The increase in complexity owes much to the strangely compelling relationship between Roxana and her shadow figure, Amy, a doubling that originates in the servant's excessive attachment to her mistress but that over time becomes mutually defining. Unlike Moll's, Roxana's background is privileged and since her relatively late fall into poverty is a result of a spendthrift husband, she has the accumulated experience and the sophistication to argue that institutions like marriage offer no protection to dependent wives; as she asserts, "be any thing, be even an Old Maid, the worst of Nature's Curses, rather than take up with a Fool" (25). Her alertness to gender inequities, her sense of entitlement, and her antipathy to marriage (the first brewer husband having inherited a lucrative business, very nearly runs it aground, and then after he has sold it and squandered the proceeds, decamps leaving Roxana and their five children destitute) encourage her pursuit of more self-directed forms of partnership, as courtesan with a string of wealthy and often titled men and, most enduringly, as mistress of and collaborator with her maid, Amy.

Amy's role as double – both thematically as Roxana's agent and keeper of her secrets, and structurally as a stable point of reference – differs on a number of fronts from that of the series of male partners. After the brewer's abandonment of the household, Amy assumes powers far in excess of the norm for her position, advising and sometimes inventing measures to forestall disaster. While her "Kindness and Fidelity" (32) align her with qualities valued in later eighteenth-century fictional servants, the latter tend to function as straightforward mirrors of their employers' leading traits. In positive representations, good and unquestioningly loyal servants reinforce the virtue of the master or mistress (Tobias Smollett's Humphry Clinker, Annette in Ann Radcliffe's *Mystery of Udolpho*) or of fellow servants (Mrs. Jervis in Samuel Richardson's *Pamela*), with comic capital occasionally being made of a figure like Partridge in Henry Fielding's *Tom Jones*, whose service is partially self-interested though still well intentioned; alternatively, wicked and unquestioningly obedient servants (Mrs. Jewkes in *Pamela* or Mrs. Sinclair in Richardson's *Clarissa*) carry out their employers' immoral persecution of the victimized heroines. Amy, the most active of Defoe's doubles, not only projects and performs for Roxana plans of her own devising, she also attempts to shelter her mistress from potentially disastrous public scrutiny. Secrecy, then, is crucial to Roxana's success and Amy is its indispensable manager.

The seeming dependence of mistress on maid to which the first-person narrative testifies is consciously manipulated by Roxana in ways that sometimes unintentionally reveal key aspects of her character and motivations. Self-exculpation is a strong element in her representation of her history and Amy occasionally serves as a convenient stalking horse for her own rationalizing of questionable actions. When, for instance, Roxana wants to divest herself of full responsibility for her conduct, she will cite the extenuating pressure of an immediate calamity and the willingness of Amy to seize control (and thus remove from herself the burden of choice). As in *Moll Flanders*, deference to the actual, often criminally inclined double – the Governess in *Moll Flanders*, Amy in *Roxana* – will also be justified by contrasting it, in turn, with its spectral alternative, "dreadful Poverty" (48), a figure apparently powerful enough to undermine familial ties, whether blood or chosen. At the beginning of the novel, Roxana thus sets the abandonment of her five children with the brewer within the dual contexts of financial ruin and Amy's regulation of her. In claiming that the "Misery of my own Circumstances hardned my Heart against my own Flesh and Blood," and then agreeing to "leave the Management of the whole Matter [the desertion of her children] to my Maid, *Amy*" (34), she effectively transfers her own liability to her servant. Elsewhere, she pursues a contrary – though equally self-interested – blurring of the distinction between mistress and maid, as when, wishing to ensure an equal moral culpability, she contrives her lover's rape of Amy, declaring that "as I thought myself a Whore, I cannot say but that it was something design'd in my Thoughts, that my Maid should be a Whore too, and should not reproach me with it" (54–5). Only at moments of extreme duress does she partially admit complicity in Amy's corruption: "I had been the Devil's Instrument, to make her [Amy] wicked … and she had but follow'd me; I had been her wicked Example; and I had led her into all." But even at this critical juncture, when death by drowning threatens divine rather than merely human judgment, Roxana concludes her seeming confession by noting, "that as we had sinn'd together, now we were likely to sink together" (114), not only retreating from full acknowledgment, but also introducing a slightly comic alliteration that takes the edge off her supposed high moral seriousness.

By this point in the narrative, as the two women follow the Dutch merchant's advice to return to England after Roxana's relationship with the Prince ends, there exists abundant proof that Amy's protection of Roxana and her willingness to act as her eyes and ears have assured their mutual survival (and the mistress's spectacular financial success). The mutually reinforcing power of secrets and doubles to preserve the protagonist's singularity has already survived a critical test in Paris, where Roxana caught a glimpse of her first husband whom she had assumed dead. She sets Amy to spy out his circumstances and when an unfavorable report is returned, resolves not to acknowledge him. This episode knits together character and event in terms that confirm Defoe's increasingly sophisticated mastery of novelistic technique. It also introduces a potential but finally unrealized plot line, a favorite narrative device of later writers. Unrealized plots exploit the interconnections between the actual and the possible both to enhance the sense of fidelity to contingent or "real" experience and to allow the shadow or speculative action obliquely to comment on the trajectory of the chosen one. Here, Roxana notes that if Amy had brought back a more promising account of the brewer husband, she might have considered returning immediately to England and living "honestly with him: But as a *Fool* is the worst of Husbands to do a Woman Good, so *a Fool* is the worst Husband a Woman can do Good to: I wou'd willingly have done him Good, but he was not qualified to receive it, or make the best Use of it" (90). The contours of this anecdote are entirely familiar: as with her responses to Amy, Roxana here makes her behavior to her husband appear straightforwardly reactive, a self-justifying tactic that coexists uneasily with the details she elsewhere provides of the measures taken to preserve her autonomy and her wealth.

Like other Defoe protagonists, Roxana worries about managing her fortune and since under ordinary circumstances marriage would entail its loss (under eighteenth-century property law, her wealth would become her husband's), her status as single woman is crucial both to her independent selfhood and her control over her riches. As these two forms of personal and propertied ownership gradually coalesce, she resists marriage on any grounds, spurning the advice of her financial advisor in London that she find a merchant wealthy enough to let her settle her money as she wishes: "seeing Liberty seem'd to be the Men's Property, I wou'd be a *Man-Woman*; for as I was born free, I wou'd die so" (148). Roxana's contentious claim to all the abstract rights of men takes her well beyond questioning gender norms to crossing sexual boundaries as a "*Man-Woman*." However culturally anomalous this authority, she is enormously successful in exercising it until, as earlier with Moll Flanders, biology apparently trumps personality. After she turns fifty, she abandons the vigilant dedication to concealment and independence that to this point has ensured her prosperity. Roxana's ongoing re-inventions of herself through name and place changes now give way to a wish to make amends for deserting her children.

This return to the past allows situations to develop that threaten the corner-stone principles of secrecy: on the one hand, continuous affiliation with the double, Amy, and, on the other, serial but temporary involvement with male partners. The distrust of Amy as counsellor and confidante leads Roxana to seek relationships with substitute doubles; and, in a culminating betrayal of precedent, she marries the Dutch merchant, whom she had years ago refused.

We grasp the interconnections between these seemingly discrete events initially through their narrative proximity and ultimately through their disastrous consequences. Toward the end of her last relationship as courtesan, Roxana reveals, in a very brief compass, her age, her staggering wealth, her lack of remorse for "six and twenty Years of Wickedness" (160), and her unprecedented effort to right a past wrong by seeking out her children. Subsequently, Amy acts decisively true to form, first when she conceals her discovery that one of the daughters, Susan, is in fact a servant in their house and later when she takes it upon herself to dismiss her. But Roxana, having once broken with her established pattern of forward-mindedness by indulging her guilty conscience about the abandoned children, revisits the past in other ways: she takes up again with the Dutch merchant and dances before him in an elaborate Turkish costume (carefully preserved from any earlier moment in her life) that will prove crucial to Susan's attempts to discover her whereabouts. These departures from her once habitual restraint and privacy leave Roxana unable to counter the threat posed by Susan's cunning in deducing her identity and unwilling to reveal herself to her children as "but a Whore, a common Whore" (175). In time, all Amy's plans to preserve her mistress's autonomy come to nought.

After Roxana dismisses Amy for proposing Susan be murdered, dissolving the uniformity of purpose and shared commitment to secrecy that sustained their relationship, Roxana becomes increasingly uncertain, confessing that "without her, *indeed*, I knew not how to go away, nor how to stay" (258). Her loss of direction is expressed formally in deviations from chronological narrative and thematically in the proliferation of doubles. The most harrowing of these is Susan who while alive "haunted me like an Evil Spirit" (252), "hunted me, as if, *like a Hound*, she had had a hot Scent" (258) and even when (possibly) dead, "haunted my Imagination … my Fancy show'd her me in a hundred Shapes and Postures; sleeping or waking, she was with me: Sometimes I thought I saw her with her Throat cut; sometimes with her Head cut, and her Brains knock'd-out; other times hang'd up upon a Beam; another time drown'd in the Great Pond at Camberwell" (263–4). After Susan's disappearance, Roxana seeks out another of the daughters and impressed by "how sweetly and modestly she behav'd," declares her, rather unaccountably, "the very Counterpart of myself, only much handsomer" (267). In a parallel trading of the good and docile for the unruly and wicked, Roxana increasingly turns to her Quaker neighbor as a substitute for Amy. But as she herself acknowledges, the exchange is only partial since she did not "let my Friend the QUAKER into any Part of the Secret History of my former Life … it was always a Maxim with me, *That Secrets shou'd never be opened, without evident Utility*" (264). The novel's abrupt ending with its hint that Roxana may have genuinely repented after she and Amy "fell into a dreadful Course of Calamities" (267) has few of the satisfactions readers of later eighteenth-century fiction will come to expect: at best, it reanimates the terms of secrecy and doubling and reinstates volatility as a guiding principle. There is no attempt here to fold the singularity of the heroine within the more inclusive contexts Henry Fielding and Samuel Richardson invoke in the novels discussed in the next chapter.

Chapter 2

The virtue of singularity

Published in the same year as *Roxana*, Mary Davys's *The Reform'd Coquet* (1724) has a quite different relationship to the mid-century achievements of Henry Fielding and Samuel Richardson. While many of the themes discussed in Chapter 1 – secrecy, doubles, mentors, female power, disguise – are taken up by Davys, she uses romance conventions to frame and then resolve these elements in terms that reinforce traditional hierarchies. In this tailoring of singularity to mesh with prevailing social norms, she anticipates mid-century fiction. Like *Joseph Andrews, Amelia, Pamela,* and *Clarissa, The Reform'd Coquet* represents virtue as "singular" by drawing on the double sense of the latter as at once an exceptional quality and a characteristic trait. At the same time, however, the adventures of the heroine, Amoranda, immerse her in the contexts of what Dror Wahrman calls the "ancien régime of identity" with its distinctly un-modern view of selfhood as "mutable, malleable, unreliable, divisible, replaceable, transferable, manipulable, escapable, or otherwise fuzzy around the edges."[1] While observing how *The Reform'd Coquet* tolerates certain transgressive energies in realizing the fluid and experimental understanding of identity it shares with *Moll Flanders* and *Roxana*, I want also to suggest how Davys's muting of other counter-normative behaviors forecasts Fielding and Richardson's novels.

Like Moll and Roxana, Amoranda crosses gender boundaries with great ease: she is described as being at once feminine in appearance and motivation – she had "all the Beauties of her Sex, but then she had the Seeds of their Pride and Vanity too" – and masculine in her daring, active intelligence and willfulness.[2] Again, like Defoe's heroines, she is removed from the immediate supervision of family; but while Moll and Roxana struggle to achieve financial independence and then dominance, Amoranda has inherited a substantial fortune that frees her from economic need. Later eighteenth-century novelists recurrently place their protagonists in comparable circumstances, often with the intent of testing the limits of individual autonomy. Because orphanhood removes the props of family security and control, it creates the conditions for an openness to experience ordinarily denied an unmarried young woman, while at the same time exposing her to the predatory libertines and fortune-hunters who instigate the novels' dramatic crises. The courtship plot further heightens the dangers and pleasures of this threshold moment. In part, the dominance of the trope reflects actual social changes, as personal rather than dynastic considerations came increasingly to drive marriage decisions. But courtship also provides a convenient structure for negotiating more general anxieties about individual mobility since the opportunity to choose allows heroines to appear simultaneously powerful and vulnerable. Wealthy, orphaned young women like Amoranda (or Eliza Haywood's eponymous heroine in *Betsy Thoughtless*, Charlotte Lennox's Arabella in *Female Quixote*, or Mary Hays's Mary Raymond in *Victim of Prejudice*, to cite examples from across the century) experience a sense of control or self-direction through courtship that they believe permanent, but we suspect is fleeting. Ultimately, a wedge is driven between their assumption of autonomy and the reality of compromise and subordination: examining where and under what terms authors impose this recognition on both readers and characters will be a recurring topic of the chapters that follow.

In *The Reform'd Coquet*, Davys maximizes the opportunities for Amoranda to display her intelligence and ingenuity not only by supplying her with the financial resources and orphan status that release her from the constraints of labor and parental supervision, but also by giving her agency to pursue her inclinations and to counter her antagonists. Like Moll and Roxana, Amoranda takes a libertine delight in the power of her attractiveness: "Her Heart was like a great Inn, which finds room for all that come, and she could not but think it very foolish to be beloved by five hundred, and return it only to one; she found herself inclin'd to please them all, and took no small pains to do so" (18). But Amoranda's situation differs markedly from Defoe's heroines: while they must exercise their wiles to trap and fleece men, she uses hers to deflect fortune-seekers who would marry and then oppress her. Removed from the Defoe heroines' early struggles simply to survive, her will to independence is fed by a privileged exemption from need.

A related distinction surfaces in the two novelists' treatment of proscribed sexuality, in particular cross-dressing and incest. Here, Amoranda's stance as commentator on Altemira's incest provides an illuminating point of comparison with Defoe and Fielding. Moll's personal involvement clearly contrasts with Amoranda's second-hand detachment, but in both novels the scenes of sexual transgression seem designed as much to highlight the protagonists' ingenuity as to elicit the reader's moral condemnation or the characters' expressions of remorse. In Moll's case, as we have seen, the assumption of male dress appears entirely fortunate since the disguise saves her from impeachment by her temporary partner. Her inadvertent marriage to her brother is treated less casually, but here too the interests of self-advancement (she continues with him for three years after her discovery of their blood ties) trump lasting punishment. *The Reform'd Coquet* combines cross-dressing and incest in an episode that similarly subordinates moral censure to admiration of the heroine's clever management of events, in this case to aid Altemira, a woman disguised as a man and victim of both incest and aristocratic seduction. Amoranda's stratagems ensure a happy marriage for the wronged Altemira, and even the lusting brother (after effecting an unusual cure for his incestuous inclinations – "*I took up a Sword which lay by me, and struck it into my Breast*") achieves absolution through his subsequent marriage to "a Creature, superiour in every Charm to her whole Sex" (91). While both authors acknowledge incest as taboo, in short, they also use it strategically to disarm untoward energies by channeling them into acquisitiveness (Defoe) or marriage (Davys). The swift reassertion of these approved activities arguably acquires an additional layer of conviction when the principal appears not as the victim (Moll) but as the manipulator (Amoranda) of illicit sexuality. Henry Fielding provides an ingenious variation on this concluding endorsement of social institutions when he invokes the threat of incest only to defuse it by revealing the true parentage of Joseph Andrews and Tom Jones, thereby allowing happy marriages for both (Sergeant Atkinson's love for his foster-sister Amelia might be seen as a further attenuation of overtly declared incest). By the time of M. G. Lewis's late-century Gothic novel, *The Monk*, both incest and gender indeterminacy are made pathological through association with the demonic.

Incest and cross-dressing represent extreme instances of the eighteenth-century novel's use of sexuality to symbolize disruptive powers that are indulged and finally repressed, sometimes by assimilating them, as here, to customary structures like marriage, or occasionally, as in *Clarissa*, by violently expelling them by way of death. As we have seen, the working out of the courtship plot in *The Reform'd Coquet* offers a relatively benign expression of such potentially transgressive energies. Davys's distinctive treatment of two other elements repeatedly used by Defoe – doubles and secrets – further supports her concluding endorsement of traditional hierarchies. Narrative point of view is crucial here. In Defoe's novels, the first-person perspective means that all information about doubles and secrets comes filtered through the protagonists' writing (leaving later critics to debate its reliability or unreliability). While Moll and Roxana present the Governess and Amy as their instruments, the corresponding figures in *The Reform'd Coquet* appear as discrete characters, their separation from the protagonists evident in their functioning more as guide figures than as doubles. The third-person narrative enhances this divestment of power by assigning control to the author rather than to the protagonist. The various turns of the plot, in corresponding fashion, exclude both the reader and Amoranda from knowledge of the secret identity of the mentor her guardian has placed on watch over her: the supposedly aged Formator is in fact the young and handsome Alanthus, the husband long designed for her by her uncle, Mr. Traffic. As he unveils his true self, Alanthus offers Amoranada two reasons for the deception: the advice he had to offer would, he assumed, be "better received from an old mouth, than a young one; next, I thought you would be more open and free, in declaring your real Sentiments of every thing to me, as I was, than as I am" (159). The revelation that she has been covertly monitored throughout the novel by her intended husband retrospectively exposes Amoranda's exuberant self-sufficiency as a sad illusion.

Davys's novel thus ends with a denial of the female agency it seemed initially to celebrate. The reversal conveys a sobering message: even when women believe themselves to be "open and free," they are subject to masculine supervision. The author's prefatorial hint that she feels beholden to readers somewhat prepares for this abrupt shift from defiance to deference. But the imperfect integration of authorial commentary and character motivation means that the potentially ironic twinning of female writer and heroine – equally objects of critical male scrutiny – remains embryonic, making the conclusion seem both rushed and forced. One of the many innovations of Samuel Richardson's first novel, *Pamela*, appears in his softening this transition from rebellion to compliance by allowing us to experience it from the perspective of the protagonist (whose combination of strength of character and susceptibility recalls that of heroines like Amoranda, despite the obvious class differences). Another distinguishing feature is the access he offers to the heroine's motivations, only some of which she herself fully recognizes. In reworking the materials of earlier fiction, in short, Richardson adapts elements from a broad range of antecedent texts using as his focal consciousness a young woman made vulnerable by the recent death of her mistress to the sexual predations of the heir, Mr. B.

The scope of Richardson's borrowings is impressively diverse: at one extreme, he draws for his representation of the heroine's perils on libertine elements (explicit and muted) in Aphra Behn, Daniel Defoe, Delarivier Manley, Eliza Haywood, and Mary Davys; at the other, he builds on the overt celebration of social and religious hierarchies in the so-called pious fictions of writers like Penelope Aubin and Elizabeth Rowe. As we shall see, traces of these sources are easily detectable in *Pamela*'s treatment of issues relating to identity and social mobility, broadly expressed through patterns of secrecy, doubles, and financial exchange; in echoing techniques for depicting moments of crisis through the contraventions of boundaries (both of behavior in cross-dressing and of space and domesticity in kidnapping and exile); and in the self-conscious awareness of its status as fiction. But Richardson's novel also differs fundamentally from its predecessors, a difference so strongly marked that the repertoire of genre features he established quickly became definitive of the form. Disentangling the inherited from the newly articulated, however, is complicated by his personal involvement in managing the reception and reputation of his work. As numbers of critics have recently argued, neither the formative influence of *Pamela* nor its huge financial success was entirely spontaneous. The business acumen Richardson had honed as a successful printer allowed him adroitly to manipulate market conditions within a rapidly changing material world and in the process to advance his own reform-minded fiction as alternative to a popular literature he wanted to discredit. This alertness to audience needs, habits, and expectations meant that *Pamela*, as Thomas Keymer and Peter Sabor document, "provoked and enabled a deluge of print," setting the terms for at least two generations of novelistic practice.[3]

The tremendous success of the novel, of course, required more than Richardson's entrepreneurial skills. The initial letters attest to the qualities that made it so attractive to its original audience, in particular the mutually reinforcing observation of social circumstance and individual character. Pamela's correspondence opens in the unsettled period following the death of the mistress who had provided her, as she writes to her father, with "Qualifications above my Degree."[4] The mistress's death represents a potentially catastrophic loss of patronage, given the inability of Pamela's family to support her and a contemporary culture of dependence that made service, and not the self-direction Defoe celebrates, the only respectable route to class mobility. Enclosed in the letter she sends to her parents are the "Four golden Guineas, besides lesser Money, which were in my old Lady's Pocket when she dy'd"(12), a substantial sum pressed on her by the heir Mr. B in a gesture we might assume was ceremonially linked to death rituals were it not for the postscript Pamela adds after she is startled by his unexpected reappearance in "my late Lady's Dressing-room." In it, she recounts that she instinctively "went to hide the Letter in my Bosom"(12), but he confiscated and then read what she had written.

His intrusion changes a finished record of filial intimacy – a sixteen-year-old girl's outpouring to her parents of "great Trouble, and some Comfort" (11) – into an open-ended seduction narrative. B's seizing of the letter initiates a pattern of textual appropriation that throughout the novel emphasizes the vulnerability of Pamela's place in the world. Using the technique he later described as "writing to the moment" to convey her provisional status, Richardson situates his reader within an unfolding experience, with just enough of a lag between immediacy and retrospective recreation to allow for the heroine's imperfect attempts to impose order on embarrassment. B's smooth flattery of Pamela after he reads her letter appears all the more specious in the face of her subsequent halting recognition that her own vocabulary of deference and apology to him had been misplaced. As she writes to her parents in the postscript to the intercepted letter: "I said, Pray your Honour forgive me; – yet I know not for what. For he was always dutiful to his Parents; and why should he be angry, that I was so to mine!" (12). These subversive claims to equivalency with him will later play an important part in the novel's adjustment of individual virtue to social hierarchies. More immediately, however, her father, recognizing B's intentions as predatory and hinting at the conventional link between social aspiration and female sexuality, expresses his fear that she may be "brought to any thing dishonest or wicked, by being set so above yourself" (13).

Twelve months and many presents later, Mr. Andrews's suspicions are confirmed when Pamela is assaulted in the summer-house as she does her needlework. B's attempt to assert his prerogatives as a gentry male entitled to possession of the young women of his household (prerogatives vigorously supported in the later Lincolnshire section of the novel by both the servant Mrs. Jewkes and the neighbor Sir Simon Darnford) foregrounds the novel's hitherto submerged contrast of residual and emergent social structures, a contrast that pits traditional codes of behavior against the individualist values of bourgeois domesticity. Pamela responds to the attack, however, not by making an outright claim to personal integrity but by decrying B's failure to live up to gentlemanly standards, a tactic that condemns libertinism as the negative expression of gentry mores while at the same time retaining the positive connotations of good birth. This preservation of social distinctions in theory if not practice has an individual complement as well: room is left for B's eventual reform by making him a curiously ineffectual seducer who yields almost immediately to Pamela's distress:

> I sobb'd and cry'd most sadly. What a foolish Hussy you are, said he, have I done you any Harm? – Yes, Sir, said I, the greatest Harm in the World: You have taught me to forget myself, and what belongs to me, and have lessen'd the Distance that Fortune has made between us, by demeaning yourself, to be so free to a poor Servant. Yet, Sir, said I, I will be so bold to say, I am honest, tho' poor; And if you was a Prince, I would not be otherwise.   (23–4)

Nonplussed by this outburst, B sends her away, ordering that she "keep this Matter secret" and "putting some Gold in my Hand" to make "Amends for the Fright I put you to" (23–4). Pamela, now cognizant (as she had not been immediately after her mistress's death) that acceptance of this gift would be "like taking Earnest" (24), a kind of promissory note for a later seduction, refuses the exchange, and then compounds her resistance by promptly disobeying his other request and telling her protector, the housekeeper Mrs. Jervis, what has happened.

In the brief span of these opening letters, Richardson sets in motion a revision of the conventional seduction plot that gives access to Pamela's inward responses while also pointing to their often inexact fit with her outward ones. As in Defoe, secrets and sexuality are integral to the development of this plot, but here their interconnections are productive of a more complex tension between discordant social visions. Michael McKeon's suggestion that the eighteenth century witnesses the migration of "honour" from a hallmark of aristocratic maleness to an internalized sign of female virtue helps to explain the novel's apparently incompatible values.[5] For the well-born Sir Simon Darnford and initially for B, the inheritance of honor by the privileged has as its complement a view of social inferiors as mere bodies. Ironically, both the older generation Mr. Andrews and his wicked opposite, the Lincolnshire housekeeper and jailer, Mrs. Jewkes, also define selfhood physically, though to very different ends. Pamela's parents declare that they would rather see her "all cover'd with Rags" (14) or even dead than dishonored, while Mrs. Jewkes enthusiastically accepts her vocation as B's pander, confident of his absolute entitlement to pursue his desires regardless of their consequences for others. Pamela, by contrast, petitions for the right to self-direction, requesting of B that "whatever you intend by me, let my Assent be that of a free Person, mean as I am, and not of a sordid Slave, who is to be threatened and frightened into a Compliance" (139). This is not, of course, to suggest that she discounts either her parents' emphasis on virginity or B's on the prerogatives of birth. But she *does* resist unthinking compliance with their contrary terms: returning home, as her parents wish, would confirm the determining power of existing structures over individual preference, while capitulating to B would verify his sense of class entitlement. In staying, she testifies to a fuller, more modern understanding of honor that respects her capacity for choice, expressed here through both physical and intellectual ownership of self. Resolutely maintaining this internally validated sense of worth, she continues throughout the period of her long "trial" essentially unchanged; B, on the other hand, undergoes a conversion marked by the acknowledgment that his attraction was always, even if unbeknownst to him, to that deeply embedded virtue.

What enables this turn (and testifies to it) is the novel's epistolary form. From early in the narrative, the process and products of writing are bound up with issues relating to being, both literal and metaphorical. Pamela's hiding of her letters by stitching them into her clothing, for example, strongly associates body and written record as manifestations of identity. Under threat, as hers is, that identity must be at once declared and kept secret. This double orientation to the expression and restraining of selfhood points to the ambivalences of the epistolary mode more generally: as revelatory of individual consciousness, letters are provisional and private; as acts of correspondence, they are social and communicative. As missives to be read by a recipient whose reaction cannot be controlled, they also expose the dangers of misinterpretation. The key limit for the novel in letters (hilariously developed in Henry Fielding's *Shamela*, a burlesque treatment of *Pamela*) is its restriction to an individual point of view, a difficulty Richardson overcomes here by finding other routes for conveying information to Pamela, including eavesdropping and crossed, misdirected, or stolen letters, and in his next novel *Clarissa*, by multiplying the numbers of correspondents and playing off their disparate observations against one another. Its strengths flow from the same source. Pamela's "writing to the moment" authenticates her grappling with contingencies she cannot control. Transcribed conversations with B also capture the glint of Pamela's intelligence and her apparently irrefutable logic, often by testifying indirectly to a highly subversive view of language as an empowering force independent of class restrictions.

The distinctive features of letters – documents written by and exchanged between individuals – are closely echoed in the novel's representation of character. B and Pamela appear as unique persons and social beings, with their eventual marriage figuring the compromise between these two impulses in ways that relate metaphorically to other patriarchal constructs of gender, family, and government. In genre terms, *Pamela* similarly assimilates and supersedes elements drawn from fable, romance, drama, and amatory and pious fiction. Two leading traits thus distinguish the novel in letters: on the one hand, the immediacy of the links between the formulation, transmission, and reception of thoughts and feelings; on the other, the intimacy of the compact between letter writer and readers – both imagined and real. On occasion, however, Richardson deliberately undermines this proximity through distancing devices, including direct addresses to the reader. Just prior to Pamela's exile to Lincolnshire, for example, the editor steps in to inform us that her "Tryals were not yet over" and produces as evidence the previously withheld information (still unknown to Pamela) that the letters she assumed had been carried immediately to her parents were previously opened and read by B: "Thus every way," the narrator intones, "was the poor Virgin beset: And the Whole will shew the base Arts of designing Men to gain their wicked Ends; and how much it behoves the Fair Sex to stand upon their Guard against their artful

Contrivances, especially where Riches and Power conspire against Innocence and a low Estate" (92).

The shift from individual girl to archetypal "poor Virgin" at this critical juncture recalls the transition from person to precept announced in the title *Pamela; or, Virtue Rewarded*. That the actual novel far exceeds in complexity this conduct-book didacticism is due in part to Richardson's steady enlargement of focus to encourage scrutiny of the variables of interpretation: not simply what happened, but how perception of it might be altered by changes in place, time, and character. In accordance with this process, repetition and recapitulation periodically stall the forward impulsion typical of "writing to the moment" with its enhancing of tension through the register of passing events. Disruptions of this ongoing chronicle become increasingly frequent after Pamela agrees to relinquish to B the secret cache of papers Mrs. Jewkes has discovered through her keyhole spying. From this point forward, narrative momentum steadily slows to accommodate written and oral recapitulation: on the one hand, Pamela orders and summarizes her previous writings in preparation for his inspection of them and, on the other, she and B discuss the letters' content and implications at each of the staged releases of the documents. Over the course of these repeated returns to the past, a slow transfer of authority takes place: from Pamela to B, from writer to reader, from female paragon to reformed gentry male. We have seen how Daniel Defoe uses repetition in *Moll Flanders* and *Roxana* to signal transitional moments in his protagonists' lives as they shed one assumed identity for another, often with the intent of preserving independence by concealing their real histories. Here, by contrast, repetition *disables* secrecy since the various iterations follow from her decision to submit the confidential letters and journal to the scrutiny of B. With the end of secrecy comes the end of Pamela's spirited defense of an intact, separate identity (as the course of Defoe's novels with their converse emphasis on the connections of secrecy and selfhood could have predicted).

Richardson further emphasizes the shift from private writing to social reading by offering multiple versions of single events: in one of the most important of these, Pamela's contemplated suicide, we have access to her original account, to the moment when she unstitches that account from the "Under-coat" where she has concealed her journal, to the précis of this "vast Quantity" (236) of papers, to the handing over of the docketed papers to B, and to his walking through the garden recreating, as he reads, her first transcription of the scene. Pamela had initially feigned drowning by throwing her clothes into the pond, then when momentarily overwhelmed by her failure to escape had considered suicide, until a "Ray of Grace" convinces her that "God can touch his [B's] Heart in an Instant" (172–3). In a testament to the reformative powers of narrative, B finds himself so moved by her turn away from sin that he himself considers at this point whether he "will endeavour to defy the World, and the World's Censures, and make my *Pamela* amends, if it be in the Power of my whole Life, for all the Hardships I have inflicted upon her" (241). After their marriage, continued references to the nexus of pond and garden maintain its significance as a site of mutual temptation, redemption, and reform.

The beginning of B's conversion not only marks the slow diminution of Pamela's agency and independence, but also a tonal change, product in part of the eclipse of idiomatic expression by standard English (Pamela's language becomes noticeably more proper as the novel unfolds), in part of the expansion of audience. Although she continues to address her writings to her parents, the knowledge that B will ultimately read them assigns him a powerful mediatory influence. The tacit pressure he exerts over her written representations is paralleled in his visual management of her person. Thus when Mr. Andrews unexpectedly arrives in Lincolnshire, "full of Grief, to see his daughter, for he fears she is seduced" (292), B informs his assembled friends he wishes to "make you all witness to their first Interview" (293) and then without telling Pamela of her father's presence, stages the reconciliation of father and daughter. The urge to make the private public appears again in his response to Mr. Andrews's concern that he lacks the appropriate dress for attendance at chapel. B begins by gently chastising him – "I thought that you knew that the outward Appearance was nothing. I wish I had as good a Habit inwardly, as you have" – and then re-literalizes "habit" by providing his future father-in-law with a "whole Suit" (312) of clothes from his own wardrobe. The next day, Mr. Andrews participates officially in the Sunday services, performing well enough, Pamela reports, that Lady Jones "whisper'd me, That good Men were fit for all Companies" (314). The scene nicely captures the confluence of a number of important themes relating to the novel's depiction of individual and social identity. Most broadly, it touches on the aspirational impulses of readers who, having followed Pamela's struggles against B's presumptive right to tyrannize, may wish vicariously to experience what seems the sudden elevation of the heroine and her family. Richardson, however, is at some pains to note that status inconsistency has not been overcome by any revolutionary assertions of equality. Instead, the exceptional inward virtue of the Andrews family validates their absorption by the gentry, with the passing reference to Mr. Andrews's having taught Psalmody "in the little School he so unsuccessfully set up, at the Beginning of his Misfortunes, before he took to hard Labour" (313) further softening the apparently unprecedented spike in the family's status by pointing to earlier institutional ties.

The social compact enacted here – in the reconciliation between Pamela and her father, in his re-garbing, and in the gathering of neighboring worthies for Sunday services – confirms the control B exercises as a result of his restored moral authority. Each of these instances importantly involves an audience observing the adjustments he effects in the spheres of family, class, and religion. This element of display recalls the argument of the influential Marxist historian, E. P. Thompson, that a carefully managed "theatre of the great" in mid-eighteenth-century England allowed patrician society to maintain its privileges through "cultural hegemony" rather than brute force.[6] The relation between these and earlier scenes of performance in the novel verifies the connection between order and spectacle, dramatized in *Pamela* by Richardson's technique of repeating clustered images. On the two occasions when the heroine readies herself to leave Bedfordshire and return to her parents, for instance, Mrs. Jervis arranges for B secretly to observe preparations that in both instances revolve around adjustments in clothing. Pamela's exchange of her elaborate dress for the plain one better suited to her future condition as laborer's daughter, accompanied by commentary on the symbolic resonances of her "metamorphos'd" (55) appearance, confirm her integrity and (particularly since B is cast as a concealed spy) its superiority to his libertinism. Her downwardly mobile episodes of virtue displayed through change of dress have a negative correlative in B's disguising of himself as the servant Nan in pursuit of a bungled attempt to rape Pamela. *His* dressing down in an act of class and sexual reversal renders him powerless. It is only when he invites Pamela shortly afterwards to walk with him in the Lincolnshire garden and, beside the pond where she earlier considered suicide, asks her to tell him "what you think I ought to do, and what you would have me do" (213) that the recovery of proper authority can begin. The process involves each articulating what might logically be considered the self-interested position of the other: Pamela urges B to "regard the World's Opinion, and avoid doing any thing disgraceful to your own Birth and Fortune" (214), while he in turn declares, "I have known in this agreeable Hour more sincere Pleasure, than I have experienc'd in all the guilty Tumults that my desiring Soul put me into, in the Hopes of possessing you on my own Terms" (218).

Despite the rapprochement signaled by this exchange (one given additional weight by its position at the end of the first volume), B continues for some time to maintain that he "cannot marry" (218) her. It takes another repetition of her experience by him fully to effect his conversion: the reading of Pamela's journal as he walks by the pond and through the Lincolnshire garden, referred to above. One further symmetrically conceived pairing cements B's commitment to virtue: as Pamela travels back to her parents, she receives a letter from B asking her to return. The coupling of settings is appropriate: he reads her account as he walks through the garden, emblem of the power he possesses through estate ownership; she his letter, while on the road, the eighteenth-century novel's favored metaphor for the processes of change. Her return and the marriage that follows situate the possibilities for virtue within a gentry order renewed by its commitment to overt displays of moral authority as B insists that others bend to his will to have Pamela treated with the respect due to his wife. The strong resistance of his sister, Lady Davers, offers B further opportunities to prove his mettle while also serving as a target for the wit that Pamela can no longer direct at B himself. As in other eighteenth-century novels, the heroine's absorption into a gendered economy that places husband over wife makes her earlier energy redundant; here that energy is channeled into the verbal pummeling of Lady Davers and her nephew Jackey, while the sexual suspense is redirected to the subplot of B's former relationship with Sally Godfrey and their child whom B maintains.

Clarissa or The History of a Young Lady

Pamela, in combination with Richardson's second novel, *Clarissa*, is used by Nancy K. Miller to outline two paradigmatic structures for women's experience in eighteenth-century fiction: the first, as we have seen, traces a pattern of ascent as the heroine's rise in social status and consolidation of identity are rewarded with a concluding marriage. The second, as the discussion following will document, charts a reverse trajectory of descent from personal integrity and an established worldly position, through violation, to death. While Pamela advances from a position of near invisibility as servant to become the subject of neighborhood accolades and the manager of gentry reform, Clarissa's standing as her grandfather's beloved heir has even prior to the novel's opening brought her unwelcome attention. This public prominence surrounds Clarissa's singularity with distinctive, often dangerous, connotations. The first letter from her closest friend, Anna Howe, in requesting details of the most recent "disturbances that have happened in your family," hints at some of these in remarking that "it must hurt you to become the subject of the public talk," while also expressing an entitlement to knowledge that verges on possessiveness: "it is impossible but that whatever relates to a young lady, whose distinguished merits have made her the public care, should engage everybody's attention."[7] These allusions to both the negative and positive aspects of fame set the groundwork for the unfolding of the plot and introduce the problem of exemplarity as a key ethical and social issue.

That Clarissa's remarkable virtue should be the source of the family "disturbances" is an irony raised by Anna's letter and subsequently deepened by our delayed recognition that the moment of the novel's opening marks the end of Clarissa's ability to continue with the good works that formerly brought her renown. Significantly, this critical turn depends not on anything she has done, but on the actions of a constellation of characters motivated by malignant self-interest. The libertine, Lovelace, attracted by the challenge of her beauty and reputation, had mistakenly been formally introduced to her sister, Arabella, as a possible suitor; in extricating himself from that entanglement, he humiliates Arabella and then her brother, James, who seize the opportunity to league against Clarissa, whom they already resent because of the preference shown her in their grandfather's will. While Clarissa might aspire, in her words, to "slid[e] through life to the end of it unnoted" (40), the sheer bulk of the letters that make up this epistolary novel testifies to the expanding circle of those given access to the intimate details of her kidnapping, rape, and death. With her privacy destroyed and death imminent, she attempts through the designing of her own coffin and the gathering together and circulating of the collected letters to secure at least posthumous control over her representation. If not an example to be followed, she can stand as a warning to others. But what kind of warning is presented by the spectacle of undeserved suffering, especially of one who has so assiduously questioned the grounds of both her own actions and those of others?

In *Clarissa*, to a far greater extent than in *Pamela*, Richardson complicates the supposed transparency of the first-person point of view by raising in our minds questions about individual motivation that even the characters themselves cannot reliably answer. Our capacity to puzzle out the relation between intention and action that access to the thoughts of all the letter writers makes possible serves as foil to their more limited grasp of events. The comparative and evaluative reflection demanded of readers, in turn, has as its negative counterpart in the novel the various degrees of single-mindedness possessed by those unable to empathize with the persecuted heroine. Arabella, for instance, falls in with James's avaricious plans for advancement because, like him, she begrudges their sister's unsought distinction and recognizes that both their parents and uncles are manipulable. Under the cloak of family interests, they plot first to marry Clarissa off to Solmes, a man she rightly despises, and then after her escape from Harlowe-place, to ensure her permanent alienation and exile. The primary correspondents, Clarissa and Lovelace and their favored addressees, Anna Howe and Belford, have a speculative inwardness that the secondary characters lack. But in probing the motives of others, the principals also reveal unacknowledged or suppressed facets of their own natures that our comparative reading of all the letters allows us to comprehend. At times, these layers of involution threaten to undermine any possibility of genuine self- or readerly knowledge. But because the questioning Richardson encourages extends well beyond individual characterization to encompass larger social structures, in particular that of the family, the novel does finally suggest alternatives to the conflicting requirements of autonomy, on the one hand, and unthinking conformity, on the other.

In both *Pamela* and *Clarissa*, family has a determining influence on individual behavior. Ruth Perry describes family relations as the "master narrative" of contemporary writing, the matrix within which she and other critics locate such models for thinking about fiction as the courtship plot, mentors, siblings, inheritance, generational conflict, and the newly important domestic sphere.[8] Significant social and economic changes, as well, are registered in the novel's attention to the diminished importance of blood as opposed to conjugal relationships, of the given over the chosen family, of dynastic over companionate marriages. In their unstable compound of aristocratic and bourgeois impulses, the Harlowes epitomize the strains of their historical moment, revealing in their attitudes to property in particular the difficult transition from given hierarchies to a more self-directed modernity. Possessed of great wealth but seeking the additional cachet of "rank and title" (77), Clarissa's two uncles and her father have decided to pool their resources and then to augment their holdings by forcing Clarissa's marriage to Solmes, whose estates border theirs. James, the chief beneficiary of these ambitions to secure a peerage, draws on the worst aspects of the new monied and old patrician orders to further his selfish ends. Since the growing acceptance of spousal choice for women reduces the dynastic value of daughters, making them in his crude formulation, nothing more than "chickens brought up for other men's tables" (77), he insists that Clarissa accept the arcane terms of an arranged marriage despite her personal, physical, and moral aversion to Solmes. Traditionally, of course, such arrangements would be the father's prerogative, not the brother's, a fact that alerts us to the Harlowes' complicity with James's twisting of patriarchal ideals to fit his self-interested nature. The departure from precedent also highlights one of the novel's central ironies: the person who most resoundingly articulates and embodies the best aspects of the old ideals is Clarissa herself (even as she is at the same time their pre-eminent victim).

The broad parallels between the social aspirations of the Harlowe and Lovelace families make additionally futile Clarissa's attempts to honor inherited principles while remaining true to her own self. She has leagued against her the combined forces of an autocratic father, a mother whose ineffectual peacemaking encourages collusion in the harrying of her daughter, intense sibling rivalry, and a brother who cunningly plots to usurp his elders' power. The maneuvers of Lord M, his two half-sisters and his nieces to secure a title for their relative Lovelace cast further doubts on the aristocratic codes of probity and filial authority by which Clarissa defines herself. Both families, in short, despite their differences of birth, scheme in highly interested ways to achieve the public status that membership in the nobility offers. And while Lovelace proclaims his absolute distinction from the Harlowes, his victim recognizes their mutual entanglement in her persecution. Alienated from her family and trapped in London after Lovelace tricks her into leaving Harlowe-place with him, she charges him with having become the "*cruel implement of my brother's causeless vengeance*" (935).

The view of women as pawns in their families' corporate advancement is deeply rooted in a misogyny that, although differently articulated by James and Lovelace, binds these two together and aligns them with a cohort ranging from irredeemably dissolute libertines to the ostensibly principled Harlowe cousin, Morden, whose deferred return from the Continent deprives Clarissa of a possible protector after she leaves Harlowe-place. The libertines' contempt for women finds expression in the rake's code with its assumption of an absolute male entitlement to sexual possession. Lovelace's early declaration that "to carry off such a girl" as Clarissa would be a "triumph over the whole sex" (147) suggests further that male solidarity is at least as powerful a motive for his predatory behavior as individual desire. The letters he writes to Belford reinforce this sense of a gendered complicity realized through the performance of a self – or multiple selves – for his friend's admiration. And because the emergence of Lovelace's private thoughts is deferred, they appear additionally shocking when they are finally revealed. The opening volumes of the novel are dominated by Clarissa's struggles to reconcile an intrinsic sense of self-worth and her own partially acknowledged attraction to Lovelace with her father's prohibition against communication with him and her brother's threatened violence. It is only in the third volume (of the first edition's seven) that Lovelace's actual intentions erupt into the text as he triumphantly crows to Belford that having effected Clarissa's removal from her family, she is now "securely mine! – mine for ever!" (386). When Morden finally reaches England, too late to prevent the drugging and rape of his cousin, he is thwarted in his attempt to take the moral high road by Lovelace's reminder that he too is a "man of gallantry" (1280). After some verbal sparring, as Lovelace relates, "a fresh bottle of Burgundy and another of Champagne being put upon the table, we sat down in good humour after all this blustering, in order to enter closer into the particulars of the case" (1286), particulars Lovelace carefully edits to palliate his responsibility. Morden, now confirmed as "one of *us*" (1291), then writes to Clarissa to "condole those misfortunes which have occasioned so unhappy a difference between you and the rest of your family" and to recommend that "forgetting past things, let us look forward" (1299), reinforcing Anna's earlier suggestion to her that, "since what is past cannot be helped, let us look forward" (1043).

Morden's and Anna's advice contains the defining elements of an alternate novel ending, a novel like Richardson's *Pamela* or Frances Burney's *Evelina* in which reconciling the personal and the social leads to the making of a new family through marriage. At that point, the "forgetting" of earlier offenses (B's attempted rape or Lord Belmont's abandonment of his pregnant wife) inaugurates a forward-looking perspective and the presumption of the characters' continuing happiness allows the contented reader to close the book, satisfied that virtue has been truly rewarded. The frustration of such expectations for *Clarissa*, however, is by this point so entrenched that Morden's hollow attempts to patch over a terrible violation in the name of family solidarity appear entirely misguided. Comparison of Richardson's first two novels confirms that careful plotting has laid the groundwork for these contrary endings. Both works employ the same broad strategy for testing the resilience of the heroine: exile her from the protection of the nuclear family, provide negative and positive substitute figures, and then observe how the documenting of her experiences contributes to a deepening self-awareness and commitment to the preservation of an uncontaminated version of social order. But the challenges faced by Pamela are hugely aggravated in the later novel: Mrs. Sinclair, for instance, resembles Mrs. Jewkes in her antipathy to innocence, but the former heads a household of prostitutes bent on Clarissa's degradation and possesses a power over Lovelace that leads to her being creditably described as "the true mother of [his] mind" (1433). And while Mrs. Norton is, like Mrs. Jervis, an alternate mother and Anna a "more than sister" (1312), neither of these surrogate family members acts decisively to help Clarissa, in part because each is divided between loyalty to her and an instinct for finding the middle ground that Clarissa's absolutism, in its own right as all-encompassing as Lovelace's, disallows. In the moral and social economy of this novel, the principals' inability to co-ordinate the demands of self-knowledge with the expectations of the larger world means that Clarissa and Lovelace must die. Those who remain may be distinctly less compelling, but as the final flurry of marriages documented in Belford's "Conclusion" suggests, negotiation is a condition of survival.

The structure of the two novels underscores the importance of such compromise by following the critical moment in the heroines' worldly fortunes – B's turn to virtue in *Pamela*, rape and then death in *Clarissa* – with protracted denouements that minutely note the success or failure of concession. In *Pamela*,

this entails some forgiveness of B for his attempted seductions and much attention to the initially grudging and finally enthusiastic acceptance of Pamela by
B's sister, Lady Davers, and by the neighboring gentry. The shift of focus from
Pamela as personality to Pamela as social being within an expanding web of
relationships supports the representation of marriage as an inclusive figure for
the ascendancy of traditional values. The constriction of Clarissa's experience
of time and space after the rape has (in the short term) an equal but opposite
effect. From the moment that she leaves Harlowe-place, through her shelter-
ing in London where Lovelace installs her at Mrs. Sinclair's brothel, her flight
to Hampstead, her departure from there with what she mistakenly believes
are Lovelace's noble relatives but are actually Mrs. Sinclair's disguised minions, to her return to the brothel where she is drugged and then raped, each
of Clarissa's entrapments in rooms and houses helps to evoke her psychic as
well as physical isolation. Ultimately, that isolation will be transfigured into an
inwardness that renders the claims of the world so entirely secondary that her
own mind, shaped by the dictates of Scripture, becomes the exclusive arbiter
of meaning. She thus counters Lovelace's offer of marriage and his plea that no
one need know of the rape by replying that he has "Ruined me in my *own* eyes,
and that is the same to me, as if *all the world* knew it" (909). Yet, at the same
time, she continues to respect an institutional ideal to which most others in the
novel merely pay lip-service. For the sake of his "ancient and splendid house,"
she will not allow Lovelace to marry one whom he has "levelled with the dirt
of the street, and classed with the vilest of her sex" (912).

Her commitment to abstract principles that only she unequivocally hon-
ors and her correspondingly steady retreat from definition by the customary
signposts of novelistic experience – space, time, and narrative – are fully in
evidence in the famous "father's house" letter that Clarissa sends to Lovelace
to deflect his pleas for an interview with her. In it, she writes that she is traveling to her father's house, a reference that he, in common with all to whom
he shows the letter, interprets literally, but that Clarissa intends allegorically
to signal her hoped-for arrival in heaven. This turn to a language that prefers
sacred to secular meaning is echoed in her self-designed coffin. Decorated with
iconographic emblems and Scriptural tags, it provides a culminating figure for
one strand of the novel's critical exploration of language. The questioning of
the relation between language and meaning is impressively various. It takes
in the central contrasts of Clarissa's commitment to clarity and singleness of
purpose with Lovelace's delight in plots, stratagems, and inventions and the
setting of her "standard" English against others' vernacular usages (from Lord
M's tags and proverbs, through the accidental lapses into low expressions by
Mrs. Sinclair's minions, to the more complex secret code that Lovelace and

Belford use in their correspondence). It is given material form in the torn fragments of Clarissa's "mad papers," written after the rape and reproduced as type running aslant the page. Most plangent, however, in one of the longest novels in English, is the brevity with which both Clarissa's rape and her death are communicated: the former, through Lovelace's notice, "And now Belford, I can go no farther. The affair is over. Clarissa lives" (883), the latter, through Belford's note to Lovelace: "I have only to say at present – Thou wilt do well to take a tour to Paris; or wherever else thy destiny shall lead thee!!!" (1359).

In the event, Lovelace is killed in a duel with Morden, a stark denial of the hope expressed in Clarissa's will that her executor, Belford, will be able "to promote peace with, and suppress resentments in every one" (1417–18) and a further contravention of her faith in the power of example. Yet the existence of the collected letters is presumptive evidence of a more diffuse realization of her ethical commitment to making the hidden visible. In *Pamela*, momentum slows in the novel's latter stages as an expanding circle of readers for particular letters marks the folding of the private into a social domain whose meanings the reformed B both illustrates and controls. Here, the gesture in the direction of collectivity occurs through Clarissa's will: by charging Belford as executor with the gathering of the letters, she makes his earlier literal translation for her benefit of the secret, coded correspondence with Lovelace the forerunner of a wider, legally sanctioned, and (arguably) more disinterested rendition of her experience as a warning for other young women tempted to resist paternal authority.

The History of the Adventures of Joseph Andrews and Amelia

Henry Fielding seems in many ways less sanguine about the power of example than Richardson, or perhaps simply more inclined to tincture his praise for exemplarity with a measure of irony. While *Joseph Andrews* opens with the flat statement that "Examples work more forcibly on the Mind than Precepts," the claim subsequently withers under the force of the author's arch consideration of two recent cases in point, the actual life of the actor, playwright, theater manager, and poet laureate, Colley Cibber, and the invented one of Pamela (the egregious self-promotion of *An Apology for the Life of Mr. Colley Cibber … Written by Himself* is echoed in the mocking title of the Richardson parody, *An Apology for the Life of Mrs. Shamela Andrews*).[9] Fielding's tactic here – assertion followed by qualification – is central to his fiction. It is most broadly evident in the way that his novels gain leverage from an earlier work (or event, as we will see in *Tom Jones*'s use of the 1745 Jacobite rebellion): *Shamela* and *Joseph Andrews* use *Pamela* as foil, *Amelia*, although in different ways, *Clarissa*. Intriguingly, the final works of both writers also experiment with their rival's major themes, so that *Amelia* adapts *Clarissa*'s inwardness, while Richardson's *Sir Charles Grandison* reworks the national concerns of *Tom Jones*. Like *Pamela* and *Clarissa*, Fielding's *Joseph Andrews* and *Amelia* are also connected as more and less sunny approaches to the possible relation between the individual and the social. In the "comic Epic-Poem in Prose" (4) that is *Joseph Andrews*, this is positively expressed as the ideal conjunction of the "Good-Humour and Benevolence" (5) exhibited by the hero and a number of fathers and father figures, including Abraham Adams, Mr. Wilson, and the third-person narrator.

The omniscient third-person perspective is an essential element in Fielding's survey of various levels of authority ranging from the wholly legitimate to the corruptly assumed and administered. His own aristocratic connections (as opposed to Defoe and Richardson's bourgeois ones) make him a proponent of civic humanism, a discourse derived from Machiavelli's republican ideal and widely supported in the early eighteenth century. The central figure in civic humanist politics is that of the landowner, a gentleman whose admired impartiality is a product of good birth, classical education, possession of real (not monied or mobile) property, and reasoned control over the passions. Such gentlemen assume a directive role in what Alexander Pope calls in his poem, *An Essay on Man*, the "Vast chain of being" (I.237), an inclusive figure for the ordering of the universe in which all created things fulfill their divinely assigned functions. The landed estate operates as a microcosmic instance of this macrocosmic principle and hence the restorations of identity at the end of each of Fielding's novels are accompanied by the protagonists' re-establishing themselves in the country. The opposite of a bounded rural existence is the fluid, urban one that *Joseph Andrews* alludes to when it replaces the figure of the "chain of being" with the "Ladder" of "Dependance" where "those bordering nearly on each other, to-wit the lowest of the High, and the highest of the Low, often change their Parties according to Place and Time; for those who are People of Fashion in one place, are often People of no Fashion in another" (141). The emphasis here on the mutable over the stable, the diverse over the uniform, and the eccentric over the universal accords with the terms set out by Bernard Mandeville's *Fable of the Bees* where the notion that "private vices" generate "public benefits" finds paradigmatic expression not in the estate, but the mechanistic hive.[10]

Fielding's opposition to this provisional understanding of identity and his support for civic humanist values are flagged for readers of *Joseph Andrews* in a variety of ways: in the control exercised over the world of the novel by the obtrusive, omniscient narrator, in the circular structure (intimating perfection) that takes the characters from country to city and back to the estate, in classical references that point to the social homogeneity of his readers, and in the allusive naming of characters. The latter is an aspect of his commitment to "describe not Men, but Manners, not an Individual, but a Species" and is typically orchestrated to align good characters with Biblical archetypes (Abraham Adams, the patriarchal innocent, or Joseph, like the son of the Biblical Jacob and Rachel, a type of male chastity), and negative ones with a prevailing defect (Lady Booby, Tom Suckbribe, Slipslop). To direct attention away from the "individual" and toward the generic, he also adapts the period's favored metaphors to narrative purposes, not only the "Vast chain of Being," but also that of "Order in Variety," pithily rendered by Alexander Pope in the phrase, "tho' all things differ, all agree."[11]

Seen from the limited perspective of particular characters (or of readers who have not yet come to the end of *Joseph Andrews*), the novel's multiple incidents of threatened rape, possible incest, false arrest, and random violence conjure a world governed by chance. But underlying this apparent chaos, Fielding emphasizes, there is a providential order directed by divine benevolence. Its textual avatar is the omniscient narrator, counterpoint to the aggressive self-interestedness of Joseph and Fanny's adversaries. Secrets, as later in *Clarissa*, provide a means of comparing ethical motives, here distinguishing the benign intentions behind the narrator's withholding of information from the damaging ones of others. In Richardson's second novel, as we have seen, all characters engage in versions of concealment, although only the iniquitous use their covert knowledge for purely selfish ends heedless of the pain of others. In *Joseph Andrews*, the wealthy indulge in clandestine pursuits (as in Lady Booby's attempted seduction of Joseph), while spying dependants like Slipslop work to feather their own nests by making themselves indispensable instruments of their social betters' corruption. But the emphasis here falls on inexpertly concealed actions (rather than on deeply buried psychological flaws as in Richardson) and, consistent with the novel's social comedy, even the wickedest stratagems are ultimately foiled.

The third-person perspective allows, in addition, for the elaboration of an entirely positive view of secrets. Their constructive possibilities are identified with the obtrusive narrator, in his role as simulacrum of divine authority. His keeping from us information vital to the conclusion – the true origin of Fanny and Joseph is only the last of a series of deferred revelations – reinforces his role as a shaping intelligence whose benevolent intentions we must accept on trust in the created world of the novel, just as it is assumed we do those of divine agency in the real world fiction imitates. The high artifice of the novel's resolution at once asserts and qualifies the parallels between invention and actuality. The unashamed reliance on coincidence, the flurry of events that precipitates the ending, the classical and romance allusions (including the hackneyed device of the strawberry birthmark by which Joseph is identified as the Wilsons' stolen child), the realignment of families through the recovery of lost children, and the explanation of the formerly unaccountable signs of the hero's gentility: each testifies to the way in which apparent differences only temporarily obscure a more fundamental "Order in Variety."

The easy fit between the mapping of human and divine relations in Pope's poetry and in *Joseph Andrews* owes much to the novel's exuberant embrace of neo-classical principles, evident in its co-ordination of precept with practice and in its organizing of experience through such figures as analogy, allegory, and satire, figures that tend to hypothesize an underlying and coherent set of values. Fielding's last novel, *Amelia*, also focuses on the singular virtue of its titular protagonist, but its approach to the problem of goodness in a corrupt world is both darker and more exploratory. This is in part a consequence of the turn from *Joseph Andrews's* didacticism toward the sentimental, a turn emphasized by *Amelia*'s contrasting of two distinct spheres: on the one hand, the masculine domain of sexual competition evident in the overlapping worlds of the military and the aristocracy; on the other hand, the feminine domain of affective relationships, both given and chosen. Family is central to the novel's comparative evaluation of these realms, and representations of women as sisters, friends, daughters, and wives help Fielding to probe the social, institutional, and gendered implications of domestic life.

Amelia herself serves as nexus for this exploration. Her affiliations exceed any other character: Booth's wife, mother of six children, daughter of Mrs. Harris, sister of Betty, foster-sister of Atkinson, surrogate daughter of Harrison, friend of Mrs. James and Mrs. Bennet/Atkinson. The internal dynamics of other families, as in the contrast between good and bad sisters and daughters (respectively, Mrs. Bennet/Atkinson and Miss Mathews), act as foils to Amelia's steady refusal to dwell on what appears to be her mother's callous disinheritance of her (eventually exposed as the forgery of the other daughter, Betty Harris). The same patience will be demonstrated in the discreet silence she maintains in the face of her husband's adultery (and his gambling, jealousy, vanity, and headstrong refusal of advice). Since only the members of her extended *chosen* family appreciate her virtues, maternal and sisterly opinion is effectively discredited, leaving marital choice and the judgments of surrogate relations as the more trustworthy gauges of individual worth. One further effect of this privileging of choice is its vindication of female self-determination. Even if the wisdom of marrying Booth despite her mother's prohibition of their relationship is not finally confirmed until after his eleventh-hour conversion, Amelia's preference for him is from the beginning ratified as a socially acceptable form of female independence. Ironically, given the once-standard critical contrast of a reactionary Fielding and a liberal Richardson, it is the former's novels that repeatedly place limits on parental control in relation to marriage, as here and in *Joseph Andrews* when the hero denies that "my Parents have any Power over my Inclinations; nor am I obliged to sacrifice my Happiness to their Whim or Ambition" (271), and in relation to female mobility, as in the rewarding of Sophia Western for escaping confinement by her father and departing for London in *Tom Jones*.

Fielding's depiction of Amelia combines direct representation of her virtues with the indirect testimony to them provided by the loyalty and admiration of her foster-brother, Atkinson, and surrogate father, Dr. Harrison. More sophisticated still is his tactic of obliquely conveying her positive qualities through Booth's partial grasp of them (a limitation made more glaring by her generous tolerance of his vanity and narcissism). Booth's blindness to Amelia's merit is compounded by his habitual shirking of responsibility and tendency to blame others for his own failures. Yet despite these faults, she maintains her faith in his better nature. Such mutually revealing interactions are a departure from the more static, quasi-allegorical characterization of *Joseph Andrews*, with its favoring of the genus or "species" over the individual. Traces of the earlier mode survive in the stock names of functionaries (Bondum the bailiff, Thrasher the magistrate) and in the depiction of Dr. Harrison as a representative patriarch of the old order. Here, as later with Villars in Frances Burney's *Evelina* and Sandford in Elizabeth Inchbald's *A Simple Story*, his vocation as priest distances him from the competitiveness, both sexual and fiscal, that defines most other men in the novel. Booth, however, is from the beginning enmeshed in that alternate realm and hence insufficiently committed to what should be his proper role as paterfamilias.

The first third of the novel is set in the prison to which Booth has been sent after justice Thrasher, who "had too great an Honour for Truth to suspect that she ever appeared in sordid Apparel; nor did he ever sully his sublime Notions of that Virtue, by uniting them with the mean Ideas of Poverty and Distress," rejects his account of stopping to help a man attacked by two "Men of Fortune" both of whom, not coincidentally, are released after paying off the arresting constable.[12] As in *Joseph Andrews*, the contrast between what should ideally be the complementary domains of law and justice highlights the perils of innocence in a corrupt world. (Smollett's *Adventures of Sir Launcelot Greaves* (1760–1) similarly exploits this disparity.) While Booth's instinctive disregard for his own safety in the attempted rescue suggests innate virtue, his growing intimacy in prison with a former acquaintance, Miss Mathews, quickly overshadows this first impression. After they exchange detailed histories – he, ruined by his profligate spending, has left his family in the country and come to the city; she traces her life up to the moment of her arrest for stabbing the man who kept her as mistress – the narrator steps in to "lock up … a Scene which we do not think proper to expose to the Eyes of the Public" (153). A week later, Miss Mathews receives a letter containing a £100 bank bill with which she purchases Booth's discharge from prison. Her expectation that they will leave together ends when a "female Spectre, all pale and breathless, rushed into the Room, and fell into Mr. *Booth's* Arms, where she immediately fainted away" (159). This first direct view of Amelia (previously encountered only through the filter of Booth's retrospective narrative to Miss Mathews) relies for its power on the contrast between her genuine distress and Miss Mathews's scripted performance of emotion. In eighteenth-century novels, fainting, like blushing, provides incontrovertible evidence of sincere feeling: as bodily registers of sensibility, neither can be willed and both reinforce the alignment of women and sensation, men and reason.

Amelia's unexpected appearance recalls to Booth's mind his family responsibilities and makes more real to him the shame of the illicit connection to Miss Mathews. But his guilt is not yet sufficient to cause a complete reformation or even to provoke a confession of his misbehavior to his wronged wife. The pattern of concealment has obvious links to the repression of information central to the plots of *Joseph Andrews* and *Tom Jones*. All three novels explore the relation between public and private spheres through linked forms of secrecy: on the one hand, dynastic or cross-generational secrets – that is, those concerned with official forms of entitlement including inheritance and birthright – and, on the other, affective secrets – that is, those that bear on emotional connections between individuals. Over the course of the novels, these two realms often appear to operate independently. But in each instance, they are merged with the concluding full disclosure of dynastic secrets and the rewarding of those individuals whose essential goodness has been formerly unrecognized or even punished.

In *Amelia*, the working out of this double structure involves more complex interconnections between plot and character than previously seen in Fielding's novels. Booth's conversation, shortly after his release from prison, with what he believes to be his closest friend, Colonel James, provides a good example: the exchange has its source in a clandestine act and generates a far-reaching sequence of events. Having accidentally encountered James in the park, Booth tells him, "I will now acquaint you with my Shame, provided you have Leisure enough to give me a Hearing: for I must open to you a long History, since I will not reveal my Fault, without informing you, at the same time, of those Circumstances, which, I hope, will in some measure excuse it" (172). The conjoining of "Shame" and "excuse" exposes Booth's attempts to wriggle out of accountability for his adultery. But Col. James has a secret of his own: he purchased Miss Mathews's favors with the £100 bank bill sent to the prison and enraged by this revelation of her free distribution of them to Booth, subsequently works in concert with the Noble Lord to ruin Booth and rape Amelia. As this episode makes clear, intrigues are most dangerous to the least guilty and, in particular, to chaste women whose innocence Fielding repeatedly equates with their being entirely unaware of illicit sexuality (thus Fanny in *Joseph Andrews* is attacked after she sets off alone at night across a field and is, providentially, rescued by Parson Adams). Amelia's assertion that "a Woman's Virtue is always her sufficient Guard" (251) restates the premise, but she, unlike Fanny, has worldly assistance that enables her to frustrate the Noble Lord's plan to assault her at a masquerade. He had previously used the same setting to trap, drug, and rape Mrs. Bennet, an attack of which she was oblivious until her husband caught the syphilis with which she had been "polluted" (299). In a gesture of female solidarity, she reveals this history to Amelia and together they concoct a plan to thwart the Noble Lord by adopting masquerade disguise and exchanging identities.

The period following this escape from ruin is marked by an escalating series of additional abuses of male power, followed by the unanticipated reappearance of Dr. Harrison and his ostentatiously rapid resolution of all difficulties: while visiting the imprisoned Booth (now reformed after reading the sermons of the seventeenth-century Anglican bishop, Isaac Barrow), Harrison fortuitously hears a death-bed confession from another inmate who exposes the forgery that disinherited Amelia. As Harrison announces to Booth, "Your Sufferings are all at an End; and Providence hath done you the Justice at last, which it will one Day or other render to all Men" (522). The reversion to Fielding's standard coupling of "Providence" and "Justice" highlights the sudden turn from the novel's earlier focus on quotidian, individualized experience. The triumph of traditional meanings is complete when the Booths leave London for a country estate that, as in *Joseph Andrews* and *Tom Jones*, emblematically connects marital, familial, political, and divine orders. As the next chapter will suggest, the retrograde literary artifice through which secrecy and concealment are defeated here is differently handled in the more typically experimental fiction of the 1750s and 1760s.

Chapter 3

The punishment of singularity

The increasing complexity and narrative importance of Henry Fielding's heroines from the 1740s to the 1750s point the direction for much subsequent eighteenth-century fiction. But the high note of affirmation on which *Amelia* closes is rarely repeated. That novel's ending, by subordinating Amelia's individual struggles to the reassertion of traditional hierarchies, makes Booth's commitment to the government of his family appear the object of, and reward for, her much-tested faith in him. This chapter opens with a series of works that respond with more skepticism than Henry Fielding does to the social implications of women's capacity for refined emotion: Charlotte Lennox's *The Female Quixote* (1752), Sarah Fielding's *Ophelia* (1760), Frances Sheridan's *Sidney Bidulph* (1761), and Jane Austen's *Sense and Sensibility* (1811). In each, sensibility complicates even as it confirms existing hierarchies, at once exposing the gender inequities on which social authority rests and insisting on the need for the heroines' final and self-conscious compliance with that authority. This double schema means that alongside the depiction of excessive feeling as untenable – variously conveyed through the novels' use of tragic endings, satire, irony, or overt didactic commentary – runs a sympathetic examination of the deep appeal of sensibility for young unmarried women. When Austen's Elinor Dashwood regrets "the too great importance placed by her [sister Marianne] on the delicacies of a strong sensibility," the error is thus notably one of degree, not kind.[1] From Lennox to Austen, this registering of culpability is achieved by setting personal failings within the contexts of institutional ones.

In these fictions, sensibility incubates most aggressively in relative isolation. All four novelists tie their protagonists' emotional singularity, cultivated in solitude, to conditions dictated by the previous generation's disappointments in either politics or property settlements (when men's interests prevail) or love (when women's at least nominally do). The limits placed on the early lives of these young women thus stem from the actions of their elders: in *The Female Quixote*, Arabella's father, having fallen "at last a Sacrifice" to court intrigues, isolates himself in the country where he "never admitted any Company whatever"; when Ophelia's aunt discovers that her private marriage to the Noble

Lord was a sham, she retreats with her infant niece to remotest Wales; Lady Bidulph imposes on her daughter an excessively high-minded code of behavior that originates in her own thwarted first engagement and in doing so hobbles Sidney's powers of choice.[2] In each instance, the heroine's plot, as sketched in the opening pages, is predicated on an intemperate action by an older male. *Sense and Sensibility* underscores the enduring influence of masculine entitlement by developing its legal connotations. Since the heroines' father, Henry Dashwood, is bound by the terms of a strict settlement that guarantees the patrilineal transmission of property, the decisions he makes regarding the long-term support of his family are crucial. When Norland, the entailed estate, passes at his death to the son of his first marriage, John Dashwood, the inadequacy of these provisions is exposed after John circumvents his father's dying wish that the latter's second wife and three daughters be shielded from the full consequences of their legal disinheritance. Austen's attention to the specifics of the strict settlement – an attention to material details that exceeds that of the previous novels – emphasizes the human costs of preferring dynastic to affective relationships. Marianne, Elinor and Margaret Dashwood, no less than the earlier heroines referred to above, are profoundly affected by the personalities of their elders, but in their case, corporate forces sanction the exile from the familiar with which *Sense and Sensibility* begins.

The initial plot contrivances that define the heroine's exceptional status foreshadow wider male coalitions that will continue to shape her experiences. The leaguing together of men either in compacts of shared interests or in competitions over disputed ones are common to all four works, although only the heroines of *Sidney Bidulph* and *Sense and Sensibility* are conscious of these machinations. In *Ophelia* and *The Female Quixote*, by contrast, the heroine's extreme otherworldliness means that she can be charged neither with enticement when she attracts the protection of the powerful, nor of complicity when she becomes the object of predatory behavior. From the occasional musings of the mature Ophelia in Sarah Fielding's novel, we learn that her sequestered upbringing in Wales left her entirely unable when a young woman to recognize the sexual motives of her kidnapper, Dorchester: "Since I have learnt how his Mind was corrupted by the Depravity of Custom, I have often wondered at his Command over himself; but, perhaps, he was fortunate in having none to observe him, but one so blinded by Ignorance, that she could not easily suspect him of ill."[3] The thinness of such gestures toward plausibility, made additionally transparent by Fielding's reworking of stock devices from early eighteenth-century seduction fiction, invites us to consider more closely her use of the libertine plot. Ophelia's ingenuousness allows her to function as something of a counter-picaro, a traveler through a corrupt society, but one whose extreme innocence shields her from the attempted seductions she uncomprehendingly describes. For much of the narrative, her role as exotic, naïve tourist (the epistolary form recreates the immediacy of her youthful experiences with occasional retrospective comments) makes her virtue appear the outgrowth of a lack of worldly knowledge, rather than an inwardly defined quality to be tested and confirmed. That simplicity ends abruptly when she overhears Dorchester boasting of his rakish strategy: "I have gained her Heart … the sure Road to her Person. It is impossible a Woman should always resist both her Love and her Lover" (233).

From this point forward, as Ophelia prepares to follow the course set years before when her aunt escaped her seducer by retiring to Wales, the novel abandons episodic social observation and focuses instead on the sexual double standard that underpins libertine culture. Dorchester's apologists try at first to convince her that "consummate Virtue" cannot survive "among a degenerate People" and that marriage is little more than an expedient "political Institution" (261). Her aunt in turn insists that the supposedly natural love he proposes is entangled in gender privileges that work against women's interests: "With all the abandoned Rhapsody of voluptuous Vice," she charges Dorchester, "[y]ou talk of Freedom and Equality, in a Situation which entirely abolishes both. What can render a Woman so much your Slave, as having given up her fair Fame … to gratify your mean Passions? Where then is the Equality between you?" (272). The positions are carefully drawn, but just as quickly elided once he decides on marriage, the aunt supports him, and since "her Opinion gave a sanction for my yielding," Ophelia seizes on the "Opportunity of so agreeably deceiving myself" (274) and yields to her passion rather than holding to her principles. Dorchester's assertion that he need only gain her heart to gain her person is thus verified, though the gain requires both a wedding ceremony and a collective willingness to repress the aunt's earlier opinion that nothing but "Repentance [can] succeed a Marriage with a Rake" (275). The sudden reversal that sees the novel's contending impulses – amatory, libertine, didactic, proto-feminist – displaced by the heroine's semi-ironic endorsement of the marriage ending has an oddly unsettling effect. While Ophelia's transition from naïve to ironist marks out the inescapable need for women to accommodate themselves to existing power structures, the resolution also, and more problematically, endorses the male competitiveness that the novel had earlier questioned.

The Female Quixote effects a less jarring adjustment between the heroine's distinctiveness and the male interests leagued against her, in part by establishing Arabella's intended suitor, Glanville, as the hinge between two contrasted groupings: on the one hand, the various men who compete for her attentions, in particular, Glanville and the libertine, Sir George Bellmour; on the other, the compact of family members – her father, the Marquis, and uncle, Sir Charles – who privately advocate Arabella's marriage to her cousin (and Sir Charles's son), Glanville. Like Fielding, Lennox subjects her heroine to rakish plots, but adds to the motif of competition between Glanville and Bellmour, the other, more benign confederacy of male relatives that potentially allows for change in both protagonists. It is a confederacy that, unusually for the eighteenth-century novel, makes the older generation more tolerant than the younger. Thus, when Glanville regrets after the death of Arabella's father early in the novel that the Marquis had not "laid a stronger Injunction upon [Arabella] in his Will to marry him," Sir Charles reminds his son that "The Marquis has certainly had a great Opinion of his Daughter's Prudence; and I hope, she will prove herself worthy of it by her Conduct" (65). That confidence is eventually confirmed not only in relation to Arabella, but also to Glanville. In keeping secret the family's support for their marriage (to which the obedient daughter would, it is assumed, have capitulated without hesitation), Glanville agrees to be governed by the Marquis's more robust faith that his daughter will eventually acknowledge her false assumptions. The generational lag means that the prospective husband's growing trust in the maturing of his spouse-to-be can be contrasted with the cynical attempts of the libertine suitor, Bellmour, to exploit her quixotism, attempts that in turn suggest that only a swift transition from daughter to wife can protect young women from sexual predators. While the endings of both *Ophelia* and *The Female Quixote* circumscribe the heroine's independence, the latter makes her restriction seem less lop-sided by schooling the hero to recognize the value of her refined emotion.

The reformative powers of women, evident in *Ophelia* and *The Female Quixote*, give way in Frances Sheridan's *Sidney Bidulph* to a much bleaker vision that sets the heroine's exalted sensibility against the narrowly self-ish motives of a family modeled on the Harlowes in Richardson's *Clarissa*. Like James Harlowe, who acts on his conviction that daughters are "chickens brought up for the tables of other men"(77), Sir George Bidulph regards his sister Sidney as a "piece of goods that was to be shewn to the best advantage to a purchaser" and intends to marry her to his close friend, Falkland.[4] In both novels, the brothers' eagerness to assume this traditionally patriarchal function is presented as suspect. Here, as in Eliza Haywood's *Betsy Thoughtless*, the aggressive appropriation of paternal authority overlaps with patterns of male sociality that reinforce the young women's vulnerability. When the intended dynastic marriage is foiled by another perversion of conventional family structures – Lady Bidulph insists that her daughter reprise her own first failed engagement and refuse Falkland – the domestic forces leagued against the heroine are complete. The family compact is confirmed when Lady Bidulph, a strict interpreter of primogeniture, deeds the entire family estate to her son, by this point married to a "vain, weak, and imperious" wife who "governs him totally" (332). They ignore Sidney's penury until she is rescued by a long-lost, wealthy relative. Only then does Sir George renew contact, a reconciliation that the ever-ingenuous heroine sees as evidence of "something wonderfully powerful in the natural affections" (380).

Our fluency with such motifs – the consolidation of family interests to advantage the son at the expense of the daughter, the mother's uneven hand-ling of her children, the son's manipulations of his sister to fulfill his own material ambitions – depends not only on their recalling of Richardson (and of his imitators), but also on their subsequent, often ironic, treatment by Jane Austen. The depiction of John Dashwood in *Sense and Sensibility*, for instance, builds on the narratives of unwarranted fraternal power in Sheridan, Fielding, and Lennox. His failure to honor the death-bed promise to care for his step-mother and -sisters results in their exile from a comfortable gentry existence at Norland, with little hope of future relief given the bleak marriage prospects of the insufficiently portioned daughters. But even as Austen aligns John with earlier instances of scheming brothers, she diminishes him through her satiric treatment of the self-congratulatory platitudes he mouths to paper over his covetousness. While his ability to affect his sisters' material circumstances per-sists, the thinness of his inner life relative to their more speculative habits of mind increasingly makes him an object of ridicule. The difference between his petty avarice and their emotional depth is particularly evident in Austen's adaptation of the dynastic ambition theme, positively resolved in Lennox's conclusion with the marriage of Arabella and Glanville, tragically in Sheridan's revelation of her heroine's unintentional bigamy and the probable suicide of her husband. Here, by contrast, John Dashwood's sudden attention to Elinor whom he mistakenly believes is being courted by the wealthy Col. Brandon makes familial aspiration appear a cipher of small-mindedness. And since his schemes to advance the Dashwood interests by advantageously marrying off his sisters are directed by the domineering and fiercely status-minded Ferrars women, dynastic ambition becomes associated with emasculation.

The ultimate failure of the would-be matriarchs to preserve and extend family possessions by controlling their sons' choice of partner – not only Mrs. Ferrars with Edward and Robert, but also, though more obliquely, Mrs. Smith with her dependant, Willoughby – represents yet another of Austen's adjustments to received novel conventions. In *Sense and Sensibility*, Mrs. John Dashwood, Mrs. Ferrars and Mrs. Smith function as proxies for institutional forces like the strict settlement whose goal is the consolidation and enlargement of inherited properties. While these structures remain intact at novel's end, the matriarchs' schemes have been either foiled or questioned, and more important, the characters they opposed have been materially and emotionally rewarded (variations on the pattern can be seen in *Pride and Prejudice*'s Lady Catherine de Burgh, *Mansfield Park*'s Mrs. Norris, and *Persuasion*'s Lady Russell). The individual and social happiness that comes to Elinor and Marianne at the end of *Sense and Sensibility* stands in sharp contrast to *Sidney Bidulph*, where the complicity of older women in the power compacts of men continues unchecked and alternatives to the status quo are disallowed. In Sheridan's novel, this collaboration with forms of male privilege is made additionally striking because women pursue it to the detriment of their own daughters' well-being. The novel's multiple plot lines numbingly repeat a pattern in which mothers regulate the flow of family property to advance already wealthy sons, while daughters meekly accept their increasing poverty and unhappy marriages.

The bad mother – a reversal of the more usual positive view of maternity as counter to worldliness – is coupled in *Sidney Bidulph* with another inversion of a customary pattern, that of friendship between women. Novels of sensibility typically suspend the heroine between female advocates and adversaries (the latter often unrecognized by her). In *The Female Quixote*, Charlotte Glanville schemes to effect Arabella's public humiliation in London, but her hopes are overturned when the Countess begins the process of reform that is then completed by the Doctor at novel's end; Ophelia escapes from imprisonment in the Gothic castle of the wicked Marchioness of Trente with the aid of the latter's disenchanted female companion. The positive change in the heroines' circumstances depends in both instances on the meliorating effects of conversation. In *Sidney Bidulph*, however, contact with like-minded women, whether direct or epistolary, offers the heroine only the limited comfort of expressing her commitment to the course of virtue. Against the combined force of Lady Bidulph's favoring of her son and substitute daughter, Miss Burchell, Sidney's sensibility is entirely ineffectual. Austen's novel offers muted versions of these familial imbalances in Mrs. Dashwood's attention to Marianne over Elinor and in Lucy Steele's manipulation of a sequence of surrogate mothers. But while Sheridan's epistolary narrative grimly records the onslaught of disasters from the point of view of the unjustly afflicted Sidney, Austen's plays off against each other the perspectives of a range of characters from the obtuse to the insightful, granting to Elinor, in particular, a complex inwardness that, together with the narrator's engaging of the reader through omniscient commentary, highlights the importance of conversation as a means of reconciling intimacy and decorum. In the novel's final paragraph, the reference to the "constant communication" that now exists "[b]etween Barton and Delaford" (431), the residences respectively of the Edward Ferrars and the Brandons, heralds the end of the sisters' earlier estrangements. The metonymy of place – houses stand here for the concordance of personal, familial, and social identity – confirms the high value assigned to Marianne and Elinor. As expected in a celebratory conclusion, their achievements exceed in permanence, continuity, and pleasure those for which John Dashwood, the Ferrars women, and Willoughby so demeaningly schemed.

"Constant communication" also signals a disabling of the secrets that these novels make pivotal to the abuses of power they catalogue. The varying effects of secrecy – positive or negative – are governed by a sliding scale of intention: Glanville's withholding from Arabella the information that he is the spouse favored by her father means that her choice of husband can be deferred until she discovers for herself the limits of her romance fantasies; contrarily, when Dorchester conceals his libertinism from Ophelia, he conspires to advance his planned seduction not by expanding but by restricting the boundaries of her knowledge. In *Sidney Bidulph*, as in its antecedent *Clarissa*, the crushing effects of secrets on the heroine of sensibility depend on others' intractability. Sidney may communicate the "inmost secrets of my soul" to her "second self" (136–7), Cecilia, but the intensity of their epistolary friendship is no match for the scheming of the hard-hearted narcissists who surround her. Sidney's mother provides a particularly glaring instance of selfishness when she papers over the treachery of her protégé Miss Burchell. Having once accepted at face value Miss Burchell's avowals of truthfulness, she refuses afterwards to alter her opinion. Sidney becomes an unwitting party to the women's stratagems when she promises to keep secret a supposedly "candid confession" (307) that Miss Burchell divulges in order to trap Faulkland into marriage. Austen at once rings the changes on this pattern with Lucy Steele – who similarly advances her devious plans by first securing the silence of her rivals – and more speculatively addresses the ambivalent place of concealment in a culture that prizes decorum and limits women's ability to act independently.

In Austen's novels, secrets give us access to the peculiar mix of intimacy and antagonism that shapes family relationships both immediate and more extended. As Tony Tanner suggests, secrets are also intrinsic to plot development.[5] In *Sense and Sensibility*, Marianne's non-engagement to Willoughby, Brandon's failure to speak of Willoughby's seduction and abandonment of Eliza Williams, Lucy's engagement to Edward and pursuit of his brother, Robert Ferrars, Elinor's painful suppression of her disappointment in Edward and entrapment by Lucy into an unwanted confidence: each concealment compounds the ripple effects of the others. Careful attention is paid to the means by which access to hidden knowledge is gained. In the case of Marianne and Willoughby, the tone of an overheard conversation convinces Elinor that they must be privately engaged. When Willoughby then offers Marianne a horse and she in turn covertly provides him with a lock of her hair, the two gifts – clustered in a single chapter – seem to make semi-public and consensual a relationship not otherwise formalized. But the contiguous discovery that they have made a clandestine visit to the estate of his patron, Mrs. Smith, troubles Elinor since it suggests a "strange kind of secrecy … wholly contradictory to their general opinions and practice" (83). When his sudden departure from the neighborhood aggravates her doubts, her mother derides them (and by extension Elinor), declaring in the face of clear evidence to the contrary that "no secrecy has been attempted; all has been uniformly open and unreserved" (93). Mrs. Dashwood's reluctance to speak privately to Marianne leads ultimately to her humiliating encounter with Willoughby in London.

Conversations focused on surreptitious behavior – whether accidentally overheard or shared between related third parties – make apparent the threat secrets pose to family solidarity. Gossip represents a cruder and potentially more damaging opening of private concerns to public scrutiny. Austen establishes degrees of culpability in rumour-mongering, ranging from Sir John Middleton and Mrs. Jennings's awkward prattle about suspected lovers through to Anne Steele's spiteful (and possibly collusive) announcement of Lucy's engagement to Edward Ferrars. Non-verbal exchanges offer, in turn, revelatory visual complements to knowledge understood, but left unstated. Together, these versions of disclosure – both deliberate and involuntary – contribute to the reciprocity of form and theme in *Sense and Sensibility*. Dull characters are marked by a flatness of depiction that expresses their literal-mindedness and inability to move beyond surface declarations, the more intelligent by a complexity of representation that accords with their inwardness and *its* complement, an intuitive grasp of others' intentions. The conversation with Elinor in which Lucy Steele asserts a territorial right to Edward Ferrars provides a particularly strong example of Austen's adroit use of secrets to advance plot and character in these terms.

The scene begins with Lucy asking a direct question about Mrs. Ferrars that Elinor inwardly considers evidence of an "impertinent curiosity." Austen signals Lucy's calculating foresight by having her repeat aloud this unspoken judgment: Lucy hopes that Elinor will do her "the justice of believing that I do not mean to be impertinent," personalizes the wish, "I cannot bear to have you think me impertinently curious"(147), and finally confides she is engaged to Edward Ferrars: "it was always meant to be a great secret, and I am sure has been faithfully kept so by me to this hour. Not a soul of all my relations know it but Anne, and I should never have mentioned it to you, if I had not felt the greatest dependance [sic] in the world upon your secrecy; and I really thought my behavior in asking so many questions about Mrs. Ferrars, must seem so odd, that it ought to be explained" (149). Her true motive for pursuing the conversation, it now becomes clear, was not to apologize for untoward curiosity, but to warn off the woman whom she correctly grasps Edward loves. She is thus fully prepared for Elinor's sceptical comment that she has never heard of this four-year engagement. Her reply, "considering our situation, it was not strange. Our first care has been to keep the matter secret" (150), is followed by her flourishing the miniature portrait Edward gave her (a gift that recalls other tokens of imperfect love, among them Marianne's lock of hair). With her claim authenticated, Lucy advances to her ultimate objective: "I have no doubt in the world," she says, "of your faithfully keeping this secret" (151). Elinor agrees, but with a significant qualification. She observes that while she "certainly did not seek your confidence … you do me no more than justice in imagining that I may be depended on. Your secret is safe with me; but pardon me if I express some surprise at so unnecessary a communication. You must at least have felt that my being acquainted with it could not add to its safety" (152). Lucy, having shrewdly calculated that Elinor's sense of honor would prevail, has nevertheless withheld two further proofs that she now produces to counter these residual doubts: first, a "correspondence … by letter [that] could subsist only under a positive engagement" (154) (again anticipating Marianne's situation in London), and second, the lock of hair in Edward's ring that Elinor had believed hers but that Lucy now trumpets as her own.

Volume I ends with Elinor "mortified, shocked, confounded" (155). At the beginning of Volume II we are given access to her thoughts as she reviews the "body of evidence" (159) presented and decides against divulging it to Marianne or her mother. But she, unlike Sidney Bidulph, is not entirely passive in the face of female enmity. Under cover of a busy social gathering, she pursues a conversation with Lucy that both unequivocally discredits the schemer and suggests Elinor's own resourcefulness. Descriptive details – Lucy's "little sharp eyes" – combined with her fulsome phrasing – "If you knew what a consolation it was to me to relieve my heart by speaking to you of what I am always thinking of every moment of my life" (167) – suggest that her wiliness may not be supported by genuine intelligence. But it is the careful transcription of gesture that, in conveying the unspoken currents shaping the exchange, opens the possibility for the future redressing of the power imbalance. When we are told that "Lucy here looked up; but Elinor was careful in guarding her countenance from every expression that could give her words a suspicious tendency" (168), we understand that Elinor has begun to practice some of her antagonist's guile. Eventually, as so often in eighteenth-century novels, female presumption oversteps itself and with Lucy's unmasking, the now-exposed secret can be directed to new purposes. One of these is the schooling of Marianne, who responds to the revelation by asking her sister, "how have you been supported?" (297) in what now appears to be Elinor's parallel betrayal by Edward Ferrars. Elinor's impassioned account of her long and lonely suffering corrects her family's self-serving assumption that her sense can be taken as presumptive proof of a lack of sensibility. From this point, Marianne makes an effort to conduct herself with dignity. "Such advances toward heroism in her sister," the narrator comments, "made Elinor feel equal to any thing herself" (300). If the confirmation of Sidney Bidulph's "heroic soul" (462) is her passive endurance, the brush of irony in Austen's phrasing indicates a more critical understanding of its place in her heroines' lives.

Throughout *Sense and Sensibility*, the active cultivation of secrets to self-interested ends is aligned, as in Daniel Defoe's novels, with material and social aspiration. More recent Gothic and radical fiction had invested concealed knowledge with new narrative purposes, in particular the exploration of psychological interiority, as in Ann Radcliffe's *The Italian*, M. G. Lewis's *The Monk*, or William Godwin's *Caleb Williams*. Austen develops a contrary tack by using secrets as foils to the shared confidences that, as we have seen, anticipate the protagonists' final reward of "constant communication." Since inwardness is the signature of a positive character, we do not enter Lucy Steele's mind; instead, she (like Willoughby) temporarily blocks the sisters' intimacy (a loss we experience through our continued access to Elinor's subjectivity). One further instance of the artful development of correspondences between form and meaning can be seen in the treatment of Lucy's manipulation of audience, her inventiveness, and, most damagingly, her facile "cleverness." Together these traits represent a counterfeit version of narratorial authority, and thus, by a process of inversion, help to authenticate the means by which Austen expresses positive values.

Austen builds on established novelistic practice when she assigns to a negative character certain of her own attributes as writer. Each of the fictions considered in this chapter includes a convincing but unethical story-teller who plots to inveigle the innocent. The libertines, Sir George Bellmour in *Female Quixote* and Dorchester in *Ophelia* (like Vallaton in Elizabeth Hamilton's *Memoirs of Modern Philosophers* [1800] or Fitzosborne in Jane West's *A Tale of the Times* [1799]) opportunistically pitch their stories to the romance expectations of the naïve heroines. Miss Burchell and Lucy Steele in turn exercise the narrator's prerogative of allocating information selectively, creating imbalances of knowledge that affect the actions of others. The trope acquires more subtle resonances in the stories told by Willoughby and too easily accepted by Marianne. As the first male in the novel to unite "a manner so frank and graceful" with an "uncommonly handsome" person, he appears to Marianne to be "equal to what her fancy had ever drawn for the hero of a favorite story" (50–1). The fact that he is also the first character to offer detailed physical descriptions of the Dashwood family seems retrospectively to hint that his attention to surface appearances is achieved at the expense of the novel's most valued attribute, empathy. His inventiveness, his charm, his eagerness momentarily to please: these suggest a heedlessness about consequences that runs against the grain of the self-knowledge and social responsibility extolled by Austen.

The stories told by Bellmour, Dorchester, Miss Burchell, Lucy, Willoughby, and (in part) Marianne differ in one crucial regard from the narratives in which they are embedded: their ostentatiously derivative language. While Lennox, Fielding, and Sheridan identify this imitative rhetoric with romance delusions, Austen typically establishes a broader spectrum of usages. On one hand are minor characters whose stock phrases – anticipating Dickens – make them memorable, as in Mrs. Palmer's repetition of "so droll" to describe her husband's unfunny rudeness. Sir John Middleton's vernacular expressions for husband-hunting – "setting your cap at him" (53) or "well worth catching" (52) – give a mordantly comic turn to the often desperate need for women to secure their financial futures through marriage. As "flat" characters, both Mrs. Palmer and Sir John thicken the texture of the novel, but they do not fully engage with the protagonists. On the other hand, the selective marking of "rounded" characters by derivative language signals not the absence of ability (as in Mrs. Palmer and Sir John), but much more culpably, a shirking of its responsibilities. Marianne claims in a discussion of picaresque beauty that she "detest[s] jargon of every kind" (113), but here as in other contexts, fails to recognize how it infiltrates her own comments. Willoughby understands that he uses "hackneyed metaphor[s]" (368) when he attempts, after his marriage to the heiress Miss Grey, to describe to Elinor his earlier treatment of Marianne. That understanding, however, aggravates the nature of his offense: in choosing to conform to the tired plot of marrying for money, he has become something of a cliché himself and in the process betrays not only the Dashwoods' trust, but also his own potential. His speech reproduces the bathos of his situation, without offering any possibilities for excusing it. Elinor's rhetorical range situates her usage between these two extremes of deficiency and excess of self-consciousness. Her occasional proverbial turns of phrase, while formulaic, reflect a positive respect for common experience, as when she struggles to explain Edward Ferrars's hesitations by seeing them as a product of the "old, well established grievance of duty against will, parent against child" (118). Elsewhere, she approaches the narrator's standard of discourse in her measured phrases, her analytical power, and her recognition of the dangers of enthusiastic reading, particularly Marianne's. In this negative appraisal of compulsive reading, Austen again participates in a long-standing trope: from the early eighteenth century, novelists use characters' responses to books as a way to address the habits of their actual audiences. Reading, in short, is a form of "metacommentary" embedded within texts in order to direct interpretation and foster appropriate practices.

In novels of sensibility by women, the effects of unusually wide reading are often exacerbated by the heroines' isolation. While their remote situations shield them from worldliness, the combination of seclusion and erudition appears to impede self-knowledge and to entice predators. Early in *The Female Quixote*, Glanville implores Arabella to use "your own Language, I beseech you; for I am sure [no other person's] can excel it" (116). His concern is well founded: Arabella's inability to speak in her own voice leaves her susceptible to ventriloquizing libertines who spout romance phrases as part of their attempts at seduction. When Ophelia's aunt in Sarah Fielding's novel limits her library to works of divinity and history, she pursues a policy different from the Marquis's allowing of unchecked access. But since her tacit censorship proves no more effective in protecting the heroine than the Marquis's absence of supervision, Lennox's point is confirmed: women must develop interpretative skills that can be transferred from books to experience. In both novels, the act of conversing enables this transfer. *The Female Quixote* defers the transformative conversations to the novel's end when Arabella discusses romance first with the Countess, then the Doctor; in *Ophelia*, the epistolary form, combined with the frame narrative, makes conversation an intrinsic element of the novel's structure. (Smollett's *Sir Launcelot Greaves*, by contrast, is cured of his knight-errantry once he accepts the rule of law over that of chivalry.) Ophelia's written account of her youth has been solicited by a curious, unnamed "Lady"; the letter in response that makes up the substance of the novel incorporates a further internal dialogue between the mature, first-person retrospective writer and the ingenuous early self who describes her initial impressions of the world after her abduction from Wales. In novels written from a more overtly masculinist perspective, female reading tends not to be identified as here with acclimatizing young women to adult married life, but with ruin and seduction. Thus the history of Miss Wilkins in Smollett's *Roderick Random* (like Emily Atkins's in *The Man of Feeling*) charts her descent into abject poverty and prostitution through her rejection of her aunt's "good books" for the philosophers Shaftesbury, Tindal, and Hobbes and her subsequent credulous belief that she will enjoy "all that I had read of love and chivalry" in romances.[6]

Frances Sheridan's *Sidney Bidulph* develops further the thematic potential of Sarah Fielding's use of preliminary matter in the form of a frame narrative by multiplying the levels of epistolary and conversational exchange. The "Editor's Introduction" recounts the elaborate process by which the manuscript was compiled and conveyed: as part of a reading circle, the Editor had years before participated in a discussion centered on the audience's possible "disappoint[ment] in the catastrophe of a fable, if every body in it be not disposed of according to the sentence of that judge we have set up in our own breasts" (7) (an allusion, perhaps, to the "man within the breast," the phrase used by the philosopher Adam Smith in his 1759 *Theory of Moral Sentiments*, to explain how conscience collaborates with empathy to limit self-love and enable social benevolence). Cecilia, their aged host, produces as counterevidence to the ethical imperatives of poetic justice her youthful correspondence with Sidney Bidulph, letters that the Editor inherits after Cecilia's death and now publishes. The scene of collective reading and edifying communal judgment staged in the "Editor's Introduction" provides an evaluative standard against which the alternative representations in Sidney's letters can be measured: among them, her husband's demand that she give up Horace for needlework and, more culpably, Lady Bidulph's inattentive skimming of texts that is the source of the plot's most disastrous turns. Here, as in *The Female Quixote*, *Ophelia*, and *Sense and Sensibility*, the dangers of solitary, enthusiastic, uncritical, or inattentive reading shade into considerations of genre in which disparaged forms – romance, secret history, amatory tales – contrast with the more sociable form of the novel itself.

Male-authored novels of sensibility such as Laurence Sterne's *Tristram Shandy* (1765–7) and *A Sentimental Journey through France and Italy* (1768), Henry Mackenzie's *Man of Feeling* (1771), and William Godwin's *Fleetwood* (1805) tend to retreat from overt didacticism and emphasize instead the eccentricities of character and circumstance that motivate and, on occasion, paralyze their protagonists. In Sterne's novels, this focus on idiosyncratic behavior means that satiric undercutting often coexists with sentimental affect. As a result, familiar genre conventions take on a distinct coloring that recurrently destabilizes the reader's relation to the narrative. This can be clearly seen in Sterne's reworking of the generational plot used by Sheridan, Lennox, and Sarah Fielding to trace their heroines' plights back to the often thoughtless or selfish actions of their elders. *Tristram Shandy* simultaneously observes and parodies the problem of origins by having the hero consider whether Mrs. Shandy's punctuating the very moment of his conception to ask her husband about the winding of the clock might have influenced his "HOMUNCULUS," the embryonic human form microscopically visible in sperm. Referring to this nascent self as "our fellow-creature" and as fundamentally "alone," he initiates the novel's paradoxical representation of identity as at once determinate and contingent, time-bound and freely associational, alienated and communitarian, solipsistic and empathetic.[7]

Tristram's ability to trace in near-burlesque terms the question of formative influence back to the moment of his own conception itself testifies to the compound of intimacy and emotional detachment that defines the Shandy family. The "anecdote" of interrupted congress comes to him third-hand from his father Walter through his uncle Toby. Its enduring power to affect his father's view of Tristram is confirmed by uncle Toby through a linked story he also repeats to his nephew: when he and Tristram's parents a few years later observe a "most unaccountable obliquity, (as he [Walter] call'd it) in my manner of setting up my top," Walter comments that "his heart all along foreboded, and he saw verified in this, and from a thousand other observations he had made upon me, That I should neither think nor act like any other man's child: – *But alas!* continued he, shaking his head a second time, and wiping away a tear which was trickling down his cheeks, *My Tristram's misfortunes began nine months before he ever came into the world*" (7). The "obliquity" that Walter transposes from the spinning top to his son is both physical and psychological. We in turn experience it formally in the decidedly non-linear structuring of Tristram's story. Signifying an angle neither parallel nor perpendicular, an indirect course, or a character flaw, "obliquity" describes the seemingly haphazard course of the narrative, the typographical oddities of the text's material presentation (including marbled, blank, and flourish-marked pages), and the mechanism on which all the Shandy men rely to deflect intimacy, the "hobbyhorse" that Tristram will later define as

> the sporting little filly-folly which carries you out for the present
> hour – a maggot, a butterfly, a picture, a fiddle-stick – an uncle
> Toby's siege – or *any thing*, which a man makes a shift to get a
> stride on, to canter it away from the cares and solicitudes of life –
> 'Tis as useful a beast as is in the whole creation.   (471)

The opening pages of the novel prepare us for the distinctive traits of the individual family members: Walter's theorizing of everything from procreation to child-rearing, Mrs. Shandy's knowing "no more than her backside what my father meant" by the reference to "nine months," Toby's naïve (or not) relaying to his nephew the "anecdote" (7) of the conception, Tristram's own attempts to articulate order through a sly mixture of bawdy and sentiment. In the "life and opinions" that follow, the "course" of "excentricity" (53) set in the first chapters will shape the hero's arch manipulations of identity, time, and narrative structure.

This self-conscious play with the literary conventions of representation has been seen as proto-modernist, but *Tristram Shandy* is, in fact, both indebted to the past and reflective of its own period: it draws on the Renaissance learned-wit tradition of Rabelais, Montaigne, Cervantes, and Burton, while also exhibiting the leading traits of formal realism that Ian Watt defines as attention "to the particularisation of time, place, and person; to a natural and lifelike sequence of action; and to the creation of a literary style which gives the most exact verbal and rhythmical equivalent possible of the object described" (291). More specifically, the novel responds to contemporary anxieties about the grounds of individual identity in terms familiar from works considered earlier in this chapter: Arabella's conceit that books shape experience has its echo in Walter's obsession with names, his belief that "there was a strange kind of magick bias, which good or bad names, as he call'd them, irresistibly impress'd upon our characters and conduct" (43); Sidney Bidulph's inability to escape a family history defined by narcissism and intractability resembles the Shandys' individual and collective entrapment; Clarissa's documenting of her exceptional circumstances in prolix "writing to the moment" relates not only to Tristram's artful play with the disjunctions between recorded and lived experience but also to Sterne's evolving themes over the course of the novel's staggered release (Volumes I–II in January 1760; III–IV in January 1761; V–VI in December 1761; VII–VIII in January 1765; IX in January 1767).

Yet however close the connections between *Tristram Shandy* and 1750s and 1760s fiction, Sterne outpaces his fellow novelists in his pressing of thematic and formal devices to the point of mockery of himself as writer and his readers as reliable interpreters. Henry Fielding's *Shamela*, *Joseph Andrews*, and *Tom Jones* had registered authorial insecurities about an increasingly unknowable reading public by embedding references to distinct audiences within the novels; Sarah Fielding offers a variation in *David Simple* and its sequel *Volume the Last* when she simply refuses to countenance readers who lack her characters' virtues: "Indeed, to such I *cannot* write, concerning *David*, and his Company; as no Words are equal to the raising in such Minds, any true Image of the Pleasures of our happy Society."[8] In the case of both authors, the unwavering ethical position of the intrusive omniscient narrator at least potentially adjudicates the conflicting views of their imagined readers. The predicament to which Sterne attends in *Tristram Shandy* is closer to that of *Pamela* and *Clarissa* since the first-person perspective removes the Fieldings' centralizing consciousness. But while Richardson works on methods to control errant interpretations, Sterne foregrounds their centrifugal force by having Tristram address both personal friends ("Eugenius" and "Jenny") and the anonymous public, particularly women with "a vicious taste" for reading "straight forwards, more in quest of the adventures, than of the deep erudition and knowledge which a book of this cast, if read over as it should be, would infallibly impart" (48).

Typically, the irony here cuts both ways; if "Madam" errs by skimming through the plot, the alternative of intensive reading too closely resembles the obsessive detailism that immobilizes the Shandy men. Much as Tristram aspires to a "conversation" in which he pays the "truest respect" to "the reader's understanding" (87) by allowing latitude of response, he is finally unable to achieve the rhythms of genuine exchange because "[i]n a word, my work is digressive, and it is progressive too, – and at the same time" (58).

The difficulties of managing the disparate needs of a wider public recur in the painful private attempts of the novel's inscribed writers, interpreters, and storytellers to shape their own experiences. The principal characters (and more peripheral figures like Slawkenbergius) carry out the task in distinct, but ultimately equally ineffectual, ways. Corporal Trim suggests to his master that constructing battlefields to scale might ease the "many perplexities" that face Toby as a result "of the almost insurmountable difficulties he found in telling his story intelligibly" (67). Characteristically, Toby does not build models of the 1689–97 King William's War in which he was actually wounded, but chooses instead to recreate the ongoing 1702–13 Queen Anne's War in his Yorkshire bowling-green (pausing briefly after the Treaty of Utrecht for the failed "amours" with the Widow Wadman before returning to military re-enactment). The sublimated sexuality evident in his initial response to Trim's proposal – "[n]ever did lover post down to a belov'd mistress with more heat and expectation than my uncle *Toby* did, to enjoy this self-same thing in private … [for] the idea of not being seen, did not a little contribute to the idea of pleasure preconceived in my uncle *Toby*'s mind" (80) – acquires additional point when the bowling-green battlefield is considered as a displaced form of narrative. Uncle Toby's construction projects offer a material equivalent of what Sterne's contemporaries called "secret history," that is, history filtered through a subjective consciousness to give an insider's perspective, often salacious, on public events. Tristram himself indulges in a comparably marginal version of historiography when he assembles his "life and opinions" from fragmentary sources, among them Yorick's notes on his sermons. These antiquarian methods are no more likely than Walter's equally voluminous "Tristapaedia" to produce a shapely, reliable, or even finished account. Walter had launched his educational treatise "with as much devotion as ever my uncle *Toby* had done to the doctrine of projectils" (298) after all his plans to control his son's destiny (through conception, birth, and naming) were thwarted. But his urge to comprehensiveness and tendency to learned digression mean that the child's life quickly outstrips his progress in writing, rendering the project a compounding exercise in futility.

The inarticulate Toby and prolix Walter commonly fail to find a balance between language and life, experience and knowledge, memory and progress.

Tristram's near-parodic description of the problems he encounters in recording his own history testifies to a shared affliction:

> I am this month one whole year older than I was at this time twelve-
> month; and having got, as you perceive, almost into the middle of
> my fourth volume – and no farther than to my first day's life – 'tis
> demonstrative that I have three hundred and sixty-four days more life
> to write just now, than when I first set out; so that instead of advancing,
> as a common writer, in my work with what I have been doing at it – on
> the contrary, I am just thrown so many volumes back – was every day of
> my life to be as busy a day as this – And why not? – and the transactions
> and opinions of it to take up as much description – And for what reason
> should they be cut short? as at this rate I should just live 364 times
> faster than I should write – It must follow, an' please your worships,
> that the more I write, the more I shall have to write – and consequently,
> the more your worships read, the more your worships will have to
> read.   (228)

Earlier in the novel, our reading time had been wittily correlated to Toby and
Walter's conversation in terms that comically underscored the artifice of narrative conventions and our unthinking compliance with them. But just as
satire gives way to an increasing emphasis on sentiment over the course of
the novel, so too does Tristram's bravado question here ("And for what reason
should [my "transactions and opinions"] be cut short?") have a darker and
very personal undertone.

The recurring references to the distinct cadences of experienced and
recorded time that have throughout conveyed the limits of memory, history,
writing, even comprehension itself, are gradually made subject to a receding
horizon of completeness as Tristram's disease gains hold. By the final Volume
IX, mortality has emerged as a major theme:

> I will not argue the matter: Time wastes too fast: every letter I trace
> tells me with what rapidity Life follows my pen; the days and hours of
> it, more precious, my dear Jenny! than the rubies about thy neck, are
> flying over our heads like light clouds of a windy day, never to return
> more – every thing presses on – whilst thou art twisting that lock, – see!
> it grows grey; and every time I kiss thy hand to bid adieu, and every
> absence which follows it, are preludes to that eternal separation which
> we are shortly to make – Heaven have mercy upon us both!   (498)

Tristram's aspirations toward expressive clarity are, like his father's and uncle's,
blocked. The conviction that "his life was put in jeopardy by words" refers in his
case, however, not merely to the recalcitrance of language and the slipperiness

of identity, but to death itself. As the narrative advances, so too does his disease, lending an additional measure of desperation to his attempts to fix on paper a coherent version of selfhood. Whether slowed to match exactly the duration of our reading to the activities of his family, or accelerated to convey his imaginative sense of death's imminence, time finally triumphs over Tristram's ability to continue articulating his often baffled sense of love and intimacy.

A Sentimental Journey (1768) shares many features with *Tristram Shandy* beyond the most obvious one of Parson Yorick, the protagonist of the titular journey, author manqué, and here as in the earlier novel associated (through Shakespearean allusion) with death and jesting. Like its predecessor, *A Sentimental Journey* avoids linearity, favors the episodic over the causal, and demonstrates considerable ingenuity in creating the illusion of personal and perceptual immediacy. The novel opens in mid-conversation with Yorick's interjection " – They order, said I, this matter better in France – ," after which he jumps up from the table in England, crosses the Channel, and by "three I had got sat down to my dinner upon a fricassee'd chicken."[9] But "order," whether institutional, national, narrative, or individual, finally seems less interesting to Yorick than immediate and sensational experience. Sterne employs various techniques for heightening the sense of proximity that Yorick values. These include his habitual description of scenes as if they were "this moment before my eyes" (7) (a mode of visualization reinforced by painterly references), his fixation on passing gestures, and, as in *Tristram Shandy*, his repeated distinctions of "experienced" from "mechanical" time. The sound of the town clock striking four thus recalls to mind that he has been "little more than a hour in Calais," and prompts the observation: "– What a large volume of adventures may be grasped within this little span of life by him who interests his heart in every thing, and who, having eyes to see, what time and chance are perpetually holding out to him as he journeyeth on his way, misses nothing he can *fairly* lay his hands on" (38–9). Melvyn New and W. G. Day, in annotating this passage, point to its expression of Sterne's belief in the plenitude of the world, a plenitude that, as indicated by the compressed references here to illicit sexuality ("adventures") and to scriptural phrases (Mark 8:18, Matthew 13:13, Luke 8:10, Ecclesiastes 9:11), effortlessly incorporates body, mind, and spirit.

Ranged against this plenitude is the potential for egotism in one who "interests his heart in everything." The opening episode with the mendicant monk, Lorenzo, probes this possibility by representing the unsavory dynamics of gift-giving and charity. Having initially refused alms to Lorenzo, Yorick subsequently tries to recoup his amatory interest in the widow, Madam de L***, with an overly generous compensation for his earlier meanness, a gesture that the monk manages gracefully to turn from a "contest" into a more equitable "exchange" of snuffboxes. The "little horn box" that Yorick retains from this encounter has a mnemonic power capable of impressing his "affections" to the point that it makes him "burst into a flood of tears – but I am as weak as a woman; and I beg the world not to smile, but pity me" (28). Weeping acquires more salacious overtones in his anticipated response to hearing Madame de L***'s story, an event he suggests will "crown my journey" in the opportunities it offers of "sharing in the sickening incidents of a tale of misery ... in wiping [tears] away from off the cheeks of the first and fairest of women, as I'm sitting with my handkerchief in my hand in silence the whole night besides her" (61). Such displays – actual and prospective – remind us that his expressions of sympathy remain private, unlike Harley in Mackenzie's *Man of Feeling* who more often realizes his benevolence in acts of kindness with positive social consequences.

Yorick's hyperbole conveys Sterne's awareness of the prurient aspects of sentiment. But unlike the newly founded mid-century philanthropic institutions that sought, like the Magdalen Houses for penitent prostitutes, to regulate illicit behavior by repressing carnality, he revels in the paradoxes generated by the inseparability of body and mind. Yorick's first view of Paris epitomizes the visionary possibilities of this ironic self-consciousness:

> I walked up gravely to the window in my dusty black coat, and looking
> through the glass saw all the world in yellow, blue, and green, running
> at the ring of pleasure. – The old with broken lances, and in helmets
> which had lost their vizards – the young in armour bright which
> shone like gold, beplumed with each gay feather of the east – all – all
> tilting at it like fascinated knights in tournaments of yore for fame and
> love. –   (69)

Plangent in its evocation of mortality and loss, the passage characteristically leavens its bleakness with wittily obscene references to the ring of pleasure and broken lances.

The episode that most engaged contemporary readers, Yorick's threatened imprisonment, builds on these techniques of pictorialization and spectatorship both to heighten and question sentimental responsiveness. Mid-way through *Sentimental Journey*, Yorick faces incarceration within the Bastille because he has heedlessly entered France (with whom England is at war) without a passport. Oppressed by the thought of confinement, he responds to the refrain of a caged starling, "I can't get out, I can't get out," by launching a paean of praise to liberty (typically, his tentative efforts actually to release the bird are fruitless). He then retreats to his room and, drawing on the principle that collective visualization is considerably less powerful than individual projection (a thesis outlined in Adam Smith's *Theory of Moral Sentiments*), he imagines how imprisonment might feel:

> I was going to begin with the millions of my fellow creatures born to no inheritance but slavery; but finding however affecting the picture was, that I could not bring it near me, and that the multitude of sad groups in it did but distract me – I took a single captive, and having first shut him up in his dungeon, I then look'd through the twilight of his grated door to take his picture.   (103)

By the time he finishes his exercise in sympathetic conjuring, he has so reduced the distance between himself and the imagined prisoner that he dissolves into tears. The moment is both intensely affecting (particularly to contemporaries who reproduced it in a variety of media, including Joseph Wright of Derby's c. 1775–7 painting, *The Captive, from Sterne*) and a precisely rendered image of the dangers of our own vicarious reading. At the other extreme from this representation of second-hand emotion is the more sensational gesture with which the novel abruptly closes. Yorick, forced by a late arrival at a small inn to share a room with a fellow traveler, enters into "treaty" negotiations to preserve decorums. Unable to sleep, he and the woman from whom he is separated by a temporary curtain begin a spirited argument that concludes when Yorick "stretching my arm out of bed by way of asseveration ... stretch'd out my hand [and] caught hold of the Fille de Chambre's END OF VOL. II" (173). The droll and bawdy play on the materiality of texts and corporeality of bodies recalls Richardson's typographical experiments (Pamela's double-columned response to B's "Articles" or Clarissa's mad papers) and their finessing in *Tristram Shandy*'s marbled page and variable fonts. But the swing between the sentimental and the ribald, high and low, body and mind is uniquely Sterne's.

Set against the edgy satiric reflexiveness of *Tristram Shandy* and *Sentimental Journey*, Mackenzie's *Man of Feeling* seems a much tamer exercise in sensibility: its fragmentariness, intense emotion, and political subtexts more obvious and less exploratory. The fiction on which the novel depends – that it is a discarded hand-written record of Harley's life compiled by a person dubbed the "Ghost" and only partially recovered from its use as gun-wadding by local hunters – builds on the long-standing trope of the "discovered manuscript" as an authenticating device (Mackenzie repeats this in *Julia de Roubigne* [1777] where the sheets of the narrative are rescued from their use as wrapping for groceries). But while the *Man of Feeling* ostensibly begins at the eleventh chapter and pauses frequently to note missing pages, its plot is straightforward. Occasional literary allusions to Shakespeare, Pope, Johnson, Otway, Richardson, Marmontel, and the Bible and to the philosophers Hume and

Berkeley are equally accessible; unlike the coterie knowledge demanded by Sterne's work, these references mark out common ground shared with a broad range of novel readers. The reflective intimacy of the tone further heightens the sense of the narrator as a familiar and suggests that the institutional abuses he criticizes are also obnoxious to his audience.

At the same time, however, he aligns himself with a highly idealized standard of past excellence that seemingly determines his current state of alienation. One of the most potent emblems of contemporary decline he cites is the diminished status of books, which appear here most often as merely physical objects, rather than imaginative or ideational resources. References to books are ubiquitous: from the volume carried by Miss Walton, through the *Complete Accountant or Young Man's Pocket Companion*, the *Coke upon Lyttelton* (Edward Coke's influential 1628 commentary on Sir Thomas Littleton's property law *Treatise of Tenures*) that Harley's aunt uses to press her linens, the religious writings owned by Mrs. Atkins and discarded by her family after her death, to the plays and novels that contribute to the seduction of her daughter Emily. The restriction of most of these texts to functional or highly interested ends suggests that improving or contemplative reading is unusual. The conceit that we have access in the retrieved pages of the *Man of Feeling* only to the tattered remnants of the Ghost's original biography of Harley reinforces the idea (confirmed by the edition of one of the "German Illustrissimi" carried by the curate's hunting companion for use as gun-wadding) that the devaluing of "bookishness" in the world they once inhabited has more recently accelerated.

Harley's experiences as recorded by the Ghost anticipate this hastening moment of crisis through their emphasis on oral narratives and story-tellers: the beggar encountered in the novel's opening pages whose autobiography comments on authorial pandering to audience expectations, the mad men and women in Bedlam, the penitent prostitute Emily Atkins, and most particularly Old Edwards. Harley responds to each of these stories in turn with tears that authenticate his status as a "child in the drama of the world."[10] But his passivity is not treated with the irony of Tristram and Yorick's; the fault here lies entirely with a culture too corrupt to appreciate his irreproachable virtue or to learn from his "manly tone of reason" (83). Even his one foible – an "inclination to physiognomy" (76) that convinces him he can interpret the motives of those he encounters – ultimately confirms the eclipse of integrity by hypocrisy, aspiration, consumerism, and fashion. In London, he is thus repeatedly gulled by sharpers whose honest appearance he trusts, a pattern that culminates in his losing the lease he sought for some crown-lands to a gauger who pimped his sister to secure them.

On his journey back to the country from this failed excursion, he encounters a childhood acquaintance, Old Edwards, whose story gives global significance to Harley's speculation that "the world is in general selfish, interested, and unthinking" (128). In a scene awash in domestic sentiment, Edwards describes how he offered himself as substitute for his press-ganged son and then witnessed first-hand in the East Indies the consequences of imperial brutality and greed. The hardships he encounters after he is discharged from his regiment for freeing an aged Indian prisoner (who was sentenced to fifty lashes each morning to force him to reveal the hiding place of an assumed treasure) leads to sharp criticism of colonial oppression. But as with Goldsmith's *Deserted Village*, published the previous year, it is the relation between nabob wealth, metropolitan consumerism, and the erosion of traditional hierarchies that defines this episode. Coming near the end of a novel that depicts the victimization of both Harley and the objects of his sympathy by the forces of a new monied economy, the vignette focuses on the sad remnants of a residual order whose commitment to real property and defined social roles once guaranteed collective stability. Years before, Edwards had been driven from the farm "possessed by [his] father, grandfather, and great-grandfather" when the local squire listened to the financial advice of his new steward, a "London-attorney" (87). In less overtly material but equally formative ways, Harley too experiences a changed culture, particularly in relation to his belief that disparity of fortune prevents his courting his beloved, the very wealthy Miss Walton.

Harley recreates for Edwards and his orphaned grandchildren a diminutive version of the world both have lost (just as Trim does for Toby). The narrator comments:

> Harley had contrived to lead a little bubbling brook through a green
> walk in the middle of the ground, upon which he had erected a mill in
> miniature for the diversion of Edwards' infant-grandson, and made a
> shift in the construction to introduce a pliant bit of wood, that answered
> with its fairy clack to the murmuring of the rill that turned it. I have
> seen him stand, listening to these mingled sounds, with his eye fixed on
> the boy, and the smile of conscious satisfaction on his cheek, while the
> old man, with a look half-turned to Harley and half to heaven, breathed
> an ejaculation of gratitude and piety.   (101–2)

The pastoralism recalls the Wilson estate in Henry Fielding's *Joseph Andrews*, a place of retreat from worldly corruption that to Parson Adams captures "the Manner in which the People had lived in the Golden Age" (204). More recently, Henry Brooke's *The Fool of Quality* (1766–70) used the same vocabulary in posing the question, "Did any poets or philosophers ever place their golden acres or golden scenes amidst such a town as London? A man can scarce be himself; he is confused and dissipated by the variety of objects and bustle that surrounds him." Only the country, Brooke answers, provides the "health, pleasure, and spirits" essential to true independence.[11]

But Edwards's rustic garden in *The Man of Feeling* is what the present-day hunters of the novel's opening frame narrative encountered in ruins. Its impermanence is conveyed here by the narrator's elegiac tones and anticipated by a related earlier episode of masculine communion. After Harley rescues the starving Emily Atkins, he meets her father, a Captain reduced to half-pay who once "'fondly imagined'" that his daughter would continue to be "'the joy of my age, and the pride of my soul! – Those things are now no more! they are lost for ever! Her death I could have born! but the death of her honor has added obloquy and shame to that sorrow which bends my grey hairs to the dust!'" (73). Emily, seduced by an "eldest son … home from his travels" (38) and then abandoned to prostitution in London, represents the culture of decline and exchange fatal to the stalwart few whose authentic masculinity and commitment to family render them immune to the taint of money. In both scenes, the suffering inflicted by women – whether literally in the case of Emily or more figuratively in the effeminizing effects of new money – leads inevitably to the extinction of the old order. Unlike *Joseph Andrews*, where Harriet Hearty accompanies the repentant Wilson from debtors' prison to pastoral estate, women in *The Man of Feeling* are associated not with regeneration but with a degrading materialism. The few men – Harley, Edwards, Atkins – who resist its lures are fated like the Ghost who records their history to a merely spectral existence.

Underpinning Mackenzie's novel is a conservative politics that laments the decline of hierarchies based on gender, birth, and inherited real property. While the late-century William Godwin is equally critical of contemporary institutions, his radical stance orientates him to the future rather than the past. Godwin was a central figure in the revolutionary decade. His doctrine of perfectibility, detailed most closely in his philosophical treatise, *An Enquiry concerning Political Justice* (1793), but informing as well such novels as *Caleb Williams* (1794) and such biographies as *The Lives of Edward and John Philips* (1815), holds that the dissemination of truth through reasoned discussion between individuals will ultimately lead to the withering of government and introduction of an enlightened anarchy capable of defeating sickness and even death. As a result, the lonely singularity of the first-person narrator of Godwin's 1805 novel, *Fleetwood; Or, The New Man of Feeling* is not a positive signifier of moral integrity in a corrupt world (as it was in Mackenzie's *Man of Feeling*), but a negative mark of the protagonist's failure to participate in a wider human community. Only gradually, however, do we realize that Casimir Fleetwood is an unreliable narrator.

Fleetwood's childhood places him in the familiar territory of *The Female Quixote*, *Ophelia*, and Elizabeth Inchbald's more recent *Nature and Art* (1796): parental death or disappointment has caused the family to withdraw to a remote estate. From the beginning, his retrospective narrative is cast as confessional, the writing of it "an act of my penitence and humiliation."[12] But his commitment to unadorned disclosure is repeatedly complicated by appeals to the reader's sympathy and claims to exceptional genius (with the implication that this entitles him to a different standard of judgment than that imposed on lesser beings). In recounting his childhood experience of "reverie" in nature, for instance, he reveals that he

> acquired a habit of being absent in mind from the scene which was before my senses. I devoured at first with greedy appetite the objects which presented themselves; but by perseverance they faded on my eye and my ear, and I sunk into a sweet insensibility to the impressions of external nature. The state thus produced was … [like] a living death, which, at the same time that it is indolent and inert, is not destitute of a certain voluptuousness.   (56)

The closeness of this passage to William Wordsworth's description in "Tintern Abbey" of "that serene and blessed mood,/In which the affections gently lead us on,/Until, the breath of this corporeal frame,/And even the motion of our human blood/Almost suspended, we are laid asleep/In body, and become a living soul" (ll. 42–7) casts doubt on Fleetwood's supposed truth to his own experience, suggesting that his recovery of the past may be more derivative than authentic.

The turn inward that defines his childhood appears in adulthood as a self-absorption that, far from being inherently poetic or a mark of genius, is represented as culpably anti-social. When Fleetwood leaves the remote Welsh estate of his youth for university in Oxford, Godwin activates a set of contrasts widely used in 1790s novels to indicate the consequences of unthinking autonomy: nature and art, true and false education, benevolence and tyranny (the latter exemplified in the cruel trick played on a fellow student that results in his suicide). The alternative to narcissism appears in the interpolated narrative of the family benefactor, Ruffigny, whom Fleetwood meets in Paris at the beginning of his postgraduate Grand Tour. Ruffigny tells a history in which the terrible adversity and injustice he suffered as an abandoned child fed his "restless imagination" (158) and pleasure in thinking he "belonged to no one" (175), a frame of mind overcome by the loving kindness and gratitude of Ambrose Fleetwood who rescued him from near-starvation. Ambrose (Casimir's grandfather) educates the waif, sets him up in business, and years later when Ambrose is ruined through no fault of his own, Ruffigny repays his debt of gratitude by transferring his fortune to the Fleetwoods. What might well in an earlier novel have been presented as a providential plot of restitution is used here to convey the ethical power of individual choice.

Ruffigny's narrative also serves as foil to Fleetwood's in its treatment of the doubles motif. The contrast of Ruffigny's evil uncle, the "malignant demon, the recollection of whom haunted my thoughts, waking and sleeping" (158), and Ambrose Fleetwood, the "guardian genius and better angel" (190), is resolved by Ruffigny's decision to model himself on the latter and carry through his stewardship to future generations. Casimir represents the effects on him of Ruffigny's narrative as transformative – "[f]rom this period I became an altered man" (213) – and seeks to substantiate the change by claiming affinities with a series of benevolent father figures. But his assertions of exceptionality and entitlement undermine the parallels he asserts and further distance his biographical arc from Ruffigny's. Presenting himself as heir to the republican virtues of Ruffigny and the social benevolence of his father, he at the same time suggests that his historical belatedness makes constructive action impossible. The lengthy disquisitions on the state of the nation that punctuate his confession echo the passages of overt moral commentary found in mid-eighteenth-century novels. But Godwin, unlike Mackenzie, makes his anti-hero's theorizing appear a specious rationalizing of passivity. Instead of acting purposively, Fleetwood "formed projects, – sometimes of investigating the progress or decay of national genius and taste, and sometimes of following through its minutest ramifications a certain memorable period of history" (218). But none is actually carried to fruition and the result is a paralysing "*ennui*" (228).

Fleetwood's self-deceptions in many ways anticipate those of the protagonist of *Frankenstein*, written by William Godwin's daughter, Mary Shelley. Both men desire a friend who will serve "as another self, who joys in all my joys, and grieves in all my sorrows" (229). Sarah Fielding's mid-century *David Simple* offers an instructive contrast: while David seeks a friend to confirm the presence of virtue in a vicious world, Fleetwood and Victor want only a mirror of their own flattering self-images. The crisis of the novel that reveals the fatal consequences of this solipsism begins with Fleetwood's encounter with Macneil, the last in the series of father figures whose sceptical appraisals offer the reader an alternative to the narrator's tendency to represent himself as heroic. Macneil tells Fleetwood that he is "wayward, and peevish, and indolent, and hypochondrical" precisely because he "weakly hover[s] on the outside of the pale of human society, instead of gallantly entering [him]self in the ranks, and becoming one of the great congregation of man" (259). But his proposed solution – marriage – unfortunately considers Fleetwood's needs over those of his future wife, Macneil's own daughter, Mary.

Even seen through the distorting lens of her husband's narcissism, Mary appears to the reader to possess a depth of character denied Miss Walton in *Man of Feeling* or Jenny in *Tristram Shandy*. But while she asserts her equality, telling her husband (in an echo of Mary Wollstonecraft's *Maria*) that "[i]n me you will have a wife, and not a passive machine" (281), he persists in considering her an appendage: "My tenants loved me, because I had power; my acquaintance, because I could contribute to their entertainment; the poor who dwelt near my mansion, for my wealth; but my wife would love me in sickness or in health, in poverty, in calamity, in total desolation!" (287). The echo of the marriage service from the *Book of Common Prayer* locates her value to him in the institutional structures of religion and the state, a forecast of the possessiveness that leads him ultimately to madness. In the *Man of Feeling*, Harley dies just after voicing his love for Miss Walton; Tristram never fulfills his promise to describe his relationship with Jenny; Frankenstein's wife is murdered by the monster before their relationship is consummated. *Fleetwood's* pursuit of the narrowing effects of an overactive sensibility into the terrain of marriage allows Godwin to address the full social and familial consequences of his hero's misanthropy and misogyny.

The final complication of the narrative follows from the introduction of yet another set of paired figures, these ones heavily indebted to the Gothic tropes of 1790s fiction: the ingenuous Kenrick and his illegitimate half-brother, Gifford, "a youth of a dark complexion, and elegant figure, sagacious, shrewd, supple, and insinuating" (332). Fleetwood is soon inveigled by Gifford who "flattered me in my notions and weaknesses, with the greatest imaginable address" (337). While these fraternal contrasts recall Henry Fielding's Tom Jones and Blifil, Godwin's exploration of psychological depths is fully indulged in the pathological edge he gives to Gifford's satanic pleasure in destroying virtue and reducing others to his own miserable state. As Fleetwood's demonic alter ego, he capitalizes on his host's imperfectly veiled tendency to "revile and abhor" (114) women. He convinces him that Kenrick and Mary have an adulterous relationship, presses him to divorce her, and once he has been named Fleetwood's heir, arranges for his assassination. The distributive justice of the ending – Kenrick rescues Fleetwood, a deeply veiled

Mary enters her ex-husband's room at dusk, invites him to "take my heart" and then "fell into my arms" (422), Gifford "dies by the public executioner" (423) – strains credulity. But it also confirms Godwin's political argument: the singularity, secrecy, and excessive sensibility of the "new man of feeling" are inimical to the realm of benevolent action to which family affections should properly be directed.

Part II

Sociability and community

Introduction

This part explores the forms of community that eighteenth-century novels envision as complement to the exceptional, isolated, and sometimes autonomous selves explored in the first three chapters. Chapter 4 opens with one of the period's most celebratory accounts of relationships secured by kinship and marriage, Samuel Richardson's last novel, *Sir Charles Grandison* (1753–4). Its orthodox articulation of a "family of love" provided a point of reference for numbers of succeeding works, including Oliver Goldsmith's *The Vicar of Wakefield* (1766), a far less sanguine representation of the social power wielded by fathers. In another complementary pairing, Eliza Haywood's *Betsy Thoughtless* (1751) and Jane Austen's *Emma* (1815), it is the subjects, rather than the agents, of domestic patriarchy that are of primary interest. While each of these novels specifies grounds for criticizing the family, they all end by validating its authority to define individual, social, and political behavior. Chapter 4 closes with two works from the 1790s that use earlier novels to gain a purchase on their own far bleaker assessment of the politics of family: Eliza Fenwick's 1795 *Secresy* adapts elements from Samuel Richardson's *Clarissa*, while George Walker's 1796 *Theodore Cyphon* re-writes the 1794 *Caleb Williams* (a work itself heavily indebted to *Clarissa*).

Chapter 5 pursues the characteristically broad eighteenth-century understanding of family to investigate novels that advance alternative forms of sociability independent of the patriarchalism central to the novels considered in Chapter 4. Sarah Scott's *Millenium Hall* (1762) and *Sir George Ellison* (1766), Clara Reeve's *School for Widows* (1791) and *Plans of Education* (1792), and the anonymous *Henry Willoughby* (1798) and *Berkeley Hall* (1796) focus on utopian collectives as substitutes for the nuclear family. Two further groupings that explore issues relating to community by invoking geographically distant cultures are then considered. The first includes Aphra Behn's *Oroonoko* (1688), the anonymous *Female American* (1767), Frances Brooke's *Emily Montague* (1769), Phebe Gibbes's *Hartly House, Calcutta* (1789), Elizabeth Hamilton's *Hindoo Rajah* (1796), and two novels by George Cumberland, *The Captive of the Castle of Sennaar* (1798) and *The Reformed* (c. 1800). These novels address vulnerable constituencies – women, colonial subjects, and religious iconoclasts – and identify possibilities for their reconstituting of sociability in ways suited to their distinctive beliefs. The second grouping, Ann Radcliffe's *Mysteries of Udolpho* (1794) and *The Italian* (1797) and Matthew Gregory Lewis's *The Monk* (1796), is used to consider the failures of sociability central to Gothic fiction. Finally, Chapter 6 both enlarges on and further abstracts the notion of family to argue that eighteenth-century writers – including Jane Barker in *The Galesia Trilogy* (1713–26), Sarah Fielding in *David Simple* (1744) and *Volume the Last* (1753), Frances Burney in *Evelina* (1778), Elizabeth Inchbald in *A Simple Story* (1791), Amelia Opie in *Adeline Mowbray* (1805), William Beckford in *Modern Novel Writing* (1796), Eaton Stannard Barrett in *The Heroine* (1814), and Jane Austen in *Northanger Abbey* (1817) – invite novel readers to imagine the affinities between books as reciprocally mimicking and encouraging wider forms of sociability.

Chapter 4

The reformation of family

Distinctions between "given" and "chosen" families and between nuclear and extended ones are crucial to both the unfolding and resolution of plots in period fiction. In most novels, given families – the ones individuals are born into – tend to impede the protagonist's progress and are usually either renounced or superseded by chosen ones, most often through the device of a concluding marriage that represents the newly wed partners as figures for compromise, the resolution of past injustices, and the promise of future happiness. Orphaned heroes and concealed kinship offer interesting variations on this pattern. Temporary freedom from the customary limits of the inheritance trope – including the fixities of class position, birth order, and paternal control – seems to enhance the likelihood of independence and of rewards based on merit rather than birthright. In fictions of concealed kinship – including Henry Fielding's *Tom Jones*, Tobias Smollett's *Humphry Clinker*, Frances Burney's *Evelina*, and Eliza Fenwick's *Secresy* – the disclosure or acknowledgment of paternity in the final chapters curbs the self-direction indulged in the narrative proper, allowing the status quo to be reasserted. But even in the relatively unusual instances of protagonists growing up in complete nuclear families, as in Austen's *Pride and Prejudice*, parents are most often liabilities who serve as negative foils to the advancement of the younger generation.

This chapter opens with a discussion of Samuel Richardson's *History of Sir Charles Grandison*, one of the few novels of the period to represent family – understood both affectively as the nexus of domesticity and genealogically as the sign of inherited status – in unequivocally celebratory terms. As we will see later in this and also in subsequent chapters, the obligations of family relationship are more often honored in the breach than the observance, affirmed in the closing pages of novels rather than appearing throughout as an achieved ideal. But from the beginning of *Sir Charles Grandison*, the "family of love" serves as template for the social, gender, and political values cultivated by the titular hero.[1] (A decade earlier the phrase had very different resonances when used by John Cleland's Fanny Hill to describe the group of women under the protection of the procuress, Mrs. Cole, the so-called "daughters" with whom Fanny leagues after losing the support of Mr. H –².) Instead of the cross-generational conflict of individuals struggling to reach beyond their given families, *Sir Charles Grandison* documents the willingness of all who enter the hero's orbit to accede to his view that marriage secures personal and collective harmony. While alternative structures are invoked – dynastic, libertine, religious – they are either consigned to the past or to the cultural margins, leaving the hero's conservative principles triumphant.

The novel opens with letters written by Harriet Byron to the extended family in Northamptonshire that raised her after the early deaths of her parents. The correspondence begins by describing her visit to her cousins in London and then, after Sir Charles rescues her from a libertine's attempted kidnapping, moves to an account of her prolonged recuperation at his family estate, Grandison-hall. Almost immediately, Sir Charles acts to fold Harriet into his domestic world, asking that she consider himself and his sisters as her siblings; equally immediately, her own relatives regard him as a prospective husband. He, however, has an unresolved romantic history that echoes key aspects of Harriet's own recent experiences: while on the Grand Tour, he had rescued Jeronymo della Porretta from an assassination attempt, been welcomed into his family "not only as the preserver of his life, but as restorer of his *morals*" (II.122), and fallen in love with his sister, Clementina. But he demurs when religious conversion and settlement in Italy are made conditions of their marriage. Clementina, torn between romantic and religious "enthusiasm" and harshly treated by her parents and uncles, subsequently descends into madness. Sir Charles comes back to England, leaving open a return to Italy should she and her family accept the compromises he has proposed.

The Porrettas embody many of the autocratic traits eighteenth-century novels conventionally assign to the given or birth family: severe to the point of being punitive in relation to daughters, focused on issues of property rather than sentiment, determined to make the younger generation defer to the will of the older, and, as in *Clarissa*, ready to extend patriarchal mandates to uncles and brothers. A cluster of references to the 1745 Jacobite rebellion (mounted to topple the Hanoverians and reclaim the throne for the Stuart dynasty in the person of James II's grandson, the Young Pretender, Charles Edward) politicizes their domestic enactment of absolute, hereditary power. But unlike Henry Fielding's complex, fully integrated use of the same event in *Tom Jones*, Richardson's is local and strategic, designed to identify the Porrettas with the exiled Stuarts as intransigently foreign and despotic compared to Sir Charles. The Continental location of the two censured families – invented and actual – in turn foregrounds the Grandisonian alternative as quintessentially English in its moderating and refining of traditional structures. The renovation of damaged families and formation of new ones through marriage, his particular preoccupations once he returns to England, reinforce the bonds between patriotism, community, and domesticity. But his private life remains suspended since the standing obligations to Clementina prevent any overt declaration of his growing love for Harriet. The odd dormancy of the courtship plot – an effect heightened in this epistolary novel by our having access only to Harriet's letters and not Grandison's for the prolonged period in which their nuptial prospects are widely canvassed within both their extended families – throws into sharper relief the efforts at social renewal that define his character.

The form of renewal with which he is most closely associated is marriage and his efforts here are directed, somewhat paradoxically, by the wish to reinstate the mores of "the purest times, an hundred or two years … ago" (I.211). In practice, this entails preserving and even enlarging patriarchal authority, while also paying lip-service to the notion of individual identity. His role as latter-day paterfamilias emerges in part through contrast with his late father, Sir Thomas Grandison. Sir Thomas's retrograde insistence on dynastic marriages and strict patrilineal inheritance led him to disregard entirely the needs of his two daughters and the opinions of his long-suffering wife; his libertinism tied these domestic lapses to an aristocratic culture of fiscal extravagance and sexual excess. When set against his father's tyrannies, Sir Charles's brokering of multiple marriages seems comparatively enlightened. His orchestration of the wedding of Miss Mansfield and Lord W is typical. Sir Charles himself approaches the recently impoverished Miss Mansfield with the proposal: in exchange for her nursing the gouty ex-reprobate Lord W, she, and by extension her family, will enjoy the financial security they lost in a recent law-suit. In turning the principals' self-interestedness to the broadly social end of marriage, Sir Charles appears, unlike his father, to have taken individual needs into account. But since his plans ratify both male power and a view of women as property, the difference between the two positions on arranged marriages seems in many ways more imagined than real. The emotional orientations of father and son, however, remain entirely distinct, since the former's motives are selfish and the latter's altruistic. Sir Charles's negotiations here and elsewhere allow two imperfect lives – the one a consequence of undeserved penury, the other of a willfully debauched youth – to be reconstructed as mutually supportive.

Sir Charles's efforts to restore broken families grow out of his conviction that marriage underpins social harmony, in large part because it enforces traditional hierarchies of sexual and behavioral difference. To Sir Charles, marriage provides shelter from an emerging alternative culture of public display that tolerates, even encourages, gender transgressions: "Can there be characters," he asks his sister, Charlotte, more odious than those of a masculine woman, and an effeminate man? What are the distinguishing characteristics of the two Sexes? And whence this odiousness? There are, indeed, *men*, whose minds, if I may be allowed the expression, seem to be cast in a Female mould; whence the fops, foplings, and pretty fellows, who buz about your Sex at public places; *women*, whose minds seem to be cast in a masculine one ... the women, who, at such places, give the men stare for stare, swing their arms, look jolly; and those married women who are so kind as to take the reins out of their husbands hands, in order to save the honest men trouble.   (III.247)

If the assertive gaze and jaunty walk define what Charlotte in an earlier letter to Harriet had described as this "gross age" in which women "give the men stare for stare where-ever we meet them" (II.427), the changes in her own physical appearance dramatically confirm the potentially transformative effects of marriage. Up to the point that she yields to her brother's suggestion that she accept Lord G's proposals, she has played flighty satirist to the reflective Harriet. In a standard eighteenth-century formulation – from Samuel Richardson's Anna Howe and Clarissa through Robert Bage's Maria Fluart and Caroline Campinet (*Hermsprong*) to Jane Austen's Marianne and Elinor (*Sense and Sensibility*) – the pairing of heroines sets the female protagonist's steady virtue against the livelier sensibility of her friend. Charlotte herself describes the narrative functions of such contrasts when she tells Harriet that "[o]dd characters, my dear, are needful to make even characters shine. You good girls would not be as valued as you are, if there were not bad ones" (II.414). As with the other oppositions that advance the plot in this novel – native and foreign, Protestant and Catholic, rational and enthusiastic – the power of the discredited term is first indulged and then checked. Once Charlotte agrees to marry, her appearance thus undergoes a striking change: "A charming flush had overspread her cheeks: A sweet consciousness in her eyes gave a female grace to her whole aspect, and softened ... the natural majesty of her features" (II.316). The process of feminization is completed with the birth of her first child and her full embrace of maternity.

In charting the triumph of the collective over the personal and of the sociable over the self-referential, Richardson makes full use of the expressive potential of epistolary narrative to endorse connectedness. While *Pamela* and *Clarissa* were also "told in letters," the formal adjustments here emphasize this novel's overwhelmingly communitarian ethic. In the earlier works, letters were at once private and public: on the one hand, subjective expressions of desire, on the other, documents whose transmission, reception, and interpretation were often uncertain. Such volatility is disallowed in *Sir Charles*

Grandison, where letters, like the protagonists themselves, are identified with the certainties of corporate judgment. Harriet assumes from the beginning, for instance, that even correspondence directed to individual family members will be read aloud to others. As her relationship with Sir Charles deepens, additional means of aligning the formal attributes of epistolary narrative with the characters' social impulses are developed. Letters continue to be read collectively, but their writing too is increasingly shared, a pattern that culminates in what Harriet describes as a "journal-wise" correspondence in which the jottings of others supplement her notes on daily occurrences. This composite writing reflects the enlarged responsibilities that accompany her imminent marriage to Sir Charles: "my time is not now my own, as it used to be; tho' I shall think myself very ungrateful, and undutiful too, if I permit my new duties so wholly to engross me, as to furnish an excuse for the neglect of those which from my very birth I owe to you" (III.266). As her assertion of changing allegiances makes clear, a woman's transition from her given family to her chosen one necessarily (and seemingly here unproblematically) involves a measure of estrangement from her birth relatives.

Harriet's adjustment to the terms of a shared identity has been foreshadowed by the aura of public accountability surrounding her letters from the earliest moments of the novel. Writing home when she first arrived in London, she recorded what she imagined each of her new acquaintances might say about her, a form of speculative ventriloquism in which self-examination is played off against social awareness. Sir Charles, too, habitually directs his behavior by reflecting on the possible reactions of his mentor, Dr. Bartlett. In a projected version of Adam Smith's "impartial spectator" or "the man within the breast" (215) in *Theory of Moral Sentiments*, he shapes his conduct by asking himself " 'What account shall I give of this to Dr. Bartlett?' 'How were I to give way to *this* temptation, shall I report it to Dr. Bartlett?' – Or, 'Shall I be an hypocrite and only inform him of the best, and meanly conceal from him the worst?' " (II.116). While contemporary novels routinely investigate matters of conscience by giving us access to characters' minds, self-questioning typically is voiced here in collective terms rather than introspective or personal ones. The willingness of others to regard the hero as entirely disinterested in turn advances his status as ethical arbiter and checks the tendency of epistolary narrative toward confessional. When Clementina's mother addresses him in the "third person," confident that he "will have the generosity to advise, as *such,* tho' against [him]self" (II.455), she attributes to him an authority reminiscent of Henry Fielding's obtrusive, omniscient narrator, and far removed from the idiosyncrasies of characters like Tom Jones or Captain Booth, Pamela or Clarissa.

Richardson's investment of Sir Charles with the combined attributes of disembodied commentator and individual character anticipates the technique Austen deploys when she makes proximity to the narrator serve as an evaluative gauge. In *Persuasion*, for example, Anne Elliot is largely exempted from the alienating effects of the irony to which Austen subjects Anne's father and sisters. But even this most admirable of heroines is occasionally held at a distance, her foibles displayed and gently mocked. Responsibility for criticism in epistolary novels, of course, falls to the circle of letter writers. Since all concur in praising Sir Charles's unvarying adherence to "that true heroism which Christianity enjoins, when it recommends meekness, moderation, and humility, as the glory of the human nature" (I.263), there are few opportunities for disenchanted commentary. Only once does Harriet address the chillier aspects of his disinterestedness and even then she quickly retreats from the edge of resentment in her question,

> Do you think, my dear, that had he been the first man, he would have been so complaisant to his Eve *as Milton makes Adam*? … No; it is my opinion, that your brother would have had gallantry enough to his fallen spouse, to have made him extremely regret her lapse; but that he would have done *his own duty*, were it but for the sake of posterity, and left it to the Almighty, if such had been his pleasure, to have annihilated his first Eve, and given him a second.   (II.609)

By novel's end, the restored paradise of multiple marriages renders the query inadmissible. Its implications reverberate, however, in later works centered on highly idealized characters.

Although not often read now, *Sir Charles Grandison* had a profound impact on the eighteenth-century novel, its traces apparent in matters large and small: in the representation of the family as socially constituted through chosen relationships rather than defined by given ones; in the plot of second chances (only Harriet among the principals falls in love with and then marries her first choice); in the formative influence of maternity (Sir Charles notes that his father had "great qualities," but declares his mother in all things, his "oracle" [I.261]); in the depiction of the benevolent hero defined through charitable acts, as in Mackenzie's *Man of Feeling* and Henry Brooke's *The Fool of Quality: Or, The History of Henry, Earl of Moreland* (1766–70); in the close attention to the material world and to consumer goods; in the celebration of a culture of politeness that makes the strongest temperamental bond between Harriet and Sir Charles their being "courteous to all" (I.10). More generally, its attention to social policy was transformative: the benevolent strain of its sentimental rendering of madness, of its argument for housing "fallen" women in a Hospital for Female Penitents (William Dodd, chaplain to the actual Magdalen Hospital founded in 1758 built on Richardson's case for such an institution in his own 1754 novel, *The Sisters*), and of its advocacy of Protestant nunneries to help those disadvantaged by the loosening of traditional family obligations (proposals indebted to Mary Astell and subsequently elaborated in Sarah Scott's *Millenium Hall* and Clara Reeve's *School for Widows*). The latter philanthropic projects, in addressing current humanitarian issues, suggest a mutually defining relation between literary and social change in the period.

Sir Charles Grandison also set the pattern for the pairing of the exemplary hero and heroine that Burney uses in *Evelina* and Thomas Holcroft, somewhat surprisingly given his radical politics, in *Anna St Ives*. The protagonists of all three novels occupy a middle ground of gendered behavior that avoids modish extremes, whether reactionary or aggressively forward-looking. Novelists establish that middle ground through contrast with those extremes, each of which is typically represented by conflating sexual and social deviance: libertines appear to embody the worst aspects of the aristocracy or gentry, mannish women or effeminate men of bourgeois aspiration. Gender thus indirectly serves to establish standards of ideal conduct: the libertine Sir Clement Willoughby in *Evelina* deviates from and so confirms the true aristocracy of politeness that Lord Orville represents, Coke Clifton in *Anna St. Ives* exemplifies the faults of inherited privilege that serve as foil to Frank Henley's independence. All three novels in turn prepare for the conclusions' endorsement of sexual hierarchies by representing the heroine's conduct at the outset as slightly blameworthy: the abduction from which Sir Charles rescued Harriet Byron originated in her presence at a masquerade (an emblem of disorder across the century as suggested by Henry Fielding's *Amelia*, Tobias Smollett's *Adventures of Peregrine Pickle*, Frances Burney's *Cecilia*, and Elizabeth Inchbald's *Simple Story*) and Evelina inadvertently breaks with decorum when she rejects Mr. Lovel and subsequently dances with Orville at Mrs. Stanley's. Anna, acting on her sense that "few opportunities present themselves to a woman, educated and restrained as women unfortunately are, of performing anything eminently good," commits herself to rescuing the reprobate Coke Clifton, on the assumption that his may be "a great mind, misled by error."[3] By novel's end, however, with these minor lapses corrected and the heroes' controlling influence confirmed, marriage and enclosure within an enlightened domestic sphere convey the attainment of an ideal balance between individual desire and communal stability.

One of the most powerful alternatives to this model of paired, if slightly uneven, paragons appears in fictions centered on imperfect protagonists, particularly those spirited but mistaken heroines encountered in variations on the conduct novel from Eliza Haywood's *Betsy Thoughtless* to Jane Austen's *Emma*. Before turning to these, however, I want to consider an example of their male counterpart, the fallible hero of Oliver Goldsmith's *Vicar of Wakefield* (1766), a novel that responds with scepticism to *Sir Charles Grandison*'s insular model of family and community. The point of connection between the two works is most evident in the exaggerated patriarchalism of the eponymous Vicar, Dr. Primrose, the first-person narrator whose single-mindedness – "Matrimony," he pronounces, "was always one of my favorite topics, and I wrote several sermons to prove its happiness" – is often inflected with a smug vanity.[4] While Richardson focuses on his hero's successful efforts to colonize domesticity, Goldsmith examines the inclination of patriarchal structures to impede sociability and disable the potential links between family and community.

The novel opens in a moment of crisis: a catastrophic loss of fortune caused by the contemporary equivalent of a bank failure forces the Primroses to leave their comfortable life behind and travel to a new curacy in a distant parish. As so often in eighteenth-century fiction, public spaces – inns, theaters, pleasure grounds, masquerades – provide occasions for accidental encounters, unexpected news, and the crossing of class boundaries. Here, when the Primroses stop to rest at an inn, they learn that their new landlord, Squire Thornhill, is a libertine and they meet a fellow traveler, Mr. Burchell, to whom the Vicar generously loans money (a moment recalled at the end of the novel when Primrose himself becomes object of charity). Burchell, we discover through a slip of the tongue that the Vicar typically does not hear (his negligence as both auditor and later reader lies behind many of the plot turns and is recurrently used to satirize him), is in fact Sir William Thornhill, uncle of the current squire and self-described as a lapsed hero of sensibility. In search of authentic, disinterested virtue, he appears in the neighborhood as a poor man, a disguise he abandons only at novel's end when the villainy of his nephew is unmasked. Over the following months, Primrose's actions initiate a complicated series of disasters, many of them the result of the vanity and social aspiration he claims not to possess.

Martin Battestin's influential reading of the novel maps the Vicar's downward trajectory of pain and deprivation in religious terms: from material (loss of fortune) to spiritual (the debauching of the elder daughter Olivia) to physiological (the burning of his arm in the fire that destroys their house). In this account, Burchell appears typologically as a Christ-figure, a redeemer who moves disguised among men to test and judge; later, in his final unveiling as Sir William Thornhill, he operates as a *deus ex machina* to deliver the Job-like Dr. Primrose from the satanic Squire Thornhill. Other equally compelling interpretations prefer the terms of irony to those of theology, seeing the Vicar's children, for example, as parodic extensions of their father's negative traits. As with *A Sentimental Journey* and *Tristram Shandy*, this novel's unstable compound of satire and sentiment helps to make equally credible what appear to be mutually exclusive readings. The piling up of coincidences, the fortuitous meetings, the lengthy disquisitions on political and social matters, and the eclectic jumble of homiletic, romantic, parodic, fabular, and picaresque elements also indicate parallels with Sterne.

Something close to a unifying thread, however, is found in the *Vicar*'s apparent use of *Sir Charles Grandison* as a point of contrast to its own scrutiny of familial hierarchies. Dr. Primrose shares many attributes with Sir Charles. But the discrepancies between the Vicar's pronouncements and his actions, and between his view of his family and theirs of him, combine to recast the earlier novel's ideals in unflattering ways that additionally invite retroactive scepticism about the tenor of Richardson's text. Primrose claims the disinterestedness that makes Sir Charles the ethical center of Richardson's work, but the quality manifests itself here as a vain and elitist pomposity, all the more dangerous because unacknowledged and frequently the source of actions that while flattering to the Vicar are disastrous for others. If Primrose's similarity to Sir Charles draws our attention to the rigidity of Richardson's paragon, so from the opposite perspective does Sir William Thornhill's very different social fluidity. The cumulative effect of these specific comparisons is to highlight the larger divergence between the two novels' representations of hierarchy. The patriarchal authority that in *Grandison* sanctions the translation of individual virtue into social power is subjected to pointed irony in the *Vicar of Wakefield*. Thus, while Primrose roundly asserts both his familial and professional status as father figure, he falls into despair with each succeeding disaster, forcing his children repeatedly to admonish him to practice what he preaches by looking beyond this world and accepting "the justice of heaven" (159). His lowest point comes after Squire Thornhill arranges to have him confined for debt.

Novels ranging from *Tom Jones, Amelia*, and Tobias Smollett's *Peregrine Pickle* through Godwin's *Caleb Williams* to Inchbald's *Nature and Art* also employ the trope of imprisonment, although the uses to which it is put change over time. In the late-century radical fiction of Godwin and Inchbald, it recurrently serves as a metaphor for the entrapment of individuals within a coercive social order. For mid-century traditionalists like Fielding, Smollett, and Goldsmith, however, it marks the nadir of experience *and* signals the imminent resurgence of an hierarchically ordered providential plot. Tom Jones, Peregrine Pickle, and Captain Booth thus undergo a life-altering conversion while in prison. Their acknowledgment of their offenses against divine law releases them spiritually and literally to enjoy marriage and the domestic idyll of the country estates to which both finally retreat. Goldsmith, in contrast, focuses in the prison scenes on collective reformation rather than individual conversion. In doing so, he presses beyond *Sir Charles Grandison*'s identification of family with the vested interests of the upper gentry and prepares for the more expansively social terms of his novel's ending. He also, albeit very briefly, advances a modified version of the patriarchalism Richardson makes central.

The Vicar rouses the motley group of his fellow prisoners to a sense of their mutual interdependence when he effects their moral reformation and then introduces them to the regularizing discipline of labor. Few details of the spiritual direction that ensured that "in less than six days some were penitent, and all were attentive" are provided, but the subsequent "temporal services" devised for "rendering their situation somewhat more comfortable" (148) are closely described and justified. He sets them to work "cutting pegs for tobacconists and shoemakers ... [and then] instituted fines for the punishment of immorality, and rewards for peculiar industry. Thus in less than a fortnight I had formed them into something social and humane, and had the pleasure of regarding myself as a legislator, who had brought men from their native ferocity into friendship and obedience" (148). The narrative irony that consistently pricks Primrose's vanity here sets his singular "pleasure" in being "legislator" against the collective vision of the "social and humane" new-modeled prisoners. Even after the dramatic revelations that release the family from the "gloomy mansions of sorrow" (186), the subtle undermining of the patriarch continues. At the wedding party that marks the novel's ending, as the Vicar tries unsuccessfully to dominate the proceedings with "two homilies and a thesis of my own composing" (187), his efforts to impose his own narrow and unchanged views of matrimony contrast sharply with the responses of the less doctrinaire younger generation. For them, it appears, marriage is a companionate union of individuals who have been positively altered by their trying circumstances.

In Eliza Haywood's *Betsy Thoughtless* (1751), the critique of patriarchal authority is developed not through ironic representation of an agent – the Vicar is both professionally (as priest) and domestically defined by his fatherly vocation – but through sympathetic treatment of an occasionally resisting female subject. As Betsy writes to her mentor, "I know not how it is, I cannot all at once bring myself into a liking of the marriage state."[5] In fact, her antipathy to marriage allows her to preserve the freedoms she enjoys as an orphaned heroine of means, and she puts off the moment of her capitulation for as long as possible. This tantalizing of the reader with a deferred wedding resembles – despite its contrary logic – *Sir Charles Grandison*, published two years later. Haywood was like Richardson an established author, although her career stretched further back to the wildly successful 1719–20 *Love in Excess* (an amatory fiction whose sales, together with *Robinson Crusoe* and *Gulliver's Travels*, were unsurpassed until *Pamela*). Narrative traces of this earlier period appear in *Betsy Thoughtless* alongside features that anticipate later fictions. Subsequent eponymous heroines, like Burney's Evelina and Cecilia are also left in the care of guardians – the loving Reverend Villars in the former, the trio of the spendthrift Harrells, the avaricious Mr. Briggs, and the elitist Mr. Delville, in the latter – but in these novels the custodians' leading traits relate intrinsically to particular thematic issues. Here the old-fashioned generalized naming of Betsy's two trustees, Mr. Goodman and Sir Ralph Trusty, complement their equally traditional location by place: Mr. Goodman lives in the city, Sir Ralph in the country. This contrastive structure is supported by further pairings: of Betsy's two brothers, the elder Thomas is a libertine, the second son Francis is virtuous, and she herself is coupled with an unsavory female counterpart, Flora, step-daughter of Mr. Goodman and his wife Lady Mellasin.

As in Charlotte Lennox's soon-to-be published *The Female Quixote* (1752), the overt sexuality of the false friend makes the heroine's willfulness in the courtship period seem not simply less culpable, but perhaps even necessary to the formation of a coherent female identity distinct from the terms of the body. Both novels treat equivocally the protagonists' abuses of power: on the one hand, the heroines are roundly criticized for the distress they cause their true lovers when they tolerate (here deliberately, in *The Female Quixote* inadvertently) the advances of other men; on the other, when at last they cede authority to their new husbands, they lose the autonomy that has throughout defined their personalities. Since Betsy (like the heroine of Burney's *Cecilia*) is an orphan under the direction of trustees, she is connected through legal means to a number of surrogate families who recommend but cannot mandate appropriate behavior. Lady Trusty believes that this freedom exposes her charge to dangers and advises marriage to the most promising candidate, Trueworth:

> Consider, my dear child, you have no tender mother, whose precepts and example might keep you steady in the paths of prudence; – no father, whose authority might awe the daring libertine from any injurious attack; and are but too much mistress of yourself. – In fine, thus environed with temptations, I see no real defence for you but in a good husband.   (173–4)

Trueworth has already told Betsy's brother that he feels for her "a concern, more deep, more strong, than that of father, brother, or all the ties of blood could give" (67), thus setting the terms for the development of favored

eighteenth-century contrasts between given and chosen families, dynastic
and companionate marriages, received and discovered knowledge. To these,
Betsy Thoughtless adds a distinction between real and publicly acknowledged
innocence, insisting that however well intentioned and virtuous the heroine's
motives, they must meet worldly standards of propriety since, as another of
Betsy's trustees tells her, "it is not enough to be good, without behaving in such
a manner as shall make others acknowledge us to be so" (144). To substantiate this recurring theme, conduct novels subject the heroine to the attentions
of men eager to exploit her failures of decorum for their own sexual or social
advantage. Were they successful – and these narratives repeatedly float this
as a possibility – the sullying of her reputation would effectively destroy her
marriage prospects. The eventual husband is the only one among the male
peers who refuses to take advantage of her misbehavior: Trueworth recognizes that Betsy's coquettishness is the socially unacceptable face of a more
fundamental individual integrity (Glanville similarly understands Arabella's
romance delusions in *The Female Quixote*). Later novels substantially dimin-
ish the scope for the heroines to realize and repair their faults: from Burney's
Evelina and *Camilla* through to Austen's *Emma*, social blunders increasingly
stand in for the earlier instances of sexual impropriety. The difference between
mid-century novels and their successors points to the 1750s as a transitional
decade of experimentation in relation both to form and ideas.

Betsy Thoughtless's indiscretions reach a tipping point when she narrowly
escapes being tricked into marrying a servant posing as Sir Frederick Fineer.
Her brothers now demand that she accept a partner of their choice, declaring
that otherwise she will "bring ruin on herself, and disgrace to all her family"
(406–7). This late-novel shift of attention from companionate to arranged marriage – Trueworth has long since despaired of her maturing, let his suit lapse,
and wed another – raises the stakes of female identity by tightening its connection to domestic politics. The stark representation of marriage as a check
on female sexuality makes possible some disenchanted speculation on the corporate aspects of the institution. With the slow fading of her initial pleasure in
complying with her brothers' wishes, Betsy's doubts increase:

> '… what can make the generality of women so fond of marrying? – It
> looks to me like an infatuation. – Just as if it were not a greater pleasure
> to be courted, complimented, admired, and addressed by a number,
> than be confined to one, who from a slave becomes a master, and,
> perhaps, uses his authority in a manner disagreeable enough.
>
> 'And yet it is expected from us. – One has no sooner left off one's bib
> and apron than people cry, – "Miss will soon be married." – And this
> man, and that man, is presently picked out for a husband. – Mighty

ridiculous! – They want to deprive us of all the pleasures of life, just
when one begins to have a relish for them.   (431)

In the event, her husband, Munden, exceeds all her anxieties: a misogynist
who "considered a wife no more than an upper servant, bound to study and
obey, in all things" (448), he also spends beyond his income and then accuses
her (like Berrendale in Amelia Opie's *Adeline Mowbray*) of being extravagant.
At this moment of crisis, Betsy's core virtue resurfaces: she puts herself on trial,
concludes that "all her faults, and her misfortunes had been owing either to an
excess of vanity; – a mistaken pride, – or a false delicacy" (495), and from that
point forward resists flattery.

Betsy's secular conversion and repentance earn her – eventually – the comic
resolution of a happy marriage. But her extrication from Munden must be
carefully handled to ensure a balance between female integrity and spousal
duty. She discovers that Munden has a mistress and deems herself bound to
him by neither "divine nor human laws" (526), a decision supported by the
paragon Lady Loveit who declares that remaining with an errant husband – as
both Sheridan's Sidney Bidulph and Mowbray's Adeline Mowbray do – would
be "an injustice not only to herself, but to all wives in general, by setting them
an example of submitting to things required of them neither by law nor nature"
(531). During the period of separation, the now-widowed Trueworth glimpses
her out of doors, clad in "the most negligent night-dress" and pressing a "lifeless image to her bosom" (543), a miniature portrait of him. The scene recalls
the standard garden seduction of early amatory fiction and its eliciting of a vicarious sexuality, as in the following depiction of Amena and Count d'Elmont
in Haywood's own 1719–20 *Love in Excess*:

> The heat of the weather, and the confinement having hindred her from
> dressing that day, she had only a thin silk night gown on, which flying
> open as he caught her in his Arms, he found her panting heart beat
> measures of consent, her heaving breast swell to be pressed to his, and
> every pulse confess a wish to yield: her spirits all dissolved sunk in a
> lethargy of love.[6]

The substitution in *Betsy Thoughtless* of the miniature portrait for the actual
desiring hero of *Love in Excess* redirects the narrative point of view in order to
emphasize sentiment over sex. Departing from the precedent of a novel's-worth
of coquettishness, Betsy rebuffs Trueworth's declaration of undying love, saying:
"remember, sir, I am a wife, and being such, ought never to see you more." To
this, the narrator adds, "all in general must applaud the conduct of Mrs. Munden;
till this dangerous instance she had never had an opportunity of shewing the
command she had over herself" (546). Lest her resolve be seen as improperly

independent, she returns to Munden for a death-bed reconciliation, pledging never to leave him "'unless your behaviour shall convince me you do not desire my stay'" (550). He dies, she spends the appropriate year of mourning with Lady Trusty, and then at last marries Trueworth. Francis Thoughtless, who had long ago introduced them and urged his sister's acceptance of his friend's proposal, returns from the Continent unaware of their reconciliation. In a small but telling gesture, Trueworth greets him by "lock[ing] him in his arms, saying, – 'Dear Frank, I shall at last be so happy as to call you brother'; – Heavens, is it possible!' – cried he, 'Am I awake? Or is this illusion!'" (567). Marriages at the ends of mid-eighteenth-century novels are rarely imagined as simply negotiations between individuals: as here, they are also family alliances that enable compacts between men and hence the reassertion of gender and social hierarchies.

Jane Austen's *Emma* shares a surprising number of features with *Betsy Thoughtless* beyond that of the fallible heroine: both make class distinctions central to the plot and characterization, both defer the protagonist's recognition of her true feelings, and although neither is epistolary in form, both make misconstrued or secret letters the source of many difficulties (and in the process foreground reading as a fraught activity). In addition to this broad concern with communication, *Emma* engages more specifically with language through scenes involving word games and through charged references to other texts: while Mr. Martin, for example, is familiar with the middle-brow *Vicar of Wakefield*, he does not know the more fashionable Gothic novels favored by Harriet Smith. The most striking common element, however, is the framing of the heroine's strengths and shortcomings through the use of paired characters. Haywood sets Betsy in relation to two companions, Miss Forward and Flora Mellasin, whose combination of sexuality, competitiveness, and deception contrasts with the heroine's essentially virtuous, if misguided nature. Austen complicates the positioning of her protagonist by making Emma's attraction to Harriet Smith and dislike of Jane Fairfax revelatory in a number of different ways, each integral to the unfolding of the plot. Harriet's inappropriateness as chosen friend is not – as in *Betsy Thoughtless* – principally tied to sexual misbehavior (although her illegitimacy refers obliquely to this standard trope of mid-century fiction). Instead, the unsuitability grows out of differences in intellect, taste, and class, differences that Emma's need for an acolyte lead her willfully to overlook and that, conversely, explain her resistance to the talented Jane Fairfax. Given Emma's peculiar circumstances – she is the mainstay of her valetudinarian father – the opposition between the admiring but dim Harriet and the refined but distanced Jane appears a transposed version of the courtship choices facing young heroines in contemporary novels (with gender alterations made necessary by Emma's pledge to remain single).

Emma has been driven to find a new companion after the marriage of her beloved governess Miss Taylor leaves her with only the "quiet prosings" of the amiable but tedious women who visit with her father, Mr. Woodhouse.[7] Harriet is chosen as replacement in part because she is flatteringly deferential and pliable. Her current friends, however, are problematic. Austen uses free indirect discourse – taking us inside a character's mind while retaining the ironic distance of the third-person voice – to relay the mix of snobbery, narcissism masquerading as benevolence, and self-deception that defines Emma in her self-elected role as patron:

> The friends from whom [Harriet] had just parted, though very good sort of people, must be doing her harm. They were a family of the name of Martin, whom Emma well knew by character, as renting a large farm of Mr. Knightley, and residing in the parish of Donwell – very creditably she believed – she knew Mr. Knightley thought highly of them – but they must be coarse and unpolished, and very unfit to be the intimates of a girl who wanted only a little more knowledge and elegance to be quite perfect. *She* would notice her; she would improve her; she would detach her from her bad acquaintance, and introduce her into good society; she would form her opinions and her manners. It would be an interesting, and certainly a very kind undertaking; highly becoming her own situation in life, her leisure, and powers.   (23)

The verbal repetitions and alterations – particularly the shift from "they must be" to "she would" – nicely track Emma's rationalizing self-puffery. Typically, she registers Knightley's point of view, although at this early stage, she fails to pursue its implications. Ultimately, his assessment of both Harriet and Mr. Martin proves correct, and by novel's end, Emma concurs, as we might expect given the author's forecasting of the protagonists' eventual harmony through the free indirect discourse she uses to convey their distinctive inwardness. The technique, refined and extended by Austen, functions as an evaluative gauge, an index to those charged in her imagined world with meeting a higher threshold of expectation in their translation of emotional and intellectual capability into action.

Knightley's meeting of those expectations and Emma's frequent lapses from them allow us to monitor her gradual progress toward an individual and collective awareness comparable to his. Emma at several points along the way falls short of the kindness due to her social inferiors, as when she deliberately truncates Harriet's visit to the Martins, or, much more seriously, at Box Hill when she makes a witty but cruel comment at the expense of Miss Bates. These solecisms recall earlier revelatory uses of politeness. In *Evelina*, for instance, Lord Orville's undifferentiated courtesy offers a positive alternative to the tendency of the insecure and egotistical to harass the vulnerable. In *Emma*, as elsewhere in Austen, Burney's contrast between civility and insolence is complicated by the additional demand for "openness" (311), an attribute whose enhanced importance in later novels corresponds to the growing fascination with the fictional rendering of interiority. One result of this newly prized candor is to make Orville's version of perfect politeness seem slightly untrustworthy, an effect heightened by the notoriety of Lord Chesterfield's recommendation of a mannered urbanity in the posthumously published *Letters to his Son* (1774). *Persuasion*'s Anne Elliot, for instance, feels "that she could so much more depend upon the sincerity of those who sometimes looked or said a careless or a hasty thing, than of those whose presence of mind never varied, whose tongue never slipped," and on these grounds she condemns Mr. Elliot as "too generally agreeable," one who although "rational, discreet, polished" was culpably "not open."[8] While Emma similarly suspects that Frank Churchill "knew how to make himself agreeable" (205), she nevertheless confides to him that she "'never could attach'" herself to one "'so completely reserved'" (218) as Jane Fairfax, a criticism that on a first reading seems to align Jane's manner with Mr. Elliot's and oppose her circumspection to Frank's frankness. We realize subsequently, however, that this exchange (like numerous others in this superbly plotted novel) contains multiple ironies that only become apparent with the deferred revelation that Frank has feigned interest in Emma to hide his secret engagement to Jane.

The crosscurrents generated by his apparent openness and actual duplicity, Emma's indiscretion, and Jane's repressed misery alert us to the ways in which the novel's deliberately imperfect symmetries complicate ethical judgment. Frank's manipulation of Emma, for example, echoes her tendency to manage others to her own advantage. But typically, while this parallel is reinforced by their shared responsibility for Jane's distress, it is also qualified by his calculated deceit and by the disparity between his suffering and Jane's (the acuteness of the latter in turn mitigates her guilt and establishes her moral superiority to him). The separation of Jane and Frank from their birth parents, respectively through death and adoption, offers another ostensible similarity with very different outcomes. While he enjoys the privileges of the intended heir to the Churchill fortune, she faces the more demeaning of the futures to which Emma glibly refers when she tells Harriet that a "'single woman, with a very narrow income, must be a ridiculous, disagreeable, old maid! ... but a single woman, of good fortune, [Emma's own projected future] is always respectable, and may be as sensible and pleasant as anybody else'" (91).

Spinsterhood is not, of course, the ultimate fate of the novel's trio of women. Despite Emma's conviction that she cannot marry and tend to her father,

Knightley is pegged early as a pre-eminently suitable partner. Typically of a novel that filters its representations of power through the domestic sphere, their compatibility is forecast at a family gathering at Hartfield where each manages the eccentricities of their various relatives to achieve a concord that will later be formalized in their own union. But Emma needs first to be humbled. Although convinced (falsely, as it turns out) that Frank is "undoubtedly very much in love" with her, she intuits that she cannot "altogether build upon his steadiness or constancy" (285), and plots instead to marry him off to Harriet. An earlier plan to do the same with Mr. Elton had gone sadly wrong, and once again her efforts to control others' lives are undermined when the existing relationship with Jane surfaces. Meanwhile, Emma has begun slowly to register Knightley's attractions: he dances with a "natural grace" in a "gentlemanlike" manner and, like Darcy in *Pride and Prejudice*, possesses an estate that could only be the "residence of a family of true gentility, untainted in blood and understanding" (389). The deferral of the marriage between Trueworth and Betsy Thoughtless to allow for the heroine's recognition of her faults and his virtues is echoed here, as are elements from Frances Burney's reworking of Haywood in *Cecilia*'s clandestine engagement and *Camilla*'s contrast of steadfast hero and flighty heroine (Mandlebert, like Trueworth with Betsy, knows that "though [Camilla's] understanding was excellent, her temper was so inconsiderate, that she rarely consulted it; and that, though her mind was of the purest innocence, it was unguarded by caution, and unprotected by reflexion").[9]

The multiple restorations of social difference celebrated in the weddings of Emma, Jane, and Harriet, however, exceed these earlier adaptations of the dynastic marriage motif. Harriet Smith, now known to be a tradesman's daughter without any of "the blood of gentility that Emma had formerly been so ready to vouch for" (526), contentedly marries her original suitor, the tenant farmer Mr. Martin; like many other shallow secondary figures in Austen's fiction, she does so "without a care for the past, and with the fullest exultation in the present and future" (525). The better-born Jane and Emma, in confronting and acknowledging their faults, are granted a more productive relationship to time, one that enables both individual and social advancement – although in markedly unequal terms. In a reconciliatory conversation with Frank late in the novel, Emma notes their common good fortune: "'there is a likeness in our destiny; the destiny which bids fair to connect us with two characters so much superior to our own'" (522). He chivalrously resists the comparison – "'No, not true on your side. You can have no superior, but most true on mine'" (522) – but as he enlarges on his own case with praise of Jane, he also unintentionally confirms his distance from Emma and Knightley and hence the lesser reward that will be Jane's in marrying him. His enthusiasm about having his late aunt's jewels re-set for her "'in an ornament for the head'" (523) conveys, almost bathetically, his superficial attraction to appearance over the more substantive attributes of temperament or intellect. Emma's earlier twofold conversion has prepared us for this contrast between his prizing of Jane's beauty and her honoring of Knightley's judgment. Her nearly simultaneous recognition of her errors and her romantic passion effects, in personal terms, a shift from vanity to empathy and, in familial terms, from a secondary relationship (his brother is her sister's husband) to a primary marital one. The three weddings are thus arranged in an ascending order of completeness, with the most perfect being Knightley and Emma's. What makes their nuptials possible is his agreement to leave his own estate and live at Hartfield so as not to discompose Mr. Woodhouse, a detail that lets the novel's ending preserve the coherence of elements most contemporary works treat as distinct: dynastic and companionate relationships, given and chosen families, nuclear and extended social orders. Knightley's compromise allows for the authentication of each term, harmonizing what customarily appear as contrastive structures.

The inclusiveness of the ending has generated equally persuasive readings of the novel's political allegiances as either conservative or progressive. When the issue of family representations is considered from the perspective of Austen's contemporaries, this ideological pluralism appears the result of a skillful interweaving of motifs that a decade earlier had been treated as the exclusive preserve of either loyalist or radical writers. Modern critics wishing to argue for a conservative bias note that while each of the three women "marries up," traditional affiliations are preserved through their intra-class unions. Those interested in identifying a liberal feminist strain, meanwhile, could cite the adaptation in *Emma*'s father–daughter relationship of a favored radical motif of the 1790s. In such representative texts as Thomas Holcroft's *Anna St. Ives*, William Godwin's *Caleb Williams*, Eliza Fenwick's *Secresy*, and George Walker's *Theodore Cyphon; Or The Benevolent Jew*, the contrast of a wise child with a foolish parent metaphorically suggests the potential eclipse of old tyrannies by a new social order based on a re-imagined family.

Despite its very different understanding of fiction as a vehicle for expanding political consciousness, *Anna St. Ives* shares numbers of features with *Emma*, including the pairing of possible suitors, the depiction of the heroine as lovingly tolerant of parental limitations, and the comic ending. But in Holcroft's novel, abstract principle and not personality directs the courtship plot: Anna, committed to the notion of revolution through reasoned argument, suppresses her love for the base-born Frank Henley in order to fulfill the higher duty of reforming the dissolute libertine, Coke Clifton. In the end, she marries Frank and they pledge their ongoing dedication to "guiding, enlightening, and leading the human race onward to felicity" (481). But this furthering of radical doctrine is premised on a fundamental (and unacknowledged) inequality, one that involves both the sacrifice of the feminist ideals of independent action with which the novel began and, as suggested by Anna's certainty that Frank "will not only pursue this best of purposes himself, but will through life conduct me in the same path" (382), the reassertion of gender hierarchies. Like Emma, in other words, Anna internalizes male governance through a willing embrace of her lesser status. By contrast, Eliza Fenwick's *Secresy* and George Walker's *Theodore Cyphon* forgo the possibilities of compromise emblematically conveyed in Holcroft's and Austen's marriage endings. In their fictions, revolutionary integrity is maintained by making the victimization of the blameless by tyrannical authority appear both inevitable and unequivocally wrong.

The preface to Walker's *Theodore Cyphon* spells out the links between radical doctrine and its formal correlatives:

> Tragedy has ever laid firmer hold on the mind than Comedy. Tragedy is therefore better adapted to impress an useful and important lesson, and create in us a desire of shunning similar practices …
>
> I have also to observe, that it is a common practice, in compliance with the feelings of a reader, to distort the natural progression of incidents; and thus it is, that contrary to real life, we mostly find virtue, in the end, rewarded, and vice either punished or reformed. But I would rather the reader, at the conclusion, should say – I am shocked at the consequences of passion; I will endeavour to overcome myself, and act as I ought – than that it should be said – Well, it was very tragical; but I am glad the hero is settled at last.[10]

Genre choice and narrative structure, and in particular the terms governing closure, are made integral to the novel's enactment of the radical principles of reason over passion and equality over hierarchy. The deaths of the honorable few who advocate such ideals mean that here, as opposed to *Anna St. Ives*, revolutionary theory can be preserved intact, unqualified by what Walker sees as the false imperatives of distributive justice that demand "virtue, in the end, [be] rewarded, and vice either punished or reformed." This adherence to "real life" conditions, however, does not entail rejection of other eighteenth-century fictional norms. In fact, *Theodore Cyphon* and *Secresy* not only recycle established motifs, but also incorporate detailed references to Godwin's *Caleb Williams* and Richardson's *Clarissa*. Both Fenwick and Walker censure existing structures of power through plots in which second sons respond to the injustices of primogeniture by treating their own sons – the novels' central male figures – with a despotism that galls their victims. These familial tyrannies are in turn made the source of other systemic abuses of authority, including misogyny, imperialism (both novels have subplots highly critical of British policy in India), the mistreatment of the poor by the well-born, and in *Theodore Cyphon*, anti-Semitism. But it is through detailed allusions to earlier works that their radical leanings are most conspicuously affirmed.

Theodore Cyphon offers a baroque embellishment on *Caleb Williams*, multiplying the opportunities for political declamation by pitting the hero against two Falkland figures, his father and his uncle, Theodoric Cyphon. Theodoric first turns against his nephew when he resists an arranged marriage and then contrives to have him imprisoned so that he can rape his chosen wife, Eliza. In response, Theodore murders his uncle, becomes an outlaw in the countryside, travels to London where he learns of religious discrimination through the title's paragon "Benevolent Jew," Shechem Bensadi, and then, when he discovers his father's complicity in Eliza's fate, gives himself up to justice, correctly assuming that the family obsession with rank and status will make a public trial abhorrent to them. But while the courtroom spectacle visually echoes the culminating encounter between Caleb Williams and Ferdinando Falkland in William Godwin's novel, it has none of the earlier scene's psychological complexity. A similar heavy-handedness is evident in the ironic commentary that follows Theodore's execution and his father's suicide: the successor to the Cyphon estates, eager "to testify his sorrow at the decease of his relation, blazoned his virtues in marble; and succeeding ages will wonder at his charity, parental tenderness, and exemplary piety" (II.222). Public records, like inherited titles and properties, reflect the vested interests of a corrupt culture (imaged here, as in Elizabeth Inchbald's *Nature and Art*, without the compensatory providentially ordained design to which Henry Fielding's use of memorial tributes refers in *Tom Jones*). In *Theodore Cyphon's* working out of radical doctrine, the elite family both symbolizes and perpetuates tyranny. Conversely, intimacy and true benevolence are found only in the families of shunned "outsiders" like the Bensadis.

Secresy engages more dynamically with the possibilities of its precedent text, *Clarissa*. Fenwick maintains Richardson's pairings of male and female primary and secondary characters, but prunes away those elements that contributed to the earlier work's meliorative ending. The Christian contexts that give spiritual significance to Clarissa's suffering are eliminated; the death of Arthur Murden, the Belford equivalent, disallows the return to order effected by his predecessor; the sympathetic treatment of the Clarissa figure, Sibella Valmont, despite her covert relationship with her foster-brother, the Lovelacean Clement Montgomery, at once questions the principle of a sexual double standard and makes its survival in practice symptomatic of the failure of revolutionary ideals. Sibella had solicited this unsanctified union, telling Clement that since her uncle Valmont's dynastic plans for her prohibit their marrying, "'tis our hearts alone that can bind the vow."[11] The letter following in which Clement "just arisen from her arms" boasts of his "glorious though secret triumph over this rival, this chosen, this elected of Mr. Valmont's favour" (130) invokes a favored eighteenth-century trope, that of competition among men, to indicate how unworthy he is of her pure passion.

Period fiction often represents the amorous pursuit of the heroine as a contest between male adversaries (a counterbalance, perhaps, to courtship's apparent, brief empowerment of women). In *Anna St. Ives*, the motif is put to the service of advancing radical doctrine. Coke Clifton's will to conquer Frank Henley by possessing the heroine aligns him with the aristocratic code of behavior that Frank and Anna's radical marriage of true minds symbolically defeats. In *Secresy*, by contrast, weddings – anticipated, thwarted, or completed – do not herald new beginnings or the triumph of emergent orders. Instead, they expose the flaws inherent in family structures, both domestic and social. The anthropologist's distinction between endogamous and exogamous relationships – that is, unions conducted within and outside kinship groupings – helps to illuminate Fenwick's negative identification of family with marriage. In her novel, endogamous affiliations prevail and they are universally disastrous: Valmont conceals the fact that Clement Montgomery is his illegitimate son, then secretly plots to marry him to his niece Sibella in order to consolidate the family estates and preserve patrilineal inheritance; Caroline Ashburn, the Anna Howe figure, tries to arrange the marriage of Arthur Murden, the man she wishes were her husband, to her beloved Sibella; in the only union that is actually formalized, Clement weds Caroline's mother (in the process foiling the plans of his undeclared father). Two decades later, Emma and Knightley's relationship adapts the endogamous strengthening of familial bonds to very different political ends. While in *Secresy* marrying within the tribe appears a dangerous and morally indefensible perpetuation of old-order corruption, in *Emma* it is celebrated as a key means of preserving social and cultural integrity.

Walter Scott's 1816 review of *Emma* noted that its reader would not find in it a "course of adventures of a nature more interesting and extraordinary than those which occur in his own life, or that of his next-door neighbours."[12] Scott's insight – and Austen's revisionary talents – are confirmed through comparison with Fenwick's fictional strategies and *their* amendments of inherited tropes. The resurgence of secrecy as a central thematic concern in 1790s radical fiction recalls its earlier, but quite distinct, deployment in the 1720s. For writers like Defoe whose novels are structured by competition between autonomous adversaries, secrecy is crucial to the aspiring protagonist's worldly success. In

Jacobin fiction, contrarily, secrecy has entirely negative associations: it is the instrument of an autocratic ruling class and countertype to the ideal of open, intellectual exchange within a new model of sociability defined in *Anna St. Ives* as dedicated to "the good of all" (278). The opprobrium the radicals attached to concealment has a precise legislative source in the repressive measures (among them the 1794–5 Gagging Acts and Treason Trials) the government enacted to limit their influence.

As Scott suggests, Austen's fictional world stands apart from both the melodrama and the abstract theorizing of 1790s writing (especially its extreme expression in the Gothic machinery of castles, ruins, and mysterious spectres, all of which make an appearance in Fenwick's *Secresy*). While 1790s radicals make concealment the defining trait of villains obsessed with blood relationship, sensationalizing their evil and their victims' helplessness, *Emma* domesticates and localizes the consequences of secrets. Secrecy remains problematic, but Austen's representations of its power allow for both social and individual correction by setting in motion two versions of hidden knowledge. These correspond roughly to public and private facets of experience: on the one hand, the culpable withholding of information that affects others – as in Emma's matchmaking or the engagement of Frank Churchill and Jane Fairfax – and, on the other, the cultivated intelligence that connects the ironic narrator with those protagonists capable of introspection and with the discerning reader. The result of the latter is something close to a virtual community: not the ever-expanding mass of the enlightened to whom the radicals appealed, but a more circumscribed elite directed by an omniscient intelligence. The privileged access to Emma's consciousness we gain through free indirect discourse allows us to observe through her progress the positive rewards of membership in that community: in individual terms, from selfish vanity to genuine love for an intellectual and emotional equal, and in familial terms, from independent wise child to compliant spouse.

In the posthumously published *Persuasion*, Austen departs from this characteristic late-eighteenth-century marriage ending. *Persuasion*'s Anne Elliot is defined almost entirely by her interior life, a consequence in part of her exclusion from even the limited forms of sociability other Austen protagonists experience through their relatives. Unlike Emma or the pairs of sisters in *Sense and Sensibility* and *Pride and Prejudice*, and to a greater degree than Fanny Price in *Mansfield Park*, she is isolated within her given family, her astute financial advice ignored by the father whose selfish extravagance necessitates their exile from the Kellynch Hall estate of her childhood and youth. The novel's harsh assessment of the landed gentry in the person of Sir Walter Elliot reprises the wise child and ineffectual parent of *Anna St. Ives* (and its muted

version in *Emma*), with none of the softening that the father's genuine paternal affection supplied in the earlier works. Moreover, *Persuasion* refuses in
its conclusion to override the destabilizing effects of the inadequate father by
providing the heroine with a spouse through whom orthodox social hierarchies and proper governance can be reasserted. Instead, Anne marries decidedly
outside the tribe: she rejects Mr. Elliot, the entailed heir to Kellynch (at least
in part because he lacks "openness"), and accepts Wentworth, whom she had
eight years earlier been persuaded to turn down because he was "nobody" and
"quite unconnected" (26). In the interim, he has prospered while her family
has declined, his good fortune a combination of individual ambition and the
opportunities afforded him by a naval career at a time of global war. Relative
to the retrograde landed gentry and aristocracy in this novel, the Navy appears
a thriving and purposeful meritocracy. The secondary characters associated
with it, including the redoubtable Mrs. Croft, are orientated toward the future
and connected through their active patriotism to the pursuit of national, not
selfish, interests. When Anne marries into this new order, she sheds her affiliations with outmoded family structures that are represented as literally and
ethically nearly bankrupt. *Persuasion*, in short, not only definitively rejects the
residual model of the family – both domestic and dynastic – but also sketches
in an emergent alternative premised on reciprocity between individual identity and national community.

This chapter has centered on works that use the family to explore the private, communal, and political ramifications of sociability. Family remains a
point of reference in the chapter following, but its primary concern is with
individuals and institutions that lie outside the purview of received notions
of domesticity, identity, and inheritance. Because the eighteenth-century
novel's formal features and thematic interests remained unsettled throughout
the period, many of the fictions focused on exceptional communities seem to
modern eyes experimental in both style and subject matter. As the evidence
of the next chapter suggests, experimentation, far from being unusual, was in
fact an inherent part of the new genre's efforts to articulate inclusive models
of sociability.

Chapter 5

Alternative communities

Over the course of the eighteenth century, the consolidation of the nuclear family and decline of the extended "household" one had wide-reaching consequences. As literary critic Ruth Perry and historian Naomi Tadmor have documented, kinship structures that favored the "affinal" bonds of marriage over "consanguineal" or blood connections helped to erode traditional affiliations. This reshaping of family networks occurred alongside parallel developments – a growing capital economy, urban migration, and, particularly after the 1763 Treaty of Paris ended the global Seven Years War, an unwieldy but increasingly lucrative empire – that together contributed to hone a quintessentially modern individualism. This chapter focuses on the attention paid in contemporary fiction to the human costs of these developments and to the compensatory versions of sociability they inspired. It opens with a series of novels that represent alternative orders designed to shield the vulnerable from an increasingly competitive culture: Sarah Scott's *Millenium Hall* (1762) and *Sir George Ellison* (1766), Clara Reeve's *School for Widows* (1791) and *Plans of Education* (1792), and the anonymous *Henry Willoughby* (1798) and *Berkeley Hall* (1796). The sections following examine two overlapping clusters of works that also question the pace and extent of social, political, and economic change by addressing its effects on susceptible populations. The first looks at novels that counterpoint metropolitan and imperial orders, such as Aphra Behn's *Oroonoko* (1688), the anonymous *Female American* (1767), Frances Brooke's *Emily Montague* (1769), Phebe Gibbes's *Hartly House, Calcutta* (1789), Elizabeth Hamilton's *Hindoo Rajah* (1796), and two novels by George Cumberland, *The Captive of the Castle of Sennaar* (1798) and *The Reformed* (c. 1800). The second considers Gothic's fascination with failures of sociability in relation to turn-of-the-century turbulence principally through examination of Ann Radcliffe's *Mysteries of Udolpho* (1794) and *The Italian* (1797) and Matthew Gregory Lewis's *The Monk* (1796).

Beyond marriage

Just before she leaves to attend her first London masquerade, *Sir Charles Grandison*'s Harriet Byron writes to her friend Lucy:

> If a single woman *knows* her own happiness, she will find that the time
> from eighteen to twenty-four is the happiest part of her life. If she stay
> till she is twenty-four, she has time to look about her, and if she has
> more lovers than one, is enabled to choose without having reason,
> on looking back, to reproach herself for hastiness. Her fluttering, her
> romantic age (we all know something of it, I doubt) is over by twenty-
> four, or it will hold too long; and she is then fit to take her resolutions,
> and to settle.   (I.109)

As earlier chapters have testified, the "fluttering … romantic age" with its sometimes illusory promise of freedom of choice and self-direction is favored territory for the eighteenth-century novelist. But contemporary fiction also looks beyond individual romance to consider the harsher social realities that frame the courtship idyll. The timing of Harriet's musings here, for instance, is important: the letters immediately following this one document Sir Charles's fortuitous rescue of her from Sir Hargrave Pollexfen's kidnapping, an oblique reminder of the physical dangers to which the unprotected are subject once they move outside domestic contexts. Elsewhere in the novel, the less palpable but still difficult predicament of women denied even the possibility of shelter *within* marriage is considered. As Harriet's cousin Mrs. Reeves notes to the gathered company, an enterprising man "can rise in a profession" and overcome financial setbacks, but young women who lack the dowry to attract a husband, "how can they, when family-connexions are dissolved, support themselves?" (II.355). Dr. Bartlett and Sir Charles Grandison, like Mary Astell in *Serious Proposal for the Ladies* (1694), suggest a solution: a country-wide network of "*Protestant Nunneries*" in which "numbers of young women, join-ing their small fortunes" will be able "to maintain themselves genteelly on their own income; tho' each, singly in the world, would be distressed" (II.355–6).

The nunneries "scheme," like Sir Charles's suggested Hospital for Female Penitents, responds to the problem of a surplus, nominally unproductive population not by questioning or amending the structures that make them redundant, but by recommending parallel institutions to contain and organize them. Dr. Bartlett, apparently forgetting Mrs. Reeves's emphasis on financial need, enthusiastically anticipates that "such a society as this … might become a *national* good; and particularly a seminary for good wives" (II.355). The proposals, in short, amount to little more than improvisatory stopgaps that inevitably fail to resolve the problems raised by substantial social change. The planned nunneries acknowledge the devaluing of women by the ascendancy of marital over birth identity – what Ruth Perry calls "the great disinheritance" – but, in the end, as the dizzying numbers of weddings in *Sir Charles Grandison* suggest, the plight of the spinster appears an unavoidable cost of the real business of marriage.

Sarah Scott's *Millenium Hall* represents a female utopia designed to offer a haven from the perils of the marriage marketplace, a self-sufficient estate that includes farms, a carpet manufactory, and various philanthropic projects. It had been founded many years before the novel's opening moment by a group of well-born women convinced that the world at large is modeled on "that state of war, which Hobbes supposes the first condition of mankind," and determined to put into practice their counterview of society as a "state of mutual confidence, reciprocal services, and correspondent affections."[1] As Betty Rizzo has documented, the fictional community of Millenium Hall had a real-life antecedent that originated in Scott's friendships with Sarah Fielding, Jane Collier, Lady Barbara Montagu, and Elizabeth Cutts. This group overlapped with the more fashionable, London-based "Bluestocking" circle led by Scott's wealthy sister Lady Elizabeth Montagu whose salons provided a venue for the relaxed sociability advocated by David Hume and Adam Smith. In the mid-1750s, Barbara Montagu and Sarah Scott, whose father and brothers had recently intervened to remove her from her husband, purchased a house in a village on the outskirts of Bath where they launched various philanthropic projects. By 1762, financial exigency (inadequately relieved by Scott's publishing of *Journey through Every Stage of Life* [1754] and probable motive for *Millenium Hall*) and Montagu's failing health led them to leave the Bath Easton house and settle in Bath proper where Barbara Montagu died in 1765. After plans for another community were abandoned in the late 1760s, Scott continued to supplement her limited income through writing until the deaths of her brother-in-law and father in the late 1770s made her self-sufficient.

Scott highlights the exceptional nature of the alternate order depicted in *Millenium Hall* by constructing her epistolary novel as a travel narrative: we initially see the estate through the eyes of George Ellison who, touring England with his young charge Lamont after a long residence abroad in Jamaica, seeks help when his carriage breaks down nearby. The genre and gender reversals with which the novel begins – the returned colonial shocked by the exotic otherness of what he discovers in the English countryside; the men's dependency on assistance from a self-sufficient feminocracy – verify Ellison's objectivity as witness. The subsequent discovery that he is related to one of the Hall's founders gives him a passport into this cloistered world. Now both outsider and intimate, he divides his narrative between reports on the estate's current operations and summary histories of its inhabitants, the latter centered on unhappy experiences with men that appear thumb-nail renditions of typical novel plots: innocent women threatened by libertine guardians, misanthropic husbands, and feckless lovers.

The narrative shifts between the women's past and present experiences and between the larger world and the bounded estate produce what seems initially a curiously double perspective on the opposed ways of life. Despite the far from flattering view of men within the women's interpolated histories, each one (like Frances Sheridan's Sidney Bidulph) counsels submission to, not rebellion against, patriarchal structures. Yet the new society they establish significantly reconfigures traditional roles, adjusting family relationships to assure a "reciprocal communication of benefits" (112). The once squabbling elderly women, for instance, become "sisters" to one another and "mothers again" (66) to the young children assigned to their care. What reconciles these contrary impulses – acquiescence in the context of the gentry founders' past histories and innovative governance in their present lives – is the religious conviction that "happiness consists in fulfilling the design of their Maker" (112). As wives and daughters, their duty was unstinting service to husbands and parents; as single Anglicans at Millenium Hall, they are able to work collaboratively to achieve social harmony. The new culture, at the same time, adheres to the old faith that hierarchies are part of God's plan and hence immutable. Since intelligence and judgment are the lot of the well-born and simple piety and toil that of the lowly, all activities on the estate are allocated by class on a sliding scale from high aesthetic pursuits (drawing, languages, designing) to low manual labor. As with Pope's rendering of the cosmos as a "Vast chain of being" in *Essay on Man* (a poem quoted approvingly here and in this novel's sequel, *Sir George Ellison*), to step out of one's inherited place would be impious:

> … – On superior pow'rs
> Were we to press, inferior might on ours:
> Or in the full creation leave a void,
> Where, one step broken, the great scale's destroy'd:
> From Nature's chain whatever link you strike,
> Tenth or ten thousandth, breaks the chain alike
>
> (I.241–6)

The belief that "it was the duty of every person to be of service to others" (118) turns what might seem a merely passive acceptance of one's inherited lot in life into an active and reciprocally confirming work ethic. The founders, charged by the responsibilities attendant on social position to order the lives of those in their care, make provisions for the elderly, the disabled, and the poor, each of whom contributes in turn to the functioning of the estate (itself an inclusive image of the providential design that assumes the superior intelligence and higher physical needs of the well-born).

Ellison is given a glimpse into the former experience of these laboring tenants when he questions a long-time native of the parish. Her account testifies to the mutual failures of ruler and ruled under the modern system of estate management in place before the ladies' arrival. Formerly, the aged woman tells him,

> I was almost starved … and no shame of mine, for so were my
> neighbours too; perhaps we were not so painstaking as we might have
> been; but that was not our faults, you know, as we had not things to
> work with, nor any body to set us to work, poor folks cannot know
> every thing as these good ladies do; we were half dead for want of
> victuals, and then people have not courage to set about any thing.
> Nay, all the parish were so when they came into it, young and old,
> there was not much to chuse, few of us had rags to cover us, or a
> morsel of bread to eat, except the two Squires; they indeed grew
> rich, because they had our work, and paid us not enough to keep life
> and soul together; they live above a mile off, so perhaps they did not
> know how poor we were.   (65)

When estates are treated as capital investments to be managed at arm's length, those whose work generates the squirearchy's "riches" become less "painstaking" in their tasks and lapse finally from slothfulness into ragged near-starvation. Such apathy is the negative face of the providentially assigned inability of "poor folks" to "know everything as these good ladies do." Its positive expression is the current Millenium Hall: under the guidance of its gentry founders, the formerly alienated laborers cohere as an industrious and productive community.

Sarah Scott built on the popularity of *Millenium Hall* by writing a combination prequel and successor novel that follows George Ellison from Jamaica, through his encounter with the Millenium Hall ladies, to his adaptation of their principles on his own and neighboring estates. The geographical scope of the *History of Sir George Ellison* allows for comparison of two very different communities. The first is the Jamaican plantation Ellison acquires when he marries a wealthy widow whose tyrannical exploitation of her slaves has made them mutinous and whose arsenal of manipulative tricks allows her to reduce him to "that slave which he would suffer no one to be to him."[2] His recovery begins when he introduces a combination of disciplinary and philanthropic measures that leave the slaves compliant and the plantation highly profitable (a process that generalizes the more particular account of *Millenium Hall*'s aged laborer mentioned above). The second is the English estate that he cultivates after his wife's death allows him to return home, the moment when he first visits Millenium Hall. In *Sir George Ellison*, the outsider stance he initially occupied in the female utopia is transferred to his eccentric cousin and new neighbor, Sir William Ellison, a misanthropic bachelor who begins by mocking but eventually supports Sir George's progressive measures. As each reform proves successful, other characters step in to play the sceptic, giving George Ellison repeated opportunities to defend his proposals. What might otherwise seem an extended treatise on miscellaneous subjects by this means acquires novelistic elements of dramatic conflict and serial conversion.

The turn from the earlier novel's contained group of single women to *George Ellison*'s marriageable, mobile male protagonist expands the potential for the identification and pursuit of social problems. A member of the landed gentry, he wields a power that radiates out from household to neighborhood as he reinvigorates Millenium Hall's hierarchical ideals by correcting the abuses of lax authorities. In quick order, Ellison incorporates several parishes into one entity, assigns himself overseer, and institutes reforms in government (poor relief housing and a system of unemployment insurance), church (he directs the vicar), and law (after he has himself appointed Justice of the Peace). His activism seems in part a sublimation of disappointed love; at the very least, as the narrator says, his

> conduct evidently shewed, that a passion which makes so much
> confusion in the world, owes its strength only to our weakness, and
> that if properly resisted, by the arms wherewith reason and religion can
> furnish us, it may be restrained within such innocent and moderate
> bounds, as neither to make us infamous or unhappy, though we may not
> be able totally to extinguish it.   (78)

The courtship plot, held in abeyance for much of the novel to permit the spinning out of its social program, is briefly revived when the alcoholic husband of his beloved dies, and then deferred after Ellison suffers a near-fatal riding injury. The accident allows a protracted depiction of what it appears will be a "good" death (a recurrent feature of the mid-century fiction of sensibility also seen in Richardson's *Clarissa*, Sarah Fielding's *Volume the Last*, Sheridan's *Sidney Bidulph*, and Mackenzie's *Man of Feeling*). But Ellison recovers and weds the widowed Mrs. Tunstall. The final section details in short order the marriages of children and the return of his brother from Jamaica, a dispersal and concentring of family that leaves all enjoying "the utmost felicity the world can afford." Here Scott closes down the narrative, "lest by some of those unavoidable misfortunes, which in the course of time must befal every mortal being, the scene may be overcast, and those who now are the happiest of mortals become objects of compassion" (221). Despite this final glance at the high artifice of happy endings, the novel's didactic insistence on the family as fundamental to social order remains its primary theme and point of contact with the world of Scott's readers.

The utopian strain in both *Millenium Hall* and *Sir George Ellison* supports the author's contention that reinvigorated hierarchies can limit the alienating effects of a commercial culture. In advancing this claim, Scott aligns herself with a civic humanist discourse that makes landed property and good birth the source of disinterested governance. Many of her contemporaries express similar reservations about the pace and extent of change, using fiction to register their discomfort with the model of "possessive individualism," the phrase coined by the political scientist C. B. Macpherson to describe the tendency of liberalism after John Locke to make the individual an autonomous agent, the "owner of himself" and hence understood "neither as a moral whole, nor a part of a larger social whole."[3] The contrast between conservative civic humanism and liberal possessive individualism underpins much contemporary literature. For the novel, in particular, socio-political currency becomes a defining attribute, in part because the plasticity of the emergent genre makes possible both a remarkable alertness to changes in public opinion and a willingness to represent dissenting points of view. The result is a formal and ideological diversity that recent scholars have helped to recover from the regularizing efforts of earlier critics who had excluded from their consideration works that did not fit the Whiggish rise of the novel thesis.

To modern eyes, the eighteenth-century fascination with serial adventures, interpolated histories, and economic, political, and social controversy may still seem un-novel-like in its disregard of the principles of Watt's formal realism. But for contemporary writers and readers, the co-ordination of plot and character development was clearly not a necessary or integral feature of novels. As we have seen, Sarah Scott's focus on the exemplary – individual and communal – minimizes narrative progression and psychological complexity in the interests of mapping out an ideal order. A similar reciprocally defining relation between form and meaning is found in another popular subgenre, the so-called "it" narratives that adopt the point of view of inanimate objects. The success of Charles Johnstone's *Chrysal: Or, The Adventures of a Guinea* (1760–5), which went through twenty editions in the eighteenth century, spurred numbers of imitations. Some, like the *Adventures of a Bank-Note* (1770–1), follow quite closely Johnstone's literalizing of the notion of exchange implicit in commercial culture by tracing the "lives" of a piece of currency as it moves through various social classes (although the later work substitutes for the traditional guinea, the more ephemeral paper banknotes that had been introduced after the founding of the Bank of England in 1694). Others follow a material object from owner to owner as in *The Adventures of a Black Coat* (1762), or focus on a temporarily occupied, moving vehicle as in the often salacious *Adventures of an Air Balloon* (1780). Francis Coventry's *History of Pompey the Little; Or, the Life and Adventures of a Lap-Dog* (1751) varies the anthropomorphizing by focusing on a breed of dog associated in the period with luxury, consumerism, and uncontrolled female sexuality.

The ideological leanings of "it" narratives are often uncertain since these novels typically rail against acquisitiveness even as they indulge a prurient fascination with excess. The ambiguity is familiar from Daniel Defoe's fiction, although authors after mid-century seem more inclined than Defoe to flourish the moral intentions they claim as justification for their habitually racy exposés. The heroine of the *Genuine Memoirs of the Celebrated Maria Brown* (1766), a latter-day Moll or Roxana, for instance, ends her courtesan narrative with praise for marriage and motherhood. But the novel itself takes the reader on an extended tour of Maria Brown's life within the "republic of fornication," a locale whose defining features closely follow those of the new monied economy.[4] The bawd, Mrs. G-by, for instance, tells Maria that to be successful she must "imitate the tradesman, and have no other object in view but interest and gain … [I]t is only necessary that she should seem to be enamoured with the man she proposes making her property" (II.157). The widespread cultural anxiety about the effeminizing effects of commerce (or, conversely, its erasure of gender distinctions) is nicely captured here in the image of women profiting through deceit by possessing and controlling men. Even more insidiously, Maria herself suggests that seemingly "modest" women in fact pattern themselves on prostitutes; learning from them "every new fashion, and all those little artifices which enchant, and which no one can define … they have but little reason to upbraid us, for they are only amiable in proportion as they know how to copy us, to tincture their chastity with coquetry, and to ape those they despise" (II.25–6). The unusually detailed descriptions of dress and domestic furnishings in Cleland's *Memoirs of a Woman of Pleasure* (1748–9) imply similar interests on the part of male readers.

While Maria Brown's "republic of fornication" and the Arcadian "community of indigent gentlewomen" at Millenium Hall seem at first glance to represent entirely incompatible interpretations of women and their social functions, both in fact testify to the destabilizing effects of the new exchange economy. Maria Brown offers a misogynistic fable of an upside-down world governed, directly or indirectly, by the forces of prostitution; *Millenium Hall* invokes a parallel transactional realm in its inset histories of the inhabitants' past lives, contrasting those narratives of male oppression and exploitation to the sequestered estate and its potential for recovering civic humanist mores. As publishing ventures that build on established success, the two novels also confirm authorial alertness to consumer marketing; Sarah Scott, as we have seen, designs *George Ellison* as pendant to her own *Millenium Hall, Maria Brown* less honestly claims on its title page to be written by the "the author of a W** of P**," that is, John Cleland.

Later eighteenth-century novels centered on utopian (or dystopian) projects are less likely to demonize commerce, a change suggestive perhaps of the ascendancy of middling-class values and more certainly of the polarizing politics of the revolutionary decade. Clara Reeve's *The School for Widows* (1791) and *Plans of Education* (1792) offer a particularly germane point of contrast with Scott's 1760s fiction. In both instances, a sequel elaborates on the original text by emphasizing repetition over development. But while Scott makes the landed property of the gentry crucial to good order, Reeve lauds the "*bourgeois* qualities" of "regularity and oeconomy," setting the latter against the decadence of the aristocracy (and the nouveau riche who aspire to imitate them).[5] *The School for Widows* centers on two women whose unhappy marriages forced a lengthy separation between them. Now free of constraints, they resume their correspondence with an exchange of histories, both of which advocate female deference – up to a point. When Frances Darnford's spendthrift husband ran through her fortune and was confined in debtor's prison, she assured him she would fulfill her "duty to attend you, to nurse, to comfort, to support you" (I.133); his attempt to pimp her to a wealthy lord, however, she regards as making "a divorce between us" and she leaves him. Rachel Strictland, meanwhile, writes that while she detested women who opposed their spouses, when her fear of her miserly husband's anger caused a miscarriage, she presented him with a list of demands and won a measure of independence from his control. By the conclusion, the two women look forward with great pleasure to their imminent reunion and the new life together they have anticipated throughout their epistolary exchange.

While *School for Widows* follows *Millenium Hall*'s transition from male to female orders, *Plans of Education* indicates the increasingly polemical direction of the novel in the revolutionary decade. Instead of a *George Ellison*-like reaffirmation of the precedent text, *Plans of Education* uses a coded vocabulary hostile to radicalism to argue that we must "throw aside all abstract reasoning, and metaphysical subtleties; we must simplify every thing, and bring our ideas to nature, truth, and right reason."[6] The attack on "abstract reasoning, and metaphysical subtleties" – "abstract" and "metaphysical" were among the conservatives' favored terms of opprobrium – opens into condemnation of progressive social movements, including those associated with the abolition of slavery and with Sunday schools (what is actually required, we are told, are "Schools of *Industry* … to reform the manners of the common people; where they are taught their duties *every day*, and *all the day long*" [99]). Reeve, like Scott, also notes the negative effects on women of what she sees as recent social changes, among them men's appropriation of what were once women's trades. This was in fact a long-standing complaint, particularly in relation to midwives (as *Tristram Shandy* testifies). But her overriding concern is a decline in "the national character of virtue, modesty, and discretion" (132), a decline she relates to the rise in boarding schools for the daughters of an aspirational bourgeoisie. An extended inset narrative, *A Plan of a Female Community*, proposes a series of measures to encourage young women in alternative "habits of industry and employment, to give them some business for their future support, and, finally, to make them useful and happy members of society" (139).

Beyond England

The "soft" utopianism of Scott and Reeve, with its charting of disciplined communities that protect women's interests and defy the impulses driving commercial culture, has an exotic complement in the "hard" utopias of the revolutionary decade. These build on a long tradition of imaginary voyages. Some, like Jonathan Swift's *Gulliver's Travels* (1726, 1735) provided intricately detailed satire of the current political scene. Others, like Robert Paltock's *The Life and Adventures of Peter Wilkins* (1751), tested emerging social and political theories, in Paltock's case by adopting *Robinson Crusoe*'s continuous narrative to describe encounters with the Glumms and Gawreys, a nation of "Beings as can sail on the Water in no Boats, and fly in the Air on no Wings" to whom the protagonist introduces Enlightenment principles of governance and trade.[7] Utopias of the 1790s such as *Berkeley Hall* and *Henry Willoughby* embody radical philosophical precepts when they construct ideal communities as pastoral worlds without toil. In the former, an interpolated narrative follows "Prince Pangoleen Heir Apparent to the Crown of Angola" from his impressment in Africa, through slavery in the West Indies, to a fantastic encounter with an aquatic race whose lives have been organized to furnish "leisure to improve our minds and acquire knowledge."[8] In the latter, more sustained utopia, "Anachoropolis," a sanctuary on the banks of the Mississippi, puts into practice the principles of William Godwin's "doctrine of perfectibility" in his *Enquiry concerning Political Justice* (published in 1793, weeks after the execution of Louis XVI). The expense and length of the *Enquiry* may have protected

Godwin from the fate of Thomas Paine, prosecuted (in absentia) for his *Rights of Man* (1791–2), a refutation of Edmund Burke's conservative *Reflections on the Revolution in France* that itself appeared throughout the 1790s in increasingly cheaper editions. But as *Berkeley Hall* and *Henry Willoughby* confirm, the diffusion of theories offensive to government censors was often made possible by their migration from the primary source of an elite treatise to popular fiction.

In these novels, the American settings provide both a literal and satiric distance from Britain and a point of comparison with other cultures: African, West Indian, and native American. In doing so, they testify to the increasing cosmopolitanism of eighteenth-century fiction. *Berkeley Hall* focuses in particular on the Iroquois and Mohawk tribes, anticipating the imminent eclipse of their way of life, and suggesting the advantages of commercial exchange over the brutality of imperial conquest (Sarah Scott, conversely, advocated agrarian reform as alternative to colonialism):

> The British ought to encourage [native Americans] to divide and inclose your lands [Lumeire tells Tonondoric]; and teach you to build houses, lay out gardens and orchards, and raise corn and cattle like them. This is the natural field of a commercial people like the British. They should wish not to conquer, but to civilize the globe. What a demand would open for their commodities, if the immense nations who dwell, or might settle between us and the Pacific Ocean, were civilized and used the various articles of consumption – Still more extensive, if South America and Africa were also led to peace, regular government, and civilization.   (III.192–3)

This passage echoes the "doux commerce" thesis of Montesquieu, Adam Smith, David Hume, and Thomas Paine with its argument that self-interest generates a polished, bourgeois sociability that helps to undermine authoritarian rule (a development of Defoe's *Plan of the English Commerce* (1728) that advocated global domination through trade). One of the clearest signs that the politics of *Henry Willoughby* are more strenuously radical than *Berkeley Hall's* appears in its rejection of this commercial liberalism. Trade is seen not as meliorative, but corrupting; it "fetter[s] and vitiate[s] the manners of European countries" and the community of Anachoropolis, following Godwin's prescriptions in *Political Enquiry*, therefore bans all forms of private property. Ultimately, the hero with great pleasure bids "adieu to distress and despair" (II.246) in Europe and commits himself to enjoying perpetual happiness in this imagined American realm.

The anti-imperial note that threads its way through these utopias is a striking feature of late-century fiction. Mid-century novels, like Frances Brooke's *Emily Montague* (1769), more typically adapt geographical difference to the temporal schemas used by Scottish Enlightenment writers to explain the gradual advances of civilization. The first half of *Emily Montague* develops in these terms the truism that "America is in infancy, Europe in old age."[9] As in *Robinson Crusoe*, the youthful "restlessness" of the male protagonists draws them to the new world. Once there, Richardsonian motifs of self-sacrificing love are interleaved with debates about social and economic issues, native populations, and the iniquities of the French (the 1763 Treaty of Paris that recently ended the Seven Years War, and its American counterpart, the French and Indian War, had given Canada to the British). After the characters' staggered repatriations to England and an interpolated tale of a mysterious woman whose birth seems superior to her situation, the novel ends on a conventionally sentimental note with the reunion of the heroine with her long-lost, presumed-dead birth father, multiple marriages, retirement, and cultivation of country estates.

The anonymous *Female American* (1767) also observes colonial experience through the lens of the courtship plot, but its defining terms are exuberantly fantastic rather than realist. The novel's departures from the norm are introduced in an opening feminist salvo:

> The lives of women being commonly domestick, the occurrences of them are generally pretty nearly of the same kind; whilst those of men, frequently more vagrant, subject them often to experience greater vicissitudes, many times wonderful and strange. Though a woman, it has been my lot to have experienced much of the latter; for so wonderful, strange, and uncommon have been the events of my life, that true history, perhaps, never recorded any that were more so.[10]

The heroine's casting of her life as "strange, and uncommon" is supported by a series of hybrid heterodoxies: her father is an English clergyman, her mother an Indian princess; she moves between her American birthplace and England where her "tawny complexion" and dress, "a kind of mixed habit, neither perfectly in the Indian, nor yet in the European taste" (49), attracts unwanted attention; she survives a serious illness after her male shipmates set her ashore on a deserted island by "suck[ing the] dugs" of a goat, "which she happily permitted" (67).

These breaches of racial, national, and species boundaries are recounted in a flatly matter-of-fact tone that recalls *Robinson Crusoe*, the source of many of the heroine's adventures. But in contrast to other period Robinsonades, the borrowings here have a function beyond opportune plagiarism. When Unca Eliza Winkfield anticipates a male writer taking over her "true" history to "form a fictitious story of one of his own sex, the solitary inhabitant of a desolate island" and a faux editorial footnote confirms this "prophesy" with a tongue-in-cheek citation of "Robinson Crusoe [a novel] which only is inferior to her own, as fiction is to truth" (105), the author archly plays with the novel's genre features in her ironic reference to a gender-inflected literary canon. As the example of *Tristram Shandy* and *A Sentimental Journey* suggest, such reflexiveness is characteristic of mid-century writing. *The Female American* develops a number of permutations on this self-conscious commentary on narrative concerns – the relative status of history and fiction, the nature of literary borrowing, the problems attaching to female authorship, the appropriation by male writers of female experiences and voice – with women writers and readers specifically in mind.

Comparison of particular episodes in *Robinson Crusoe* and the *Female American* also reveals another difference between them that is typical of their distinct periods: the representation of community. In re-writing the antecedent text, the later novel emphasizes Unca Eliza's social instincts at the expense of the solipsism of Defoe's protagonist. While Crusoe enslaves Friday, for example, Unca Eliza "with more than female resolution" (86) poses as a heathen god to the natives making their annual visit to her island, predicts her own arrival among them in mortal form, and after she has secured their loyalty, moves to their island and converts them to Christianity. When her cousin Winkfield unexpectedly appears with a search party of Europeans (who interpret Unca Eliza's appearance as a sign that she is a "she-devil" [129]), he asks for her guidance, they marry, and after a brief trip to England, they decide to return to the island and "never … have any more to do with Europe" (154).

The rejection of the home culture is unusual in heroine-centered novels. As we saw in *Emily Montague*, the colonial foray more often appears an exotic redaction of the standard urban experience of London: a sojourn that ends, as in Henry Fielding's *Amelia* or Frances Burney's *Evelina*, with retirement to that favored image of the well-ordered nation, the English country estate. The settings of a range of fictions beyond the relatively familiar America – the Surinam of Aphra Behn's *Oroonoko* (1688), the India of Phebe Gibbes's *Hartly House, Calcutta* (1789) and Elizabeth Hamilton's *Hindoo Rajah* (1796), and the Africa of George Cumberland's *Captive of Sennaar* (1798) – are less easily assimilated to this pattern. These novels partially bear out Edward Said's Orientalist thesis of a European tradition of romanticizing otherness in order to define the occidental as superior and to justify subjugation. But the embryonic state of imperialist practice and rhetoric in the eighteenth century allowed considerably more latitude for questioning than was possible after the nineteenth-century consolidation of a colonial discourse. In the eighteenth century, geographical distance from England tends not to be used to measure remoteness from the familiar as a means to deny the "other" coherent meaning. Instead, literal distance invites cultural comparisons that, directly or indirectly, often reflect sceptically on contemporary history and manners. Aphra Behn, for instance, recounts the enslavement, revolt, and execution by dismemberment of the warrior-king, Oroonoko and his wife, Omoinda. Their heroic suffering might well recall to Behn's readers the execution of Charles I and the brutal punishment of the regicides that followed the restoration of the monarchy in 1660. More obliquely, the stance of the woman narrator – sympathetic to the royal slave's plight but unable to change it – is linked to a revisionist interpretation of public history. Oroonoko, she suggests, demonstrated a "Personal Courage" and "acted things as memorable" as the classical Roman Caesar:

> had [his actions] been done in some part of the World replenish'd with People, and Historians, that might have given him his due [he would have shared Caesar's renown]. But his Mis-fortune was, to fall in an obscure World, that afforded only a Female Pen to celebrate his Fame; though I doubt not but it had liv'd from others Endeavours, if the *Dutch*, who, immediately after his Time, took that Country, had not kill'd, banish'd and dispers'd all those that were capable of giving the World this great Man's Life, much better than I have done.[11]

Behn's cynicism about the arbitrariness of public history opens up possibilities for other, more private, forms of memorialization (and, given that "only a female Pen" is a common modesty trope, ones presumably available to women writers). The late seventeenth and early eighteenth centuries in fact mark the onset of a period of significant change in history writing, as previously secondary forms including biography, anecdote, memoir, and later conjectural and philosophical histories challenge the pre-eminence of classical models. The novel, as we see in Behn's comments and will explore more fully in Part III, participates in this reformulation of historical genres by suggesting that fiction, too, can correct fact, complicate the historical record, and provide a more authentic insider view of public events.

A century on, Elizabeth Hamilton's *Translations of the Letters of a Hindoo Rajah* (1796) and Phebe Gibbes's *Hartley House, Calcutta* (1789) relate history to fiction in both theoretical and practical terms. Hamilton's novel opens with a "Preliminary Dissertation" that offers readers a "short and simple sketch" of Indian history shaped by the claim that the British were responsible for releasing the "long-suffering Hindoos" from subjection to the "ignorant bigotry of their Mussulman rulers."[12] Gibbes also represents Hinduism as Christianity's spiritual ally; it is "the religion of humanity" and its followers, unlike the warlike Muslims, "have hearts made for society."[13] In addition to this ideologically charged (and entirely standard) contrast of feminized Hindu and aggressive Muslim cultures, both novels allude to a more topical controversy in their

support of Warren Hastings, on trial from 1788 to 1795 for criminal misconduct while Governor General in India. Gibbes's *Hartly House* uses letters sent
to an English friend by a young woman who has recently joined her father in
India to blend details of the politics, manners, and customs of the European
settlements in Calcutta with standard sentimental themes. The novel ends
equally conventionally with a marriage that is (unbeknownst to the heroine
until she accepts her suitor's proposal) both companionate and arranged and
with the newly wed couple's imminent return to England.

Hamilton's satire alludes to contemporary events – both Indian and English –
from a more unusual vantage point. As in Montesquieu's *Persian Letters* (1721)
and Goldsmith's *Citizen of the World* (1762), the story is told from the perspective of a naïve outsider, here the "Hindoo Rajah," Zaarmilla, who comments on
English life. His changing positions over the course of the narrative – he shifts
from unwarranted idealism to an equally extreme disenchantment, to a final,
tempered assessment of national strengths and weaknesses – allow scrutiny of
a broad spectrum of social, economic, and political issues. Through contrast
with the more limited scope of history writing, this inclusiveness gradually
comes to appear a defining feature of fiction itself. Early in the novel, while still
in India, Zaarmilla thus notes that his "favourite study," the "history of states
and empires" (in eighteenth-century terms, a mode of public history) has confirmed in his mind "the weakness and guilt of mankind" in yielding to those
"whose guilty passions, and atrocious deeds have raised them to *renown,* and
to whom the stupid multitude, the willing instruments of their ambition, the
prey of their avarice, and the sport of their pride, have given the appellation
of *heroes*" (81–2). Lengthy conversations with Captain Percy (a veiled portrait of Hamilton's scholar-brother who died in 1792) whom he rescues from
Afghan brutality challenge this misanthropic world view and convince him
that England must be a utopia peopled by enlightened beings cast in the same
model as his new friend. Not even his compatriot Sheermaal's personal and
very negative account of English involvement in the slave trade, tolerance of
drunkenness and gambling, harsh game laws, and faulty education of women
can deter him from pursuing the dream of observing first-hand what he construes as this marvelous place.

Once arrived in England, Zaarmilla is at first puzzled by the gap between
expectation and reality and struggles to reconcile his romantic ideals
with what he witnesses first-hand in his visit to the wealthy Ardent family.
Hamilton fully exploits here the opportunities for social satire as the credulous (but often right-minded) narrator sends his correspondent details of a
hodgepodge of national obsessions including connoisseurship, gambling,
fox-hunting, equipage, dress, silver mines, fashionable sensibility, newspaper

libel, Methodism, and, most pointedly, Godwinian radicalism. Eventually, the chastened Zaarmilla acknowledges the "truth" of his friend Sheermaal's harsh assessment of the English. But no sooner is the concession made than he discovers an alternative to the system-mongering Ardents in the quiet virtues of the late Captain Percy's social circle: Doctor Severan, the Denbeigh family, and Darnley, a second son who balances "the amusements of elegant Literature" with those "of Agricultural improvement" (293). Together, they represent the domestic ideal that fiction, Hamilton implies, is uniquely able to evoke. Public history, constrained by its focus on "*heroes*," records the unsavory triumphs of "guilty passions" and "atrocious deeds." The novel, by contrast, provides a medium for representations attuned not only to the influence of states and empires on national identity, but also, and more importantly, to the pressures individuals can exert on the public sphere by living virtuously. The conclusion focuses on the reformative possibilities of the latter when it anticipates the social benefits that will follow from the marriage between the sensible Darnley and Emma Denbeigh, the scientific experiments of Doctor Severan, and, in a nicely reflexive gesture, the publications of Charlotte Percy, spinster sister of the deceased Captain Percy and hence Hamilton's self-portrait.

Neither *Hindoo Rajah* nor Hamilton's subsequent *Memoirs of Modern Philosophers* pursues an entirely consistent politics. While reactionary in their loyalist condemnation of radical thought, for instance, they advocate expanded opportunities for the education of women on grounds similar to those detailed by Mary Wollstonecraft. This ambivalence is not unusual in the case of women writers of the revolutionary decade, many of whom are hostile to arguments about the "rights of man," yet find the orthodox view of an absolute sexual difference disturbing (at least in terms of the well-born; the poor are still regarded by most as belonging to a distinct and very much lesser category). Otherwise conservative authors such as Jane West and Hannah More thus join partial company with the more liberal Mary Hays, Elizabeth Inchbald, and Charlotte Smith in resisting the expectation that women should confine themselves entirely to private, domestic concerns. An obverse relationship between political and gender positions, as we saw earlier in Thomas Holcroft's *Anna St. Ives*, often obtains in the work of male writers. In George Cumberland's *The Captive of the Castle of Sennaar* (printed in 1798 but immediately suppressed) and its companion volume, *The Reformed* (written c. 1800 but not printed, again to avoid prosecution as seditious material), the exclusion of women from the proposed radical extension of the franchise is more strikingly evident than in Holcroft's novel because the sequel renounces the overtly feminist principles of *The Captive*, while maintaining its commitment to a comprehensive restructuring of government.

The Captive of the Castle of Sennaar introduces its revolutionary agenda through an exchange of personal histories between two men confined in a "state-prison on the Upper Nile."[14] Both were previously exiles from authoritarian regimes: the noble Memmo from Venice, the illegitimate Lycas from a Constantinople seraglio. After Memmo briefly recounts the story of his proscribed love and banishment – Veronica is his social inferior and their marriage is therefore forbidden – the elderly Lycas launches his extended narrative. He tells his cell mate a marvelous tale of his travels to the African interior and discovery there of the island of Sophis, home to "*the happiest, the most beautiful, and the best people on earth*" (28). Lycas entered the Sophian community as a dedicated imperialist and soon laid plans to cheat the inhabitants of their "precious gems" and "purchase … some of their most beautiful females, whose charms might make my fortune in Constantinople" (28). The equation here of women and property initiates a broader indictment of commercial culture, plotted along a continuum that stretches from the brutal exchanges of imperial exploitation to the more covert acquisitiveness of nominally civilized countries. The Sophians embody the positive alternative: anarchy. Lycas's conversion to their way of life is crafted to illustrate the core Godwinian argument that if revolutions were to begin with individuals, violence could be avoided and change effected simply through appeals to reason. Because the advantages of such a process are intellectually demonstrable, the radical "doctrine of necessity" maintains that rational revolutions would lead naturally to consensual, self-regulating communities, making the present coercive institutions of government and law entirely redundant. The future state that Godwin lays out in *Political Justice* is here given a past when the Chief, having learned that Lycas responded to the "cordial familiarity" of one of the Sophian women with a sexual advance, describes the historical roots of their community:

> our ancestors made the principle of human love the basis of this
> well-ordered society: – Love first links us, as well as other animals, to
> our females; love compels us to support our offspring; our kindness
> procures us their love; and hence that which originally springs from
> self-esteem becomes the reward of its pure principle: we have no
> other criterion, by which to judge of right and wrong, but that of the
> action procuring to others either good or evil; whatever is painful or
> unpleasant to be done to others is unlawful for us to do.   (37–8)

This account closely follows Godwin's argument in *Enquiry concerning Political Justice* that human perfectibility will be best realized in societies that renounce private property (including the possession of women through marriage).

In adapting these principles to fiction, Cumberland writes against the grain of many contemporary novels. The Sophian utopia has no place for the qualities of inwardness crucial to the emergence of the modern self over the course of the eighteenth century and to the realist novel's charting of the ensuing tensions between private desire and public constraint. Nor does it subscribe to the notion that gender inequities are both socially and politically necessary. For the Sophians, by contrast, the only "sovereign good must be the good of the community" (41) and they interpret community very broadly, hence the Chief's response to Lycas's casual comment about shooting birds: "did you mean, after murdering them, to eat them! And make a *grave* of your bowels – Holy Energy! is it possible that men can coolly commit such abominable crimes merely to live!" (42).

The Captive of the Castle of Sennaar ends with the interlocutor, Memmo, determined to recreate Lycas's journey should he ever be released from prison. In the event, *The Reformed* traces not a return to the island of Sophis, but an advance to another African utopia, the society of the Jovinians, a "Christian commonwealth, on republican principles" (183). The relationship between the original text and the sequel depends on a tacit developmental paradigm in which the Greek and pagan origins of the Sophians forecast the superior Roman and Christian ones of the Jovinians. An important aspect of this "rise" in civilization is the denial of equality between men and the "softer sex." "'God has given [women] to us,'" Memmo is told

> 'for the solace and comfort of our domestic circles. The tender carefulness and love which he has planted in their hearts was not bestowed to be exposed to robust labours, but chiefly I think to soften our sterner feelings, and warmer passions. They, and our children, are the ministering angels of our habitations, their kind smiles the reward of our toils, their lively affections the solace of our sick beds, and their indefatigable attention the consolation of our mature age.' (209)

This nascent version of the Victorian "angel in the house" undergoes an interesting turn when Memmo leaves the Jovinians and, after failing to convert the Venetians to their faith, retires to his family's country estate. There he builds a model community in line with those from Sarah Scott's *Sir George Ellison* and Robert Bage's *Hermsprong*: he "laid out the village like a pleasure garden," built a "spacious manufactory for winding and weaving silk" (280) and founded a school for servants overseen by the curate. "Thus," he declares, "I became by easy means, a patriarch and legislator … a manufacturer and agriculturalist" (282). But his beloved Veronica, long retired to a convent, exerts influence only in the disembodied form of an epistolary exchange: she is, he declares, "my *Beatrice* and my *Laura* united, a guardian angel, whose presence, in my imagination, accompanied all my projects" (281). On this estate, the solitary patriarch remains childless.

The novels considered in this chapter delineate their alternative communities against a ground of contentious period issues: imperialism, colonialism, historiography, the status of women, religious faction, class formation, pedagogy, liberal economics, civic humanism, the reconstituted family. The extent of the topics surveyed reflects a characteristic feature of the eighteenth-century literary landscape: an understanding of genre interrelatedness in which inclusiveness appears the norm rather than the exception. To critics looking back at the century from the vantage point of post-1840 high realism, interruptions of narrative flow to allow for embedded discussions can seem un-novelistic, as can the blurring of the lines between the fictional and non-fictional. Such boundaries are not, however, organic; they are the consequence of a process of disciplinary division whose outcomes only become fully visible at the beginning of the nineteenth century. From that point forward, "literature" carries its current exclusionary sense of imaginative writing, having previously been understood as a form of *belles lettres* and hence to encompass all polite learning. Various separations out from the broad category of history and moral economy led to the similarly distinct strands of economics, anthropology, and sociology (and to the emergence of professional explicators, including literary critics).

An important stimulus to this process of specialization was the 1790s conservative counterblast to radical proselytizing. Thomas Paine's *Rights of Man* (1791–2) had asserted that "such is the irresistible nature of truth, that all it asks, and all it wants, is the liberty of appearing."[15] Many radicals – Thomas Holcroft, Mary Hays, Elizabeth Inchbald, Charlotte Smith, Helen Maria Williams, Mary Wollstonecraft, William Godwin – rose to the challenge by directing their writing to the widest possible range of audiences. The brevity and plain style of Paine's *Rights of Man* and *Age of Reason* (1793–4) offered one route to greater accessibility; the appeal to new reading constituencies through novels, the least prestigious of genres and hence most closely associated with popular audiences, another. Godwin endorses the latter course when he adjusts the philosophical arguments of *Political Justice* to fit the fictional form of *Caleb Williams*. As the suppressed 1794 Preface to the novel announces, his intention is to incite "reformation and change" through a plot that "comprehend[s], as far as the progressive nature of a single story would allow, a general review of the modes of domestic and unrecorded despotism, by which man becomes the destroyer of man."[16] For the arch-conservative Thomas Mathias, these incendiary words demand zealous refutation:

our weapons must be instruments of war, able to break down the
strongholds of anarchy, impiety, and rebellion, and mighty to vindicate
the powers of legitimate authority … We may (for we can) all of us
contribute to the assistance, the comfort, and the good of others, and to
the stability of social happiness. The sword, the voice, and the pen, must
be resolutely and decisively called into action, for defence, for counsel,
for admonition, and for censure.[17]

Part III will return to the contest between the overtly political novels of the
so-called English Jacobin and anti-Jacobin writers (the former was the term
of opprobrium used by the latter to link native radicals to the excesses of the
French revolutionary faction led by Robespierre). I would like here to consider
the place of the Gothic novel, and specifically Ann Radcliffe and M. G. Lewis's
contrary modes, in the context of Mathias's insistence that "we all of us" either
contribute to "the stability of social happiness" or capitulate to the forces of
"anarchy, impiety and rebellion."

Both Radcliffe and Lewis build in their fictions on an existing body of historical romances that used "other times" to represent failed or endangered social
orders (much as utopian novels use "other places" to critique the home culture).
In Horace Walpole's *Castle of Otranto* (1764), Clara Reeve's *Old English Baron*
(published in 1777 as *The Champion of Virtue*), Sophia Lee's wonderfully mud-
dled *The Recess* (1783–5) and William Beckford's *Vathek* (in English translation
1786), recurring contrasts become the vehicle for depicting the origins and consequences of the transgressive forces that threaten the worlds they describe: the
empirical is opposed to the supernatural, reason to passion, civility to savagery,
discovered manuscripts to polished texts, national to cosmopolitan identity, and
knowledge to superstition (in the 1790s an additional distinction between the
comfortably middle class and the wicked aristocracy comes to the fore). In thematic terms, Gothic assimilates elements familiar from realist texts, but exagger-
ates and psychologizes them to create a pervasive atmosphere of menace. Henry
and Sarah Fielding's novels, for instance, include incest, banished orphans, kidnapping, political violence, autocratic power, disinheritance, infractions of gendered codes of behavior, family hatreds, colonial exile, concerted evil, hypocrisy,
and confusions of law and justice. When these reappear in Gothic, no longer
contained within the providential framework that in Henry Fielding's work
subordinates them to divine order, their affective power is heightened first by
a recurring narrative – the pursuit of an innocent by an amoral figure bent on
destruction – and second by a powerful voyeuristic undercurrent that at once
elicits and questions our readerly enthrallment to fiction.

1790s Gothic, in turn, gains much of its charge from those events of the
French Revolution that seemed particularly momentous to the English: the

fall of the Bastille (1789), the Declaration of the Rights of Man (1789), the Women's March on Versailles and the forced return of the royal family to Paris (1789), the execution of Louis XVI and Marie-Antoinette (1793), the French declaration of war on England (1793), the Reign of Terror (1793–4). The castle, linked in Walpole's and Reeve's fiction with medieval barbarism, acquires a special political currency following the storming of the Bastille, an event whose subsequent interpretations by English writers ran the gamut from positive symbol of liberation from *ancien régime* tyranny to horrifying portent of mob violence. The endurance of the castle as a figure for ancestral privilege and autocratic power is evident in its many permutations in Radcliffe and Lewis: not only the literal Italian fortress of *Mysteries of Udolpho*, but also the Convent of St. Clare in *The Monk* and the chambers of the Inquisition in *The Italian*.

The terms in which each of these sites is described illuminate the leading traits of the three novels. When Emily St. Aubert first sees Udolpho, she registers that "[s]ilent, lonely and sublime, it seemed to stand sovereign of the scene, and to frown defiance on all, who dared invade its solitary reign."[18] The personification of the castle is both a negative reflection of her own threatened selfhood and image of an alienating absolute power, both juxtaposed against the lost communal pleasures of her earlier life. These destructive forces dominate the middle section of the novel as the orphaned heroine struggles for release from the control of the villain Montoni at Udolpho and from her own exacerbated imaginings. Only with the conclusion, following Montoni's death off-stage and the return of the hero Valancourt, is order restored through marriage and retirement to the "ancient domain of her late father" (672), the domestic alternative to the sublimely destructive prison. In this plot, the experience of lawlessness stimulates rejuvenation, with the younger generation's active defense of hierarchical values exceeding the melancholic defeatism of Emily's father.

The logic of revolution as indirectly affirmative in its strengthening of an active reformed sociability is entirely absent in *The Monk*. There, the description of mob vengeance against the wicked prioress St. Agatha has a graphic sensationalism that makes religious superstition the source of bestial behavior: having dragged the prioress through the street, the crowd "exercised their impotent rage upon her lifeless body … beat it, trod upon it, and ill-used it, till it became no more than a mass of flesh, unsightly, shapeless, and disgusting." Then

> the Populace besieged the [Convent] with persevering rage: They battered the walls, threw lighted torches in at the windows … The Flames rising … the conflagration spread with rapidity from room

to room. The Walls were soon shaken by the devouring element: The Columns gave way: The Roofs came tumbling down upon the Rioters, and crushed many of them beneath their weight.[19]

The brutal misogyny and grotesque sexuality of this novel (the monk Ambrosio rapes his sister and murders his mother at the urging of a shape-changing satanic agent who appears first in the guise of the novitiate, Rosario, and then as the beautiful Matilda) prepare for an equally fantastic ending as an avenging Daemon executes Ambrosio's lingering death. Dropped from a great height, the Monk is impaled on a sharp rock where he lingers in agony for six days, until finally in a reverse parody of divine creation, he is washed away on the seventh by a violent storm. While *The Mysteries of Udolpho* signals the ultimate triumph of reason by carefully explaining the supernatural occurrences that so terrified Emily at the castle, *The Monk* revels in the excesses of horror.

The Italian reconfigures Lewis's novel in tacit protest against his turning of Gothic to lurid ends wide of Radcliffe's own practice in *Udolpho*, the novel he claimed as inspiration. The monasteries and convents, even the prison of the Inquisition, are represented in *The Italian* not as uniformly malign, but as human and historical institutions susceptible to improvement. Radcliffe's equal commitment to a liberal understanding of individual agency and to the maintenance of traditional social categories leads her to emphasize the formative influence of rule by example. The autocratic abbess of San Stefano, a convent marked by "an absence of that decorum, which includes beneath its modest shade every grace that ought to adorn the female character," may echo the xenophobic anti-Catholicism of *The Monk*.[20] But *The Italian* sets against her the counter-image of the convent of Santa della Pieta, which "appeared like a large family, of which the lady abbess was the mother" (300). A benevolent female community in the tradition of Millenium Hall, this is also the place where a more literal understanding of family as the basis of good order is affirmed when the heroine Ellena discovers her true lineage and is restored to her birth mother.

The possibility held out in Santa della Pieta of an enlightened authority existing within a culture that the English habitually regarded as repressive and irrational is touched on again in the ambivalent representation of the Inquisition. As so often in this novel, the experiences of the hero, Vivaldi, shadow those of the heroine: her domestication within the private convent is replicated in masculine and public terms when he is incarcerated and tried by the Inquisition. On Vivaldi's first approach to the prison where he will be examined, the impenetrable power signaled by its façade is stressed: the "walls, of immense height, and strengthened by innumerable massy bulwarks, exhibited neither window or grate, but a vast and dreary blank" (196). But just as Ellena's first bleak encounter with cloistered life is corrected by Santa della Pieta's affirmation of family and community, so does this initial impression prove inadequate. Individual inquisitors unexpectedly exhibit a "glorious candour" (352); the trial uncovers a complex tale of murder and assumed identities; Vivaldi (and his loyal servant) are released from the prison. The discovery of truth through the repressive devices of a flawed judicial process might well have seemed to contemporary readers a comment on the British government's measures to curtail radicalism: the suspension of habeas corpus, the passage of the so-called "Gagging Acts" that defined speaking or writing against the constitution as treasonous, and the Treason Trials of the mid-1790s. Radcliffe suggests that the curtailment of certain freedoms may be necessary to the preservation of the social order as a whole.

The Gothic repertoire of visual, architectural, and topographical details (castles, decaying mansions, obscured views, labyrinthine passages, prisons, mountains), of class and gender inversions (mob violence in concert with the erosion of traditional hierarchies, powerful women driven by ambition), and of states of mind (imagination and desire overwhelming reason and restraint) owes much to the aesthetic and political writing of Edmund Burke, author of *A Philosophical Inquiry into the Origin of our Ideas on the Sublime and the Beautiful* (1757) and of *Reflections on the Revolution in France* (1790), the latter of which supplied the vocabulary for loyalist attacks on Jacobinism throughout the decade following its publication (and, as a result of its baroque rhetorical flourishes, an equally rich mine for radical satires of conservatism). Burke's *Sublime and Beautiful* contrasts the soft, feminized, pleasurable, and civilizing effects of the beautiful with the masculine, painful, terror-inducing violence by which the sublime produces "that state of the soul, in which all its motions are suspended, with some degree of horror."[21] *Reflections* develops the political implications of this contrastive structure. Even at this early moment in the Revolution's unfolding – when it was published in 1790, liberal English support for the French cause was still strong – Burke accurately predicts the violence that followed the dissolution of the *ancien régime* in France. A "philosophic analogy" based on family relationship grounds his argument for the preservation of English hierarchies as a defense against the French experience of rupture with the past: the "idea of inheritance furnishes a sure principle of conservation, and a sure principle of transmission" that gives "to our frame of polity the image of a relation in blood."[22] This divinely mandated "fixed order of things" will always be countered by men unwilling to observe "bounds to their unprincipled ambition." Drawing on the vocabulary of the sublime, Burke suggests that the views of such men "become vast and perplexed; to others inexplicable; to themselves uncertain … [I]n the fog and haze of confusion, all is enlarged, and appears without any limit" (136). Beyond these illusory distortions, however, is the unvarying certainty of that "great primaeval contract of eternal society, linking the lower with the higher natures, connecting the visible and invisible world, according to a fixed compact sanctioned by the inviolable oath which holds all physical and all moral natures, each in their appointed place" (195).

Mysteries of Udolpho, in particular, adapts Burkean tropes to depict Emily St. Aubert's victimization by her aunt's husband, Montoni. While earlier heroes and villains tend to be twinned – the avarice of Henry Fielding's Bliful, for instance, simply inverts Tom Jones's at times undisciplined generosity – Montoni is defined by a discrete and absolute solipsism. When Emily, having failed to move him through "remonstrance" or "supplication," questions the grounds of his control over her, he thus answers simply, "by the right of my will" (216). She maintains her dignity through an uncomplaining suffering that might recall to readers Burke's account in the *Reflections* of the "serene patience" with which the imprisoned Marie Antoinette endured the "whole weight of her accumulated wrongs" (169). The quiet endurance of the Queen is made additionally powerful when Burke then describes his first glimpse of her when she was still dauphiness:

> I saw her just above the horizon, decorating and cheering the elevated sphere she just began to move in,- – glittering like the morning-star, full of life, and splendour, and joy. Oh! What a revolution! and what an heart must I have, to contemplate without emotion that elevation and that fall! Little did I dream … that I should have lived to see such disasters fallen upon her in a nation of gallant men, in a nation of men of honour and of cavaliers. I thought ten thousand swords must have leaped from their scabbards to avenge even a look that threatened her with insult.   (169–70)

The craven failure of "men of honour" to protect their Queen is construed not simply as a national "revolution," but as an epochal one. "The age of chivalry is gone," Burke proclaims, and with it all the "pleasing illusions" that enabled "the sentiments that beautify and soften private society" to be "incorporated into politics." The self-interested "sophisters, oeconomists, and calculators" currently in the ascendancy have no stake in the socially meliorating effects of idealization. Instead, they rip away all "the super-added ideas, furnished from the wardrobe of a moral imagination" in order deliberately to expose to view all "the defects of our naked shivering nature." In this "new conquering empire of light and reason," a dispiriting reality substitutes for the iconic splendor of the glittering dauphiness. Now, Burke writes, "a king is but a man; a queen is but a woman; a woman is but an animal; and an animal not of the highest order" (170–1).

The contrast in *Mysteries of Udolpho* between the landed order of Emily's father, St. Aubert, and the "sophisters, oeconomists, and calculators" like Quesnel (and through their shared trait of self-aggrandizement, Mme. Cheron, Countess Villefort, and Montoni) gives way in *The Italian* to a more subtle working out of the dynamics of absolute and contractually limited power. As villain, Schedoni predictably exemplifies the former. But the aristocracy, too, becomes identified with the forces of despotism when the Marchese forbids the marriage of his son Vivaldi to Ellena on the grounds of her supposedly undistinguished birth, telling him "you belong to your family, not your family to you ... you are only a guardian of its honour, and not at liberty to dispose of yourself" (30). The overwhelming importance of definition by family denies the possibility of self-ownership and with it, the "liberty" of choice. Lying behind the Marchese's claim to absolute power is the alternative philosophical position articulated by the late seventeenth-century philosopher John Locke who argued for the contractual basis of government, and hence for the right to resist should the given authority prove ethically problematic. In countenancing Vivaldi's filial disobedience, the novel thus undermines the sovereignty of the dynastic family and supports a Lockean reading of responsible citizenship. Radcliffe also develops through the representation of her heroine the corollary proposition that individual identity involves a process of self-making. When Ellena learns of the Marchese's contempt for her, all the "imaginary honours of so noble an alliance vanished" and an alternative, essentially bourgeois understanding of selfhood comes into play. The shock of rejection throws her "sound mind" back on "its own judgment" and "she looked with infinitely more pride and preference upon the industrious means, which had hitherto rendered her independent, than on all distinction which might be reluctantly conferred" (69).

Ellena almost immediately retreats from her singular decision to pursue independence through "industrious means," recognizing that "opposition from her heart" would make it impossible for her to relinquish Vivaldi's courtship. In this continuing close observation of the tension between outwardly directed activity and inward sensibility, the novel qualifies Burke's "philosophic analogy" between familial and political structures. His assertion that an overarching principle of inheritance guarantees the stability and interconnectedness of private and public spheres presumes, as we saw, a "fixed order of things." This is opened to question in *The Italian* both by the positive value assigned to the ability to adjust to changed circumstances and by the older generation's abuses of power, the latter emphasized by Radcliffe's weaving together of the two family plots after the Marchesa Vivaldi enlists the priest Schedoni to destroy Ellena. Schedoni decides to save Ellena whom he (mistakenly) believes to be his daughter. The subsequent revelation that she is, in fact, the daughter of Schedoni's brother, whom he has murdered, erodes the implicit deference to patriarchal constructs that Burke makes central (though, significantly, Ellena herself initially demonstrated just such an acceptance when she repressed her first "astonished and doubting" reaction to Schedoni's news that he is her father and responded to him with "tenderness" [236–7]). The joyous reunion with her mother in turn gestures toward the alternative consolations of matriarchal orders. Yet such questioning remains limited in scope. The new middling order symbolized by the companionate relationship of Ellena and Vivaldi rejects the adversarial sexual politics of the previous generation with their forced marriages, adulteries, and spousal mistreatments. But as the despotism of absolute control imposed from above yields to an authority emanating from within the family, inherited structures are amended and confirmed, not replaced.

While repudiating aristocratic excess, Gothic novels find other ways to demonstrate their commitment to continuity over rupture. One of the favored means is the near-feudal representation of a domestic underclass. The comic servant – in Henry Fielding's Partridge in *Tom Jones* or Tobias Smollett's titular hero in *Humphry Clinker,* a quixotic figure who on occasion testifies to both the petty humiliations and real hardships of subordination – is defined in Gothic by an uninflected devotion to the master's cause. Indiscreet and prone to gossip, servants like Annette and Ludovico in *Udolpho* or Paulo in *The Italian* serve the useful narrative purpose of conveying information that the more modest protagonist cannot, for reasons of decorum, articulate. But their primary functions are social: just as the principals represent the triumph of middling-class compromise over Continental, aristocratic absolutism, the servants demonstrate through their fealty the difference between the loyal English subject and the treacherous French one.

Radcliffe's *The Italian* marks the high point of a strain of 1790s Gothic that probes the experience of threatened identities (individual, familial, and national) in order to affirm the power of a renovated domestic harmony. The repertoire of narrative devices she developed to stimulate and then assuage her readers' anxieties soon began in the work of her less talented imitators, however, to seem hackneyed. Within a decade, parody versions emerged and were themselves in turn rendered obsolete (one of the few parodies to retain its freshness is Jane Austen's *Northanger Abbey*). Yet Gothic survived, if not in the coherent form Radcliffe had made standard. Instead, the mode functions increasingly as a symbolic shorthand, with authors selecting motifs from the panoply of 1790s castles, subterranean passages, mysterious writings, threatened protagonists, and family violations. We can see the beginnings of this

process in radical fiction of the revolutionary decade that adapts Gothic archi-
tecture to image the repressive power of the past: the castle and the Ruin on the
Rock haunted by the mysterious figure in Eliza Fenwick's *Secresy*, the insane
asylum that the heroine of Mary Wollstonecraft's *Wrongs of Woman: Or Maria*
interprets as symptomatic not exceptional through her question, "Was not the
world a vast prison and women born slaves?," the obsessive relation to interiors that signals the persecution mania of Godwin's Fleetwood.[23]

Chapter 6

The sociability of books

If we broaden the notion of family investigated in Chapters 4 and 5 to describe relations between books as well as individual characters, eighteenth-century fiction offers much to consider. Our tendency to regard the writing and reading of novels as essentially private and singular activities is in fact anomalous within eighteenth-century experience. On the one hand, the reading aloud of novels was a customary practice, especially welcome in domestic circles. More abstractly, significant changes in literary production and consumption over the period – the decreasing importance of patronage, the professionalization of authorship, the expansion of reading audiences (along with anxieties about their diversity and the interpretive freedoms they might assume), the problems with copyright infringement and piracy that increased as the book trade grew – encouraged kinds of formal experimentation that build on the premise of the novel's intrinsic sociability. The chapter that follows explores three particular contexts in which bookish versions of sociability overlap: sequels, intertextuality, and parody. I focus initially on two sequels: Jane Barker's *Galesia Trilogy* (1713–26) and Sarah Fielding's *David Simple* (1744) and *Volume the Last* (1753); then turn to a trio of works whose intertextual references put in play a less tangible, but still compelling, notion of family resemblance: Frances Burney's *Evelina* (1778), Elizabeth Inchbald's *A Simple Story* (1791), and Amelia Opie's *Adeline Mowbray* (1805); and conclude with a brief look at parodies that demonstrate the novel's commitment to maintaining cultural currency through ongoing assessment of established conventions: William Beckford's *Modern Novel Writing* (1796), Eaton Stannard Barrett's *The Heroine Or Adventures of a Fair Romance Reader* (1814), and Jane Austen's *Northanger Abbey* (1817).

Jane Barker's writing spans two epochs in book production: the 1688 *Poetical Recreations* situates her work in the late Renaissance contexts of coterie authorship and reception, the *Galesia Trilogy* in those of modern print culture. The three novels that comprise the *Trilogy* – *Love Intrigues: Or, The History of the Amours of Bosvil and Galesia* (1713), *A Patch-Work Screen for the Ladies; Or Love and Virtue Recommended* (1723) and *The Lining of the Patch-Work*

Screen; Design'd for the Farther Entertainment of the Ladies (1726) – respond in distinctive ways to the challenge of engaging with changes in the making and dissemination of books. Structuring each novel as a conversation between the narrator Galesia and her interlocutors counters the increasing anonymity of the reading public by recreating the intimacy of seventeenth-century audience relations. As these internal exchanges draw us in to the novel, they also offset the social isolation that the author implies is the norm for most women. The conditions that govern reading and lived experience are thus understood as complementarily shaped by gender. In *Love Intrigues*, Galesia, answering Lucasia's wish for a diversion, recounts Bosvil's erratic pursuit and then abandonment of his courting of her. The more pronounced digressiveness of Galesia's biography as resumed in *A Patch-Work Screen for the Ladies* is signaled by its title. The novel opens with a number of stories told to her by fellow travelers in a coach eager to "beguile[e] the Tediousness of the[ir] Way" (55). This uninflected seriality, however, proves a false start. That journey ends, a subsequent one is interrupted by an accident, and Galesia continues on foot until she is rescued from exhaustion by a "Lady, mounted on a beautiful Steed" (73) who takes her home and "shew'd her an Appartment embellish'd with Furniture of her own making, which was PATCH-WORK, most curiously compos'd of rich Silks, and Silver and gold Brocades: The whole Furniture was compleated excepting a SCREEN." When Galesia reveals that she can contribute only "Pieces of *Romances*, *Poems*, *Love-letters*, and the like" to this creation (a feminine rendering of the classical *dulce et utile* or compound of beauty and function), the "good Lady smil'd, saying, She would not have her Fancy balk'd, and therefore resolv'd to have these ranged and mixed in due Order, and thereof compose a SCREEN" (74). In what follows, numbers of poems (most of them slightly revised transcriptions from Barker's *Poetical Recreations*) are interspersed with biographical commentary that traces Galesia's move to London from the country, the deaths of her father, brother, and mother, and the entrenchment of her position as spinster. *The Lining of the Patch-Work Screen*, the third work in the *Trilogy*, also alternates genres: like the poems in the preceding volume, the quoted proverbs in this one both segment the narrative and provide connecting links between the stories that Galesia gathers from a series of random encounters. Having concluded the business that brought her to London, she is recalled on the last page of the *Lining* to the Lady's estate in the country that provided the main setting for the *Patch-Work Screen*.

This summary account does not convey the aspect of the *Trilogy* that appears most striking when Barker's work is considered from the perspective of later eighteenth-century fiction, that is, its departures from what are often represented as standard, even defining, features of the novel, particularly those relating to genre, narrative continuity, point of view, and closure. Invented biography, for instance, is used here not to explore inwardness (as it most often is after Samuel Richardson's *Pamela*), but to account for the *Trilogy*'s impressive social range: family circumstances and Galesia's status as an unmarried woman of "Bookish Inclinations" (108) and masculine accomplishments, including a "Skill in Physick" (113), present her with opportunities for more diverse experiences than would be customary for a woman of her period and rank. The disregard for transitions between the separate adventures further heightens the episodic quality of the narrative. And finally, although the novels are based on the premise of Galesia's conversations with interlocutors, scant attention is paid to the relation either between teller and tale or between specific encounters and the frame narrative.

Two episodes, one from *Love Intrigues*, the other from *Patch-Work Screen*, stand as strong examples of the different weight early and later eighteenth-century novels assign to the amalgamation of form and theme. In the final pages of *Love Intrigues*, Galesia describes the decision of her suitor, Bosvil, to marry another woman, briefly discusses with Lucasia whether she should hold herself accountable for this shocking reversal, and then praises the "good hand of Providence [that] is ready to lend Support, that we shall not fall into Ruin or Confusion" (47). Both the flatness of the ending – it neither provides the heroine with the reward of marriage, nor offers any compelling reasons why she was denied it – and the abrupt invocation of "Providence" run counter to modern expectations of narrative continuity and closure. But they are not unusual in pre-1740 fiction. Mid-century novels, rather than simply asserting that human affairs are divinely shaped to beneficent ends, embed the concept of Providence in the working out of narrative point of view and plot. In Henry Fielding, as we have seen, analogies between authorial and divine omniscience imply that the design of the text, like that of life itself, is fully revealed only at its end. This assumption is repeated at the level of character when Mr. Wilson, Tom Jones, and Booth are rewarded only *after* a conversion experience allows them to see that they have been guided throughout not, as they sometimes despairingly assumed, by blind Fortune, but by Providence. While in *Pamela* such references to divinely mandated order begin to multiply well before the novel's conclusion, the narrative logic is the same: after Mr. B proposes, Richardson mutes the revolutionary possibilities of his heroine's self-making and slows the forward impulse of the plot by drawing frequent attention to the "wonderful Ways of Providence" (309). Later in the century, such overt references are considerably rarer. Providential direction is instead naturalized, often by making individual action the source of dramatic reversals, as when Frances Burney's

Evelina discovers (through a conversation overheard and duly reported by the intrepid Mrs. Selwyn) that her secret love for Orville is reciprocated. In short, while all of these novels chart a version of Jane Barker's contrast between "the hand of Providence" and "Ruin or Confusion" (47), the antithesis tends over time to be less abstractly rendered and more fully embodied in the specifics of personality and social behavior (although, as we will see in Chapters 7 and 8, Providence briefly resurfaces in reactionary loyalist fiction of the 1790s as a favored point of reference).

A characteristic encounter in *Patch-Work Screen* demonstrates another distinguishing feature of early novels: the authorial development of a single narrative thread without consideration of its larger emotional contexts. Galesia is visited by a young woman who has heard of her "Skill in Physick; but I [Galesia] perceiving her Distemper to be such as I did not well understand, nor cared to meddle withal, recommended her to a Physician of my Acquaintance, who was more used to the immodest Harangues necessary on such Occasions" (113). While she refuses to treat the patient's venereal disease, she does relate her "immodest" history, one familiar from contemporary amatory fiction (wholesale poaching, here of an Aphra Behn plot, was standard practice early in the century). The young woman tells Galesia that soon after her arrival in London from the country, she attended morning services at Westminster Abbey, where she observed an unusually devout elderly man. Leaving the Chapel, he spoke to her, commending her piety and offering hints on how to avoid the pitfalls of urban vice, and then, in Galesia's words, "this old Whorson play'd the *Devil for God's sake*, according to the Proverb, and took this young innocent into a House of very ill Repute" (113). Schooled by later sentimental fiction, we expect a narrative such as this to balance didactic point with compassion. Elizabeth Inchbald's *Nature and Art*, for instance, invites us to pity the betrayed maid, while Henry Mackenzie's *Man of Feeling* draws attention to the indirectly wronged father. But here, we find instead a blanket absence of sympathy for the victim, her family, or the predator, as Galesia closes the episode with a personal reference rather than "moral": "Not that I mean by this or the like Example, to condemn all who there [at church] daily make their Addresses to Heaven: But to shew you, that in all Places, and at all Times, my Country Innocence render'd me a kind of *Solitary* in the midst of Throngs and great Congregations" (115).

Sarah Fielding's *David Simple* (1744) and *Volume the Last* (1753) are (like Barker's *Poetical Recreations* and *Galesia Trilogy*) the product of two distinct literary contexts: in the 1740s, of authorial rivalry and growing consensus about the defining features of the novel; in the 1750s, of innovation and formal experimentation, spurred in part by concern with stagnating sales for fiction and by the growing power of the newly founded *Monthly* and *Critical Reviews*. But while the paired works contain trace evidence of these period differences, their leading characteristics relate them more nearly to the recurrent features of sequels as these appear throughout the century. By the mid-1700s, the practice of elaborating on an earlier text was well established, sometimes motivated by an author's wish to capitalize on a successful predecessor, as with Defoe's *Farther Adventures of Robinson Crusoe*, sometimes by the threat of a rival publication, as when Richardson countered John Kelly's attempted appropriation of the commercial success of *Pamela* with *Pamela's Conduct in High Life* by writing his own continuation, sometimes to recall the novel's action to the reader's mind after a slight delay in the appearance of a second volume, as in John Cleland's *Memoirs of a Woman of Pleasure*. The more overtly political content of late-century sequels reflects in turn the heightened ideological atmosphere of the revolutionary decade, evident in Ellis Cornelia Knight's re-writing of Samuel Johnson's *Rasselas* in *Dinarbas* (1790), or Clara Reeve's *Plans of Education* (1792), a novel presented as both an extension of her *School for Widows* (1791) and a rebuttal to the historian Catherine Macaulay's *Letters on Education* (1790), the latter impugned as radical by Reeve's attack on its "metaphysical speculations" (vii). While these examples point to diverse authorial motivations for extending the premise of an earlier work, Sarah Fielding's sequel suggests that the formal features shared by the continuations are remarkably consistent.

David Simple traces the hero's search for a true friend in London, justifying his decision to remain in his native city on the grounds that

> he was convinced, to Experience alone he must owe his Knowledge [of "the Hearts of Men"]; for that no Circumstance of Time, Place, or Station, made a Man either good or bad, but the Disposition of his own Mind; and that Good-nature and Generosity were always the same, tho' the Power to exert those Qualities are more or less, according to the Variation of outward Circumstances. (21)

In making identity predetermined and "outward Circumstances" contingent, Fielding works against the grain of progressive narratives that tend, in contrast, to rely on "Time, Place, [and] Station" as primary sources of realist detail. Virtually every aspect of her novel underscores the resistance to change that follows from the assumption "that Good-nature and Generosity were always the same" (247). David's conceptualizing and his enactment of ideal relationship reinforce his steady commitment to hierarchical principles. At the level of character, this removes him from the kinds of competition that enable worldly success; the villains of the piece, conversely, are more typically bourgeois and adversarial in their pursuit of power and wealth. Comparison of David's quintessentially eighteenth-century quest with the Romantic one of Mary Shelley's Frankenstein highlights the distinctive qualities of the former: while Frankenstein is driven by a narcissism that leads him to create a monstrous double, David's search for a like-minded friend proceeds from the altruistic hope of finding "so perfect a Union of Minds, that each should consider himself but as a Part of one entire Being, a little Community, as it were of two, to the Happiness of which all the Actions of both should tend with an absolute disregard of any selfish or separate Interest" (353). The achievement of this communal ideal occurs, moreover, not through a process of conversion, with all that that implies of an abrupt change of course, but through an immediate and grateful recognition of shared beliefs.

At the level of plot, the choice of episodic over continuous narration ensures a parallel slowing of forward momentum. As David, like Galesia, listens to others' stories and offers his own observations, pairings of various kinds further enhance the novel's tendency toward serial segmentation. Consecutive encounters based on contrasts of high and low life, juxtapositions of reverse experiences (as in the women married to uxorious and abusive husbands), emblematic names that establish connections between opposed qualities (Splatter and Varnish): all of these enforce an incremental logic that renders in prose the same relation of form to meaning found in neo-classical heroic couplets. The constraints imposed by a carefully delimited structure – whether the sequel or the couplet – encourage a dynamic that, through the display of contraries, validates compliance with a universal standard. When David's own quest is completed, Fielding adapts the same twinned pattern to the novel's ending: having rescued the siblings, Camilla and Valentine, and in a separate encounter released Cynthia from her life as a toady, David marries Camilla and Valentine his beloved, Cynthia. The two couples, at once parallel and distinct, provide yet another instance of the novel's baroque tendency to favor repetition-with-variation patterns. In this light, Fielding's terminal quote from Pope's *Windsor-Forest* – "Where Order in Variety we see,/And where, tho' all Things differ, all agree"(ll. 15–16) – captures the novel's guiding assumption that all apparent differences can in fact be reconciled for both authors within the terms of an ultimate "Order," an omniscient deity.

The commitment to a divinely mandated principle of design not only makes sense of the novel's resistance to closure both generally and in specific episodes (in the early stages of his search, David typically departs without leave-taking once he discovers the unfitness of a possible friend), but also clarifies Fielding's assumptions about her audience. In *David Simple*, she addresses her narrative to those who share with her an ethical and sentimental responsiveness that makes them "capable of the same Actions" (133) as the hero. No urging of change is necessary for such readers. *Volume the Last* more forcefully restates this congruity between author and audience, declaring that there are some for whom she simply "*cannot* write, concerning David, and his Company; as no Words are equal to the raising in such Minds, any true Image of the Pleasures of our happy Society" (247). But the bleak conclusion of the later work means that the sympathies even of these ideal readers must be redirected in order to prepare them for the author's refusal to observe in worldly terms the principles of distributive justice that reward the good and punish the wicked.

Developing the premise of "that well known Observation, that 'The Attainment of our Wishes is but too often the Beginning of our Sorrows'" (241), Fielding documents in *Volume the Last* the fatal "Timidity of Mind" that sees David "entangled in the Snare of his Love for others" (277). Anxious to avoid materially disadvantaging the expanding households that together form their "Family of Love" (293), he maintains his connections with secular branches of the law and religion (and their corrupt individual representatives). Despite his own impeccable integrity, these institutional ties prove fatal. Over the course of the novel, the two families are decimated, leaving David on his death-bed to address the only survivors, Cynthia and his daughter Camilla. In keeping with the non-progressive orientation of *David Simple* and *Volume the Last*, his dying words offer a redaction of the plot that foregrounds the ultimate truth of religious faith, in particular his "strong and lively Hope in the Revelation God has been pleased to send us." This hope allows him to "carry [his] Prospect beyond the Grave" (342), a vantage point from which the seeming opposition between *David Simple*'s discovery of community and *Volume the Last*'s painful enumeration of "Sorrows" becomes irrelevant. At the end of the novel, to recall Alexander Pope's words, "all agree" as God's transcendent "Order" subsumes difference and division.

Sarah Fielding resolves these distinct narrative trajectories – *David Simple*'s comic ending of multiple marriages, *Volume the Last*'s tragic one of multiple deaths – by allowing permanent, sacred truths to supersede transitory, secular experiences. The close fit between the author's choice of paired texts and her commitment to orthodox hierarchies also obtains for sequels discussed elsewhere in this study, including Henry Fielding's *Shamela* and *Joseph Andrews* and Sarah Scott's *Millenium Hall* and *History of Sir George Ellison*. Scott's alternative community of women, like Galesia's independence as spinster, may suggest vanguard feminism, but what finally animates these novels is the wish to conserve traditional orders. Fictions that build through careful allusion on antecedent works resemble sequels in their confidence that readers are alert to patterns and willing to draw inferences from them. But as the discussion following suggests, the comparative sensibility encouraged by such intertextuality is more often directed not to reinforcing the status quo or to validating threatened hierarchies (as sequels do), but to questioning the persistence and appropriateness of such conventions, particularly for women. While the texts under consideration – Samuel Richardson's *Clarissa* (1747–8), Frances Burney's *Evelina* (1778), Elizabeth Inchbald's *Simple Story* (1791) and Amelia Opie's *Adeline Mowbray* (1805) – encompass a period of significant genre transformation, a common thread links their portrayal of the relation between female identity and social order: all four authors emphasize the conveyance of both property and desire through wills, bequests, and legacies. The authors writing after Richardson take for granted their readers' familiarity with *Clarissa*, and internal evidence suggests that the authors of the subsequent novels also assumed that their audiences continued to register the cumulative pattern of allusions. Each work thus gains a purchase for its own distinctive representation through reference to a growing "family" of novels. Considered together, they present a layered sequence of meditations on eighteenth-century themes and structures.

Clarissa, Evelina, A Simple Story, and *Adeline Mowbray*

Wills, bequests, and legacies are conventionally understood as final dispensations, the documentary equivalents of spoken last words, and often make their appearance at the ends of novels in ways that thematically reinforce the terms of closure. Samuel Richardson thus summarizes Clarissa's virtue in the "ten posthumous letters" (1368) she arranges to have sent after her death and in the elaborately detailed will in which she disposes of her literal and metaphoric goods. The ultimate failure of her intentions casts an ironic shadow on the novel's working title, *The Lady's Legacy*, by confirming that not even self-sacrifice can effect the domestic peace she desires. This failure of ideal intent has a precursor in Clarissa's grandfather's will, a document that attempted, unusually for its time, to secure the independent identity of a beloved female relative by making her a propertied heir. For eighteenth-century writers who adapt Richardson's work as pattern for their own, the *priority* of last words, in relation to both meaning and structure, proved an especially suggestive point of reference for their own fictions, and we thus find in Frances Burney's *Evelina* and Elizabeth Inchbald's *Simple Story* a bequest used as the anterior event that sets the novel's plot in motion. For Burney and for Inchbald, the quasi-institutional contexts framing the will or bequest provide an occasion for working out the gendered relation of private to social identity in more affirmative terms than Richardson's. In addition, however, since Burney and Inchbald re-script their predecessors' work, the prior texts become part of an ongoing consideration of literary inheritance and re-making, generating an allusive web in which we can observe how novels both respond and contribute to the formation of social behaviors.

The indebtedness of Burney and Inchbald's to Richardson's work is evident in the emotional relationships that define the heroines. *Evelina* and *Simple Story*, like *Clarissa*, affiliate the heroine with a father figure at a double generational remove: Clarissa and her grandfather, Evelina and Villars, Matilda and Sandford (Opie's *Adeline Mowbray* adjusts the generational paradigm, substituting a grandmother figure for the male one, and making the bequest the practical domestic knowledge Mrs. Woodville passes on to her granddaughter, Adeline). In *Clarissa*, the sentimental and ethical bonds are clarified in the grandfather's bequest, a document that explicitly mentions the unusual over-leaping of a generation in his sense of proximity to his chosen "child":

> because my dearest and beloved grand-daughter Clarissa Harlowe has been from infancy a matchless young creature in her duty to me, and admired by all who knew her as a very extraordinary child; I must therefore take the pleasure of considering her as my own peculiar child … who is the delight of my old age, and, I verily think has contributed, by her amiable duty, and kind and tender regards, to prolong my life.   (53)

From the beginning of the novel, Clarissa extends the compliment of "amiable duty" by signaling her willingness to delegate the authority she has inherited, since, as she writes, "[t]o take all that good nature, or indulgence, or good opinion confers, shows a want of moderation and a graspingness that is unworthy of that indulgence, and are bad indications of the *use* that may be made of the power bequeathed" (104). The family's combination of ambition and close knowledge of the law, however, makes them suspicious of this ethical interpretation of power. The first plot of *Simple Story* – the one concerned with the history of Miss Milner – does not highlight such domestic jealousies, but, as in *Clarissa*, the source of the bequest is male and the consequences equally disastrous (although the disaster in *Simple Story* follows from a sexual, not ethical, choice that defines Lady Elmwood as culpable, not virtuous).

Evelina and the second plot of *Simple Story* – the plot focused on Lady Elmwood's daughter Matilda – develop an alternative to this conjunction of male testator and tragic female history. Most significantly, the wills that set in motion Evelina and Matilda's coming-of-age narratives originate with women, not men, and, while considered binding by the heirs and by their elderly male guide figures, are presented as having suasive though not strictly legal power. The pre-eminence accorded to this suasive power is underscored by the existence of other, legally enforceable routes to inherited wealth that are not finally pursued, despite the insistence of morally questionable secondary characters that they should be. A careful look at the representation of these wills and their effects will help to clarify how they at once permit and impose limits on independent female action in the two novels and, in *Simple Story,* generate in addition a pointed critique of women's uneasy position relative to fathers and husbands.

The opening letter of *Evelina* raises the issue of bequests in terms that open an unlikely connection between women two generations older than the heroine and of diametrically opposite backgrounds. In this letter, Lady Howard conveys to Evelina's guardian, Villars, the wish of the estranged grandmother, Mme. Duval, to remove her granddaughter to Paris. Using Lady Howard as intermediary, Villars refuses Duval's request to release Evelina. In offering grounds for her continued seclusion at his Berry Hill estate, he tempers the exercise of individual will by coupling it in very traditional terms with family obligations: "'it was the earnest desire of one [her mother, Villars writes to Howard] to whose Will she owes implicit duty'" (101) that Evelina remain with him. But the wishes of the two living women, and not Villars, the representative of the dead mother, prevail. Lady Howard's opening role as ventriloquist for Mme. Duval's plan to force Evelina's "entrance into the world" thus prepares for her later and very surprising support for Duval's decision to have Evelina live with her in London. Evelina's recourse to anodyne family sentiments – she admits to the pain of being "banished for ever" (230) from Lord Belmont, the surviving parent who refuses to acknowledge her as his daughter – further highlights the differences between Lady Howard's and Villars's response in this matter. Lady Howard argues from a sense of confidence in Evelina's possession of a "merit which ought not to be buried in obscurity … To despise riches, may, indeed, be philosophic, but to dispense them worthily, must surely be more beneficial to mankind" (231–2). Like Clarissa's grandfather, she urges that a young woman two generations beyond hers be allowed actively to fulfill her identity, in this instance even to the point of enlisting the law to advance her case. Villars exactly reverses this forward-looking impulse when he cites the chivalric death-bed vow made to Lady Belmont in which he had "solemnly plighted [his] faith" that Evelina *should know no father, but myself, or her acknowledged husband* (233). Burney frames his objections through metaphors that recall for her readers Clarissa's own sense of her entrapment by a world of exchange values: "to expose [Evelina] to the snares and dangers inevitably encircling a house [her father's] of which the master is dissipated and unprincipled … seems to me [Villars writes] no less than suffering her to stumble into some dreadful pit" (235). With this point – the affront to "female delicacy" were such "a child to appear against a father" (236) – he completes the gender reversals: as Lady Howard is aligned with Clarissa's grandfather, so Villars is aligned with Clarissa herself.

But even Villars shakes off his ultra-conservative affiliations and again, it is a will that prompts the change. Mme. Duval visits him in his country retirement and threatens, if he witholds permission for Evelina to accompany her to London, to leave her considerable fortune to strangers and disinherit her granddaughter. Villars now reluctantly agrees to Evelina's departure, counseling her when with Mme. Duval "not only to *judge* but to *act* for yourself: If any schemes are started, any engagements made, which your understanding represents to you as improper, exert yourself resolutely in avoiding them, and do not, by a too passive facility, risk the censure of the world, or your own future regret" (279). Like Lady Howard, he has changed course and urges his ward to act defensively and with a prudential eye to the future.

While the opening narrative summary of Evelina's family history brackets the first two letters of the novel, setting them apart from the epistolary immediacy of the ones following, *Simple Story* represents the will of the father – testamentary and behavioral – in the present. At the end of his life, Mr. Milner finds himself wracked by doubts about his vulnerable daughter and arranges to leave her in the care of the priest, Mr. Dorriforth. "When the will of her father was made known to Miss Milner," we are told, "she submitted without the smallest reluctance to all he had required."[1] But as the narrator soon after makes clear, such compliance is atypical of an indulged young woman who delights in her power over men. Dorriforth, in turn, has a "firmness of mind" verging on "obstinacy" that gives to the nature of an otherwise "good man" some "shades of evil" (33–4). In the first plot of the novel – that concerned with the relationship between Miss Milner and Mr. Dorriforth, later Lord Elmwood – the clashes between the two principals are repeatedly punctuated by references to the will of the dead father, references that enforce the cross-generational commitment of parent *and* guardian to direct (or chasten) Miss Milner. The second plot begins after the summary revelation of the now Lady Elmwood's violation of her marriage vows in an adulterous relationship with Frederick Lawnley and her and her daughter Matilda's subsequent exile from Elmwood Castle. Wills and willfulness now become central narrative concerns as Inchbald initiates a complex play between their literal and metaphoric meanings, in part through the close parallels she establishes between *Evelina* and Volumes III and IV of her own novel. The latter half of *Simple Story* develops from *Evelina* in two key ways: first, through the allusiveness of the family pattern (grandfather, his daughter, and *her* daughter) and, second, through positioning the mother's letter as a hinge to connect the retrospective generational plot and the developing present action. At the same time, however, these symmetries alert the reader to significant differences.

As we have seen, Mme. Duval and Lady Howard's unexpected agreement that the law presents the best avenue for Evelina's assertion of her claim to paternal acknowledgment by Sir John Belmont suggests that complicity between older women may have the potential to thwart their male counterparts' plans for the heroine. The men they resist are finally shown to have acted in what appeared at the time to be Evelina's best interests – Villars in confining her to Berry Hill after she turned twelve and Lord Belmont in isolating Polly Green, the substituted child he thought his own, in a French convent. Although in both instances, the sequestering preserves a false identity and stalls the transition from private to public definition indicated in the title, *Evelina, Or, A Young Lady's Entrance into the World,* the novel ultimately endorses women's willing submission to men. Inchbald at once echoes and criticizes her predecessor's conclusion by means of an extravagant intertextuality that is particularly marked at the novel's mid-point.

The history of the composition of *Simple Story* helps to explain the structural oddity that allows a mid-point to function as if it were a starting one: Inchbald began writing in the 1770s, then extensively revised in 1789–90, with the result being a "two-part novel" of which the second plot – Volumes III and IV – functions very nearly as a discrete text. The tonal changes and plot compression at the opening of the third volume underline its separation from the preceding two, an effect heightened by Inchbald's complex re-scripting of *Evelina*, published in 1778 to great acclaim. When read as a commentary on *Evelina*, the Elmwood family plot bears a striking resemblance to the generational complexities in Burney's novel; the differences, in turn, prepare for the ambiguities of Inchbald's ending. The key distinction involves the representation of literal and metaphoric wills: in *Evelina*, the disposition of persons is conveyed through documents and stated intentions; in *Simple Story*, however, the *absence* of a legally binding will and Lady Elmwood's *denial* of self-assertion are made crucial to the progress of the younger generation.

At the opening of Volume III, the narrator emerges to address directly "the reflective reader" who is to "suppos[e] himself at the period of those seventeen years" since the marriage of Lord Elmwood to Miss Milner mentioned at the end of the second volume, and to prepare to "follow the sequel of their history" (194). A quick summary account of the intervening time notes the birth of Matilda, the departure of Lord Elmwood to his West Indies estate after four years of the "most perfect enjoyment of happiness, the marriage state could

give" (196), the adultery and self-imposed exile of Lady Elmwood, her husband's banning of any mention of her or of the child whom he sent after her on
his return from the Indies, and, finally, her death-bed exclamation – "Father"
(201) – a word the attending priest Sandford interprets as a request to effect
some kind of reconciliation between father and daughter. (In a further instance
of the novel's careful symmetries, Matilda is now the age of her mother when
Mr. Milner died and she was made Dorriforth's ward and of Evelina at the
age when Villars is convinced by Lady Howard to release her to her care.)
Elmwood, safely immured on his distant estate, instructs his steward to write
Sandford and tell him "to have every thing performed as she desired. – And
whoever she may have selected for the guardian of her child, has my consent
to act as such. – Nor in one instance, where I myself am not concerned, will I
contradict her will" (205–6). But Sandford finds himself in a difficult position,
the complexities of which he explains in a direct interview with Elmwood.

> 'Your lordship … was mistaken in supposing Lady Elmwood left a will;
> she left none.'
> 'No will? No will at all?' – said his lordship, surprised.
> 'No, my lord,' answered Sandford, 'she wished every thing to be as you
> willed.'   (207)

While she has deliberately refrained from writing a legally binding document,
she does leave what Sandford refers to as a "request," contained in a letter that
Elmwood flatly refuses even to touch until he is told that his wife "'conjure[d
him] to read it, *for her father's sake*'" (208–9).

Lady Elmwood's letter has a double significance in the context of this scene's
re-writing of *Evelina*: in Burney's novel, the *daughter* hands the dead mother's
letter to her father in a climactic meeting that sees the joy of acknowledged
paternity dislodge the previous emphasis on Belmont's accountability for
Carolyn Evelyn's death. What the earlier novel combines to achieve an unalloyed
comic ending – documentary evidence of paternity, reunion of father and
child, overcoming of the past – the later one carefully separates. *Simple Story*
has the letter from the wife to the husband handed over by the elderly male
mentor Sandford at the beginning of Volume III, the daughter's disastrous first
encounter with her father at Elmwood House placed at the end of Volume
III, and their ultimate reconciliation at the end of Volume IV. These divisions
allow a careful discrimination of elements whose conflation in *Evelina* helps
to naturalize patriarchal structures. First, the changes in the conveying of the
letter – with the carrier being the male mentor and not the daughter – emphasize the ways in which a cross-generational grouping of men – Mr. Milner,
Sandford, and Elmwood – functions as a compact of specifically masculine

interests. And second, when Inchbald re-scripts Burney's encounter scene as Elmwood's later accidental meeting with Matilda on the stairway, she retains the physical resemblance of daughter to mother, but removes the documentary confirmation of identity supplied by the mother's letter in *Evelina*. In doing so, she highlights the autonomy of the father's will in deciding what punishment he will impose on Matilda for appearing before him. His absolute authority here anticipates the equally immoderate closing sequence in which he rescues the kidnapped Matilda from the threat of rape, announces his intention to banish his adopted nephew and heir Rushbrook, and then precipitately arranges Matilda's marriage to him. *Evelina* presents the heroine's final inclusion within patriarchal structures – her father's recognition and her marriage to Orville – as her reward for meeting Villars's expectation that she learn "not only to *judge* but to *act* for [her]self" (279). *Simple Story* both echoes the construct and alters its implications by representing Matilda's virtue as a fearful deference to the will of the autocratic Lord Elmwood.

But even as the revisions to the scene of encounter with the father work to consolidate masculine authority in more punitive terms than in *Evelina*, the content of the mother's letter introduces the possibility of an equal but opposite covert female power. Lady Elmwood's epistolary "request" suggests not that she has relinquished her claim to speak as an individual, but that she has intuited that the most effective means of imposing her will may be to deny that she has one. In making her posthumous appeal to her husband, Lady Elmwood thus engages in a form of self-erasure that again involves calling on the name of the father:

> 'I leave a child – I will not call her mine, that has undone her – I will not call her yours, that will be of no avail. – I present her before you as the grand-daughter of Mr. Milner …
>
> 'I do not ask a parent's festive rejoicing at her approach – I do not even ask her father to behold her; – but let her live under his protection. – For her grandfather's sake do not refuse this – to the child of his child whom he trusted to your care, do not refuse it.
>
> 'Be her host; I remit the tie of being her parent.'   (210–11)

In Samuel Johnson's *Dictionary*, "to give up or resign" is the fourth meaning assigned to "remit"; the primary definitions – "to relax," "to forgive a punishment," and "to pardon a fault" – introduce a note of motivational ambivalence to the apparently selfless act of Lady Elmwood's tending to her daughter's future. Doubts about her altruism and disinterestedness are further aggravated by the revelation that in declining to write a will she leaves not only her daughter but also Miss Woodley and Sandford entirely dependent on Elmwood's "protection" (207). Her apparent submission places all of them in the condition of "nobodiness," the state into which Clarissa and Evelina are cast by self-seeking, narcissistic men. We are, in short, invited to consider Lady Elmwood's deference as a refined form of aggression, calculated to ensure her posthumous victory over her husband's living will.

In adapting the play of literal and metaphoric wills from Richardson's and Burney's novels, Inchbald demonstrates a metafictional awareness that allows her to revisit Clarissa's question of "the *use* that may be made of the power bequeathed" (104). *Adeline Mowbray* provides further evidence of the persistence of these tropes linking wills and willfulness to commentary on acts of reading. Amelia Opie not only revives the triple generational plot of *Clarissa*, *Evelina*, and *Simple Story*, but also folds into her novel numerous points of contact with the precedent works, among them, the incest motif, the absent father, the loveless marriage (with Berrendale's faults closely resembling those of Munden in Eliza Haywood's *Betsy Thoughtless*), the metaphoric use of the library to image male power (Sir Patrick O'Carroll attempts, like the villains of 1720 amatory fictions, to ease his seduction of Adeline by having her read Rousseau's *Julie, ou La Nouvelle Héloïse*, Montesquieu's *Lettres Persannes* and Voltaire's *Candide*), the premonitory "last words," and the bequeathing of female children and adults (Caroline Evelyn and then her daughter to Villars in *Evelina*, Miss Milner and then Matilda in *Simple Story*, Adeline Mowbray to Berrendale followed by Editha Berrendale and Savanna to Editha Mowbray in *Adeline Mowbray*).

But while Richardson, Burney, and Inchbald in their various ways uphold or restore masculine authority, Opie refuses this paradigm, signaling early in the novel her deviation from her predecessors' use of the grandfather's will as premise for their fictions. In *Adeline Mowbray*, it is not the grandfather's testamentary acts that are stressed, but instead the Woodfords' – wife *and* husband's – reneging on their duty to discipline their daughter, Mrs. Mowbray, because they believe her from her birth a genius. Thenceforth, failures of parenthood and more specifically of maternity become central concerns, both given a further edge through Opie's references to 1790s controversies. Adeline's refusal to marry Glenmurray recalls both the relationship between Mary Wollstonecraft and William Godwin and key tenets of their writings, while the gap between theory and practice in Editha Mowbray's pedagogy adapts Walter Shandy's work on his *Tristapaedia* in Sterne's novel to satirize the radical idealism of the revolutionary decade. More pervasively, the novel's interest in the negative consequences of unregulated reading suggests, as do Elizabeth Hamilton's *Memoirs of Modern Philosophers* and Jane Austen's *Northanger Abbey*, early nineteenth-century concerns with mass literacy and the kinds of entitlement it might generate. The reinforcement of separate spheres doctrine that gathers strength over the course of the 1790s reflects one response to such anxieties. Adeline's dying speech thus begins by defending marriage on ethical and sacramental grounds, but quickly moves to consider in much more detail the protection it affords children. By such means, maternity comes to represent the defining feature of female identity. Here, another grouping of 1790s novels linking politics and maternity might be seen as antecedent to Opie's less vigorously feminist work, among them Elizabeth Inchbald's *Nature and Art* (1796), Mary Wollstonecraft's *The Wrongs of Woman: Or Maria. A Fragment* (1798), and Mary Hays's *Victim of Prejudice* (1799).

Novel parodies

In inviting a reading of *Adeline Mowbray* that acknowledges the persistence of structures reaching back through Inchbald and Burney to Richardson, even as she reformulates their ideas and those of 1790s radical feminists in keeping with her own later period, Amelia Opie helps us to recognize how frequently eighteenth-century fiction contemplates its own evolving literary history. By Opie's time, that history was sufficiently codified to allow for another, more explicit version of engagement through parody. Earlier novel parodies like Henry Fielding's *Shamela* tend to focus on a specific precursor with the primary goal being not to delight the reader by elaborating on familiar conventions, but to instruct the naïve in the means taken to deceive them. Parson Oliver thus counters Parson Tickletext's credulous enthusiasm for *Pamela* by providing further "authentick" documentary evidence of the low origins and scheming hypocrisy of the principal characters. Later fictional parodies, by contrast, foreground genres over individual texts. The intention is no longer the wholesale discrediting of novels, but the advancing of evaluative standards to enable better reading practices. Harry Levin's account of parody is germane here: in his dialectical model, a rejected mode (by late century, overly affective sentimental and Gothic romance) is contrasted with its opposite (history and improving literatures) in order to validate the novel as a trustworthy mediatory form. Charlotte Lennox's *The Female Quixote* provides a mid-period example in its setting of seventeenth-century heroic French romances against formal history. In works from the revolutionary decades, hackneyed language and derivative plots are once again made touchstones of the censured genres.

William Beckford's *Modern Novel Writing or, The Elegant Enthusiast; and Interesting Emotions of Arabella Bloomville. A Rhapsodical Romance Interspersed with Poetry* (1796) sends up the Gothic by threading jarringly prosaic details into a stereotypically sentimental description of the heroine:

"Alone in this dismal prison, never seeing any creature but Mrs. Dorothy Webster; from frantic fits of despair, she fell into a stupid melancholy, would frequently whistle 'Britons strike home' for the hour together, talked about the Rights of Man like a maniac, and drank lemonade like a fish."[2] Jane Austen's "Love and Freindship," written when she was only fourteen, similarly burlesques sensibilities "too tremblingly alive to every affliction."[3] Eaton Stannard Barrett's *The Heroine Or Adventures of a Fair Romance Reader* (1814) pursues more complex ends. As the self-named Cherubina copes with a daunting series of attempted abductions, assassinations, masquerades, forced marriages and imprisonments (only some of them genuine), she, like Charlotte Lennox's Arabella in *Female Quixote*, single-mindedly applies romance conventions. But the very situations that confirm Cherubina's gullibility also rouse her to displays of resourcefulness and courage that, as the hero Robert Stuart notes at novel's end, "have enabled me to judge of you more justly in a few months, than had I been acquainted with you whole years, in the common routine of intercourse."[4] Barrett's plot thus indicts uncritical reading and at the same time suggests its potentially valuable social functions. While the magnified absurdities of Cherubina's adventures deter real-life imitation, the vicarious experience of them through the medium of *The Heroine* is assumed to be salutary for actual readers. Beyond the obvious self-endorsement offered here, there are other positive consequences of extensive reading. Among them is the simultaneous acknowledgment and regulation of the independent female energy central to companionate relationships. The novel's ending confirms this connection between reading and weddings: Cherubina marries the sensible Robert and under his tutelage incorporates "useful books" (III.289) into her considerable library of established Gothic favorites.

In *Northanger Abbey*, written in 1798/9 although published posthumously only in 1817, Jane Austen adds to the local parody of Gothic and sentimental fiction a larger-scale set of references that recall the courtship plots – failed and successful – of Richardson's *Clarissa* and Frances Burney's *Evelina*. All three novels remove the heroine from the protection of family and expose her to the scrutiny of a range of classes beyond her own social order; all subject her to deficient substitute mothers on her "entrance into the world" (Mrs. Sinclair; Mme. Duval; Mrs. Allen) and to older men who misconstrue their patriarchal functions (Mr. Harlowe; Lord Belmont; General Tilney); all affiliate the heroine with women who help to advance her self-knowledge (Anna Howe; Mrs. Mirvan and Lady Howard; Mrs. Selwyn; Eleanor Tilney); all end with marriages (Clarissa as the bride of Christ; Evelina to Lord Orville; Catherine to Henry Tilney). Ann Radcliffe's novels also adapt these inherited conventions, but Austen's references to Gothic treat it as if it were a coherent and distinct genre. The effect is of two separate novel traditions: the first and enduring one binds together a community of intelligent readers, the second, as the aggressively current references suggest, aligns Gothic with fashionable consumerism.

The inherited conventions are thus layered with more pointed allusions to the voguish novels of Ann Radcliffe, particularly the *Mysteries of Udolpho*, the book that has Catherine Morland in thrall when she first arrives in Bath. She, like Arabella and Cherubina in Beckford's and Barrett's novels, applies the self-aggrandizing terms of Gothic fantasy to everyday occurrences. But her projections more often grow out of concrete moments of social unease and do not, like theirs, lead to gratuitously eccentric and very public misconduct. Instead, they are filtered through inward responses to which we are given access, a technique that makes it possible for us to observe her growth. Thus, when John Thorpe is late appearing to dance with her in the Assembly Rooms at Bath, Catherine's inflated language converts her embarrassment at being seen as a wallflower into heroic endurance:

> [S]he not only longed to be dancing, but was likewise aware that, as the real dignity of her situation could not be known, she was sharing with the scores of other young ladies still sitting down all the discredit of wanting a partner. To be disgraced in the eyes of the world, to wear the appearance of infamy while her heart is all purity, her actions all innocence, and the misconduct of another the true source of her debasement, is one of those circumstances which peculiarly belong to the heroine's life, and her fortitude under it what particularly dignifies her character. Catherine had fortitude too; she suffered, but no murmur passed her lips.[5]

Austen's heightened rhetoric calls attention to the gap between circumstance and response. But Catherine's silence here – as later when General Tilney abruptly orders her departure from his house – also relates to behavioral codes that dictate women's enforced passivity in the face of male selfishness, whether venial like John's or egregious like the General's (he is angered by the discovery that she is not, as he believed, an heiress whose marriage to his son Henry would further enhance the already considerable family fortunes). That more insidious silencing makes her imaginative retreat into heroism appear socially defensive rather than individually delusional.

The connection between these two otherwise very different moments from early and late in the novel suggests that sentimental responsiveness may in fact have prepared Catherine to act with genuine dignity and courage when she leaves the Tilneys to make the long journey home unaccompanied: when circumstances demand, she is able to rise to the challenge. As in Barrett's novel, however, the heroine's final transformation through marriage is not presented as an autonomous choice. Compliance with the hero's guidance, synoptically conveyed by his skillful managing of her reading habits, is also essential. In *The Heroine*, the moment of yielding coincides with the conclusion: Robert Stuart identifies novels that can be "read without injury, and some with profit," and as Cherubina recounts, "sits by my side, directs my studies, re-assures my timidity, and corrects my mistakes" (III.283, 293). *Northanger Abbey*, by contrast, represents reading as an ethical and inclusive criterion of value *throughout* the novel.

Information about favored books indicates qualities of mind that conversational habits confirm. Bad readers like Isabella Thorpe are driven by fashion: they lean toward single genres, usually Gothic, and dismiss out of hand works deemed insufficiently "new," as with Richardson's *Sir Charles Grandison*, by hearsay "an amazing horrid book" (35). While her brother John seems to range more widely, both the works he prefers – Henry Fielding's *Tom Jones* and Lewis's *The Monk* – and deplores – Frances Burney's *Camilla* – mark him as morally suspect. Since Catherine is not familiar with John's choices, Austen's irony in the scenes in which books are discussed assumes her audience's greater knowledge (by late century *Tom Jones* was perceived as low in its depictions of sexuality and *The Monk* as virtually pornographic). We are in turn expected to grasp the connection between Isabella's and John's carelessness as readers and as conversationalists and to see their narcissism echoed in the tête-à-têtes of their mother and Mrs. Allen. While the mirroring of younger and older generations at first appears comical, their later moral failures and lapses of responsibility are intrinsically related to their inability to participate in genuinely sociable discussion. The discrediting of self-referentiality extends as well to its textual equivalent: epistolary narrative, as in Isabella's craven letter seeking Catherine's help in winning back her brother James after she fails to entrap Captain Tilney, connects first-person writing to deceit and dissimulation.

The pairing of Isabella and John Thorpe as bad readers has its complement in Eleanor and Henry Tilney whose capacities as good readers and adept conversationalists are quickly established. The Tilneys' strengths reverse the Thorpes' weaknesses: they are familiar with an array of genres, exact in their use of language (as Henry's gentle mockery of Catherine's sloppy use of "nicest" [109] suggests), and sensitive to both direct and indirect or gestural forms of communication. Austen positions Catherine between these sibling extremes. Her own under-examined habits of speech and reading often generate faulty interpretations: at Bath, she credulously accepts Isabella's protestations of undying friendship, and at Northanger Abbey leaps to the assumption that General Tilney is responsible for his wife's death. But the "real delicacy of a generous mind" (51) that she shares with the Tilneys means that she is susceptible to amendment in the two mutually defined spheres – behavior and reading practices – on which the novel focuses. The Tilneys' positive influence is soon made evident, at least to us: Catherine's first "little suspicion" (53) of Isabella's sincerity occurs immediately after she meets and converses with Eleanor in the Assembly Rooms.

Conversation subsequently provides the medium through which Austen maps out Catherine's progress. Here again, the novel's structure affords important clues about the requisites for growth: her first independent outing with Eleanor and Henry occurs only *after* she twice rebuffs the concerted efforts of her brother and the Thorpes to make her accompany them on their excursion to Blaize Castle. In assessing her motives for resisting them, she confirms the Austen heroine's customary grasp of the reciprocity between individual and social responsibility: "She had not been withstanding them on selfish principles alone, she had not consulted merely her own gratification … she had attended to what was due to others, and to her own character in their opinion" (102). In the event, the walk around Beechen Cliff is dominated by a discussion of reading in which Eleanor and Henry gently puncture one after another of Catherine's presuppositions, beginning with her belief that "gentlemen read better books" (107) than novels. Henry asserts that men in fact "read nearly as many as women. I myself have read hundreds and hundreds," and counters a further gender truism when he comments that his response to *Mysteries of Udolpho* was so far from disinterested that "when I had once begun it, I could not lay down again; – I remember finishing it in two days – my hair standing on end the whole time" (108). These opinions were anticipated by the narrator's own earlier praise of novels for offering "the most thorough knowledge of human nature, the happiest delineation of its varieties, the liveliest effusions of wit and humour … conveyed to the world in the best chosen language" (31). At that point, Austen ironically compared the novel's diminished status to the inflated one of ready-made compilations: the abridgments, collections, and miscellanies that provided eighteenth-century audiences with shortcuts to knowledge. Here, in the Beechen Cliff conversation, Henry's reversal of stereotypical notions of men's reading is followed by Eleanor's challenging of the complementary cliché about women – that they cannot bear "history, real solemn history" (109) – when she recounts her enjoyment of the Scottish Enlightenment writers, David Hume and William Robertson.

The varied topics touched on during their walk – the benefits of a discriminating vocabulary, of reading across genres without reference to gender imperatives, of dialogue as a medium for improvement – are then combined in order to offer a practical demonstration of conversational miscues, in this case centered on novel and history. When Eleanor reacts with horror to Catherine's assertion "that something very shocking indeed, will soon come out in London" (113), Henry must intervene to correct their mutual misunderstanding. She refers, he tells his sister, to "nothing more dreadful than a new publication which is shortly to come out, in three duodecimo volumes … with a frontispiece to the first, of two tombstones and a lantern," and not as Eleanor assumed to a recurrence of the 1780 Gordon Riots that saw, in his words, a "mob of three thousand men assembling in St. George's Fields; the Bank attacked, the Tower threatened, the streets of London flowing with blood" (114). Loyalist novels of the 1790s including George Walker's *The Vagabond* depicted the Gordon Riots as the English precursor of the French Revolution in part to vindicate the current government's harsh repression of radicalism. Austen does not pursue this connection, nor does she develop the corollary argument that Gothic (with its emphasis on secrecy, tyranny, mob violence, and property seizure) represents English anxieties about revolution. Instead, she gives the conversation a comic turn as Eleanor questions whether Henry's mockery may make Catherine assume that he is a "great brute in [his] opinion of women in general" (115).

Near the end of the novel, however, Austen revisits the relation between the actual and the imaginary in Henry's reaction to Catherine's more damaging fantasy, the suspicion that General Tilney was implicated in his wife's death. Catherine's impulse to transpose scenes of Gothic violence to Northanger Abbey has already been checked after a stealthy visit to the dead woman's room reveals not a grim cell but a sunny modern apartment. When Henry unexpectedly appears and with "his quick eye fixed on her's" (202) extracts a confession, his comments unequivocally separate romance fantasy from domestic reality:

> 'Dear Miss Morland, consider the dreadful nature of the suspicions you have entertained. What have you been judging from? Remember the country and the age in which we live. Remember that we are English, that we are Christians. Consult your own understanding, your own sense of the probable, your own observation of what is passing around you – Does our education prepare us for such atrocities? Do our laws connive at them? Could they be perpetrated without being known, in a country like this, where social and literary intercourse is on such a footing; where every man is surrounded by a neighbourhood of voluntary spies, and where roads and newspapers lay everything open? Dearest Miss Morland, what ideas have you been admitting?' (203)

Henry's rhetorical questions and Catherine's habitual deference to his opinion combine to ensure a retreat from uncritical reading that in turn prepares for the novel's marriage ending. Seen from the perspective of that ending, *Northanger Abbey* appears at once a celebration and a witty parody of the eighteenth-century novel of manners. But as suggested by Henry's earlier description of the horrors of the Gordon Riots and his allusions here to the "neighbourhood of voluntary spies" that ostensibly keep them at bay, Austen's work also unequivocally refers to the pressures exerted on experience by "real history." The next part will explore the affinities between fiction, political event, and history writing over the course of the long eighteenth century.

Part III

History and nation

Introduction

The two chapters of this final part consider novels focused on particular historical events, either completed or ongoing. Walter Scott's *Waverley* (1814), often regarded as the originating point of nineteenth-century fiction, will serve here as the terminus for a discussion of three overlapping areas of interest for eighteenth-century fiction: large-scale historical change, smaller-scale sectarian politics, and the representational authority of the narratives that convey these intersections of fact and invention to readers. Throughout the eighteenth century, the traffic between history and novel writing ran in both directions, in part because genre revisions in the period kept pace with larger cultural developments. As we have seen in previous chapters, classical history writing was itself challenged by the conjectural and philosophical forms identified with the Scottish Enlightenment writers, David Hume, Adam Smith, William Robertson, Adam Ferguson, and John Millar, all authors alert to readers' increasing attention to inwardness, character motivation, and the complex connections between public event and private experience. History's importance to fiction, in turn, appears most obviously in the novel's reflex attempts to appropriate the prestige of the well-established and hence more commanding genre. The means chosen to claim parity between established and emergent genres are various. They include using a flatly descriptive style to replicate notionally eye-witness reportage of a devastating event, as in Defoe's *Journal of the Plague Year* (1722); assigning titles such as *The History of the Adventures of Joseph Andrews* (or more slyly given the difficulties of constructing a complete narrative for an abandoned infant, *The History of Tom Jones, A Foundling*); and making references to specific historical moments that counterpoint external political event and negotiations of power within the novel. Through these strategies, contemporary novels enlist history in aid of their own attempts to puzzle out the social, political, national, and even global forces that shape individual and collective identities.

The first chapter discusses early novelistic attempts to contemplate the matter of history through the exile narratives of Jane Barker, the *chronique scandaleuse* of Delarivier Manley, and the faux documentary of Daniel Defoe's

Journal of the Plague Year before turning to a more detailed investigation of the late-century resurgence of polemics and genre experimentation in William Godwin's *Caleb Williams* (1794), Robert Bage's *Hermsprong* (1796), Mary Hays's *Victim of Prejudice* (1799), Elizabeth Inchbald's *Nature and Art* (1796), Charlotte Smith's *The Young Philosopher* (1798), and Elizabeth Hamilton's *Memoirs of Modern Philosophers* (1800). The second chapter examines a series of novels that posit temporal distance as a condition for historical knowledge and understanding. Henry Fielding's *Tom Jones* (1749), Tobias Smollett's *Expedition of Humphry Clinker* (1771), and Walter Scott's *Waverley* (1814) make the first and second Jacobite rebellions pivotal to their exploration of national progress and ultimately their vindication of the novel as form. Finally, Charlotte Smith's *Old Manor House* (1793) and George Walker's *The Vagabond* (1799) testify to the powerful expressive possibilities of such detachment by adopting a converse strategy. They comment on the fraught conditions of the 1790s by setting their fictions within earlier historical moments that both authors – though to very different political ends – represent as parallel to the revolutionary crisis that defines the moment of their writing.

Chapter 7

History, novel, and polemic

The authorial worlds of Jane Barker and Delarivier Manley reflect the politico-religious uncertainties at the turn from the late seventeenth into the eighteenth century. Barker's contexts are principally religious and monarchical: the setting for the frame narrative of her 1713 *Love Intrigues: Or the History and Amours of Bosvil and Galesia* is the garden adjacent to the palace of St. Germain-en-Laye near Paris, where the deposed English king, James II, held court until his death in 1701. James had succeeded his brother Charles II in 1685, but when the birth of a son in 1688 aggravated fears of a Roman Catholic dynasty, William of Orange and his wife Mary, James's Protestant daughter, invaded England in what became known as the Glorious Revolution. On William and Mary's assumption of the throne, Barker's family, with Royalist connections reaching back to the court of Charles I, joined nearly 400,000 others who followed James into what they initially assumed would be a temporary exile. But by 1690, the Jacobite forces seemed to have been decisively routed and William and Mary joined the War of the League of Augsburg against France (which along with the War of the Spanish Succession appears in Laurence Sterne's *Tristram Shandy*). In their St. Germain conversation, Galesia and her friend Lucasia refer to this "War between France and the Allies" as being "almost like a Civil War, Friend against Friend, Brother against Brother, Father against Son, and so on."[1] Their own divided loyalties reproduce the internecine conflict: in exile as supporters of the Stuart cause, they are nevertheless tied to England through birth and upbringing. Jane Barker herself, with the exception of occasional visits to London and the family estates in England, remained at the Jacobite court from 1689 to 1704.

When Lucasia asks Galesia to distract her from these sad thoughts with tales of her early life, the stories that follow seem to swerve away from politics. Yet, suggestively, their culminating event is the failed courtship of Bosvil and Galesia, a relationship hobbled by the lovers' mutual inability to interpret the other's true feelings. Barker's biographer, Kathryn King, sees Galesia's diminishing hopes of marriage and her eventual spinsterhood as veiled references to the predicament of the loyal subject deprived of her "lost lover," the "true" Stuart monarch.[2] *Love Intrigues* was published in 1713, one year before the death of William and Mary's successor, Queen Anne. The 1701 Act of Settlement had excluded Catholics from the throne and when Anne died in 1714 without issue (despite her eighteen pregnancies), the Stuarts were superseded by the Hanoverians under George I, Anne's closest, though non-English-speaking, Protestant relative. James II had died in 1701; his son, James III, the "Old Pretender" or "Old Chevalier," attempted an invasion of England from Scotland, but this 1715 Jacobite rebellion was soon quashed. In short, between the 1713 *Love Intrigues* and Barker's next fiction, *A Patch-Work Screen for the Ladies* in 1723, prospects of a Stuart restoration had dimmed. Perhaps in response, the address "To the Reader" that opens *Patch-Work Screen* suggests a new model for political dissent that advocates tolerant acceptance of difference. Writing in "*Favour of* Patch-Work, *the better to recommend it to my Female Readers, as well in their Discourse, as their Needle-Work,*" Barker declares that though "*not much of an* Historian," she has observed that

> whenever one sees a Set of Ladies together, their Sentiments are as
> differently mix'd as the Patches in their [needle] Work: To wit, Whigs
> and Tories, High-Church and Low-Church, Jacobites and Williamites,
> and many more Distinctions, which they divide and sub-divide, 'till
> at last they make this Dis-union meet in an harmonious Tea-Table
> Entertainment. This puts me in mind of what I have heard some
> Philosophers assert, about the Clashing of Atoms, which at last united to
> compose this glorious Fabrick of the UNIVERSE.   (51–2)

In a formulation that echoes the survey of disparate items on Belinda's dressing-table in Alexander Pope's *Rape of the Lock*, large public concerns – political, religious, and scientific – are feminized and made diminutive through the tea-table setting. But while "awful Beauty puts on all its Arms" (I.139) in Pope's parody of the epic hero's preparations for battle, Barker envisions conversation working to "harmonious" ends to pacify by transcending "Dis-union." As with the exchanges between Galesia and her interlocutor that make up *Patch-Work Screen* proper, these "differently mix'd" discussions follow the associational logic of "Sentiments" rather than the linear structure of classical historical or epic narrative. A similar digressiveness, as we have seen, shapes Sarah Scott's *Millenium Hall*, although the later community does not, like Galesia's, foreground partisan politics in order to suggest that they ultimately contribute positively to "this glorious Fabrick of the UNIVERSE."

Delarivier Manley's fiction also centers on politics, though not in the elegiac terms of *Love Intrigues* or the mediatory ones of *Patch-Work Screen*. Instead, what have been termed Manley's "key-novels" take advantage, often scurrilously, of the ministerial factions that over the course of this period eroded court-sponsored aristocratic patronage. From the turn of the seventeenth century to Queen Anne's death in 1714, a number of interrelated developments in print and governance helped to reconfigure the literary field in ways that opened opportunities for "outsiders" (including increasingly large numbers of women) to participate in political culture. The lapsing of the 1662 Licensing Act in 1695 accelerated entrepreneurial activity within the print trade by encouraging a sharply competitive response to the growing demand for new books. Until the new Copyright Act of 1710 and the Stamp Act of 1712 were passed, an atmosphere of cutthroat commercialism prevailed, fueled in part by the emergence of a version of modern party politics. Between 1710 and 1714, in the final years of Queen Anne's reign, the Tory party, with strong links to Country interests and hence a deep suspicion of the Financial Revolution of the 1690s, was in the ascendant. After 1714 brought the Hanoverians to the throne, the Whigs dominated, and under Robert Walpole (from the mid-1720s until his ouster in 1742 the de facto "Prime Minister" of Great Britain) ministerial government was consolidated with the backing of monied interests.

Manley's satires supported the Tory cause by trafficking in gossip damaging to the Whigs. Her most popular work, *Secret Memoirs and Manners of Several Persons of Quality of Both Sexes. From The New Atalantis, an Island in the Mediterranean* (1709), weaves together elements from the seventeenth-century French *chronique scandaleuse* (Manley helpfully provided separately printed keys to ensure correct identification of her targets), Francis Bacon's utopia, *New Atlantis*, and Aphra Behn's seventeenth-century anti-romances to create a counter-utopia inhabited by Whig grandees of staggering greed and sexual rapacity. The pretext for this mix of political scandal and borderline pornography is the descent to earth of Astrea, the goddess of Justice, who tours the Mediterranean island, Atalantis (England), with Lady Intelligence and the banished Virtue. Lady Intelligence repeats the gossip, Astrea and Virtue comment, and the narrative as a whole settles into a complex, if predictable, play of aggression, seduction, repentance, and rumour-mongering.

Modern commentators diverge in their opinions of Manley: some see her exposure of a sexual double standard as rooted either in a nascent feminism or a spiteful misogyny; others focus on her laying the groundwork for the formulaic amatory fiction of Haywood that was in turn reshaped by Richardson in *Pamela*. In her veiled autobiography, *The Adventures of Rivella* (1714), Manley places herself in the classical tradition, using a conversation between the Chevalier d'Aumont and Sir Charles Lovemore to identify Ovid as her antecedent in the ability to "treat well of Love":

> I have not known any of the moderns in that point come up to your famous author of the *Atalantis*. She has carried the passion farther

than could be readily conceived. Her Germanicus On the embroidered bugle bed, naked out of the bath: – her young and innocent Charlot, transported with the powerful emotion of a just kindling flame, sinking with delight and shame upon the bosom of her lover in the gallery of books: Chevalier Tomaso dying at the feet of Madam de Bedamore, and afterwards possessing her in that sylvan scene of pleasure the garden; are such representations of nature, that must warm the coldest reader.[3]

This excerpt, with its traducing (among others) of the Duke of Marlborough (with his wife, Sarah Churchill, Manley's favorite target), its opportunistic promotion of herself as both personality and published author, its crude voyeurism, and its deft use of architectural and garden spaces, rehearses some of Manley's favored fictional techniques. Her scandal chronicles from the *Secret History of Queen Zarah and the Zarazians* (1705) to the *New Atalantis* were hugely successful, although even Tory fellow travelers such as Alexander Pope regarded them with contempt. Their entanglement in party faction, however, left her vulnerable to shifts in government. A foray into political journalism between 1711 and 1713, including the editing of Jonathan Swift's *Examiner*, thus ended with the extinction of Tory hopes after the death of Queen Anne in 1714 and the ascendancy of the Whigs under George I. *Rivella* was her last major prose work, a bridge between Aphra Behn's amorous novellas and the notorious mid-century memoirs of Teresia Constantia Phillips (1748), Laetitia Pilkington (1748), Lady Vane (1751), and Charlotte Charke (1755).

Although Barker and Manley work in distinct traditions, both develop Aphra Behn's argument (discussed above in relation to *Oroonoko*) that women's exclusion from power heightens their awareness of the limits of public history as a masculine mode focused on a narrow slice of privileged experience. Something akin to that sense of otherness as a provocation to insight might be attributed to Daniel Defoe on a number of different fronts: journalist, spy, Dissenter, bankrupt and highly successful entrepreneur, party hack, political agitator. The opening chapter examined Defoe's alternative histories of exemplary individuals, including the "Life and Strange Surprizing Adventures" of Robinson Crusoe, the "History and Remarkable Life" of Colonel Jack, the "Life, Adventures, and Pyracies" of Captain Singleton, the "Fortunes and Misfortunes" of Moll Flanders, the "History of the Life and Vast Variety of Fortunes" of Roxana. *The Journal of a Plague Year* (1722), like Barker's *Galesia* trilogy and Manley's *New Atalantis*, refers to a more specific moment of crisis, or in Defoe's case, two moments. The first is the prolonged episode of the witnessing and then recording the details of the 1665 Great Plague by the narrator, H. F. (possibly modeled on Daniel Defoe's uncle, Henry Foe, although there is no evidence that he kept a journal). The second is the moment of the novel's publication as plague threatens a return to England after a 1720 outbreak in Marseilles, an event that would, of course, both color readers' responses to the *Journal* and enhance the work's marketability.

Narrative treatment of the gap between ostensible first-hand experience and its prose recreation changes over the course of the century and, as the next chapter argues, these changes provide a way of understanding the increasingly sophisticated links between historical and fictional representations. Here, I want to focus on Defoe's exploitation of that gap to cast doubt on the validity of a number of other foundational eighteenth-century contrasts. Seen from the perspective Defoe offers on the catastrophic actual event of the Great Plague, these standard contrasts are made to appear merely rhetorical contrivances and hence perhaps unequal to the task of probing the complex relation between private and public experience. By way of comparison, *Tom Jones*, published twenty-five years later, assimilates oppositions between the real and the invented to the novel's concluding integration of authorial and providential plots. Fielding advances various forms of partisan superstition – individual (Partridge's gullibility), religious (Catholicism) and political (Jacobitism) – and allows their subsequent defeat to affirm the culminating figures of harmony: the true identity of Tom, his marriage to Sophia, and their retirement to the country estate. In *Plague Year*, such positive correspondences are repeatedly undermined. Historical fact and superstitious belief are not positioned as discrete categories in order that one can discredit the other, leaving triumphant an all-encompassing principle of order. Instead, *both* are treated with skepticism. "Facts" prove amenable to subjective interpretation as conflicting accounts of the death tolls, for instance, challenge the validity of empirical measures: on the one hand, the official weekly "Bills of Mortality" that H. F. reproduces; on the other, his assertion that these were at least 100,000 shy in their estimations "by what I saw with my Eyes and heard from other People that were Eye Witnesses."[4] The mystery surrounding the source of the plague (only in the late nineteenth century were rats identified as carriers) conversely makes dismissive attitudes toward signs and portents – both "publick Things," such as comets, and private ones, "the Dreams of old Women: Or, I should say, the Interpretation of old Women upon other Peoples Dreams" (40) – difficult to maintain.

As the plague intensifies, H. F. observes the breakdown of social structures that once supported hierarchies of distinct "natural" spheres, among them the individual and the family. No longer regarded as mutually confirming, these now appear fictions of more comfortable times. "It is not indeed to be wondred at," H. F. writes, if family feeling gave way to self-protection, "for the Danger of immediate Death to ourselves, took away all Bowels of Love, all Concern for one another" (111). Empathy is another early casualty of self-preservation and eventually even respect for the dead gives way to the base instinct for profit: while "at first, the People would stop as they went along" when they saw the dead lying the streets, "yet, afterward, no Notice was taken of them" and when the Bearers finally came to remove them, they would never "fail to search their Pockets and sometimes strip off their Cloths, if they were well drest, as sometimes they were, and carry off what they could get" (84). The collapse of categorical distinctions – fact and superstition, individual and family, empathy and callousness – has a visual correlative in the breakdown of the equally traditional contrast of city and country: grass begins to sprout on untraveled roads as London slowly merges with the surrounding rural communities that have barred urban travelers.

H. F. responds to these social and topographical changes by sharpening his powers of observation and recording with exactness what he sees and hears. His motivation – one several recent critics argue is inherent to the novel as form – is curiosity, in H. F's case a perpetually "unsatisfy'd Curiosity" that drives him out to range through the streets "and tho' I generally came frighted and terrified Home, yet I cou'd not restrain" it (85). At times, his inquisitiveness seems voyeuristic, even perverse, as when he repeatedly disobeys the prohibition against visiting the plague pits in the Aldgate churchyard. There, the sight of recently infected victims throwing themselves in among the corpses appears to him a measure of the desperateness of the times: "This may serve a little to describe the dreadful Condition of that Day, tho' it is impossible to say any Thing that is able to give a true Idea of it to those who did not see it, other than this; that it was indeed *very, very, very* dreadful, and such as no Tongue can express" (70). H. F. often reverts to the inexpressibility topos to signal the intensity of his wish to make the past vividly present to his readers. But the ultimate purpose of these admittedly futile efforts to recreate "the very Sound" (103) of the dying remains obscure. If Defoe were interested in inviting a politico-theological interpretation of H. F's account, there was an available (and widely credited) tradition linking the Great Plague with the 1666 Fire of London as God's punishment of the English people for Charles I's regicide and the dissoluteness of the Restoration court under Charles II. But the Great Fire does not form part of Defoe's narrative, an absence emphasized by the *Journal*'s dating the close of the plague a full year before its actual end in 1666.

Instead of evoking this standard explanatory narrative, H. F. alludes to the future in conjectural and temporally unspecified ways that stress behaviors, not events. He speculates that "Another Plague Year" might restrain the surge of factionalism that appeared in the wake of the 1665 plague: "I mention this but historically," he says, since "I have no mind to enter into Arguments to move either, or both Sides to a more charitable Compliance one with another ... But this I may repeat again, that 'tis evident Death will reconcile us all; on the other Side the Grave we shall be all Brethren again" (157). His denial of partisan politics is consistent with his projection of himself as disinterestedly object-ive and of his chosen genre as a neutral history. Intent on achieving distance from any "officious canting of religious things, preaching a Sermon instead of writing a History, making my self a Teacher instead of giving my Observations of things" (210), he chooses simply to "give Thanks" to God who elected "as it were, by his immediate Hand to disarm this Enemy" (209). Defoe's unobtru-sive artfulness here is symptomatic of his novelistic strategies more generally: the *Journal* does not "preach a Sermon" or use the rubrics by which a "teacher" would structure information. But nor does H. F. – despite his assertion to the contrary – "write a History." In filtering experience through an imagined agent, the *Plague Year* uses a known event just beyond the immediate knowledge of most of his readers to foreground the ways in which close scrutiny of others at a time of crisis at once stimulates and preserves individual identity. H. F.'s journal thus provides not only a written record of what he purportedly sees; it also affords him the opportunity to write himself into being as an authentic and unique witness whose material correlative is his text.

The "unsatisfy'd Curiosity" that drives H. F. and its partial release through the documenting of a textual self are also central to William Godwin's *Caleb Williams* (1794). The novel's original title, *Things As They Are*, seems to point like Defoe's to immersion in present experience, as do the first-person narra-tive, the undermining of traditional structures, particularly ones relating the individual to the family, and the exploration of acute psychological states. But in the seventy-year interval between the two works, changes in print culture and in the makeup of reading audiences had profoundly affected authorial strategies (and vice versa). Since mid-century, book production had increased fourfold and although exact figures for literacy do not exist, Paul Hunter argues compellingly for the novel's predominant appeal to the young, the urban, and the mobile. William St. Clair's recent quantitative analysis has allowed a more precise calibration of the publishing industry's fortunes and hence of the nature of the reading public. In the first three-quarters of the century, the monopolistic control exercised by the booksellers in what St. Clair terms an *ancien régime* of business practices limited book ownership to the affluent by fixing prices at artificially high levels. Because the restriction of reading to elite audiences helped to maintain traditional social hierarchies, it was supported by conservative commentators like Soame Jenyns who believed that encour-aging "the poor man to read and think, and thus to become more conscious of his misery, would be to fly in the face of divine intention."[5]

The stranglehold of the London cartels was broken in 1774 when the House of Lords ruled (in *Donaldson* v. *Beckett*) against the booksellers' claims to perpetual copyright, a decision that St. Clair deems the most important in the history of reading since the advent of print 300 years earlier. After 1774, he writes, "a huge, previously suppressed, demand for reading was met by a huge surge in the supply of books" (115). The ideological consequences of this sudden expansion were fully realized in the 1790s when writers across the political spectrum adapted the available media – including novels – to advance their points of view and contest those of their antagonists. The clash of radical and loyalist combatants generated an atmosphere of literary partisanship reminiscent of the earlier era of Barker, Manley, and Defoe. But the late-century print revolution with its unprecedented growth in both the production and consumption of texts raised the stakes of polemical engagement by enlarging the numbers and kinds of audiences an author could reach. Looking back on the period from the vantage point of the early nineteenth century, William Hazlitt describes the radical Thomas Holcroft's conviction that the expansion of print culture meant that society could now be reshaped from within and "below":

> He believed that truth had a natural superiority over error, if it could only be heard; that if once discovered, it must, being left to itself, soon spread and triumph; and that the art of printing would not only accelerate this effect, but prevent those accidents which had rendered the moral and intellectual progress of mankind hitherto so slow, irregular, and uncertain.[6]

A member of the Godwin/Wollstonecraft circle, Holcroft embraced the philosophical tenets of Godwin's *Enquiry concerning Political Justice*, particularly its argument that extending knowledge would gradually erode the ability of governments to coerce subjects through institutions like the law, private property, and marriage.

The appetite for proselytizing that grows out of this faith in a comprehensive transformation of consciousness encouraged novelists like Holcroft, Godwin, Mary Hays, Elizabeth Inchbald, and Charlotte Smith to adapt the sometimes arcane representations of high cultural modes including philosophy, aesthetics, and political economy to popular tastes. On completing *Political Justice* in 1793, Godwin thus began almost immediately to write *Caleb Williams*, with the intent not only of capitalizing on the notoriety of his treatise, but also of conveying the "inestimable importance of political principles" (1) to a fiction-reading public that might lack the inclination or the means to buy the earlier (and much more expensive) work. That, at least, is what the Preface claims when it asserts that *Caleb Williams* will provide its readers with "a general review of the modes of domestic and unrecorded despotism, by which man becomes the destroyer of man" (1). In broad terms, the novel fullfils this promise: the servant Caleb does become a victim of the autocratic machinations of his employer Falkland, partly through a sequence of trials that demonstrates elite (and corrupt) control of the judiciary. But unlike some of the more rote translations of radical principles to fictional form – Mary Hays's *Victim of Prejudice* or Elizabeth Inchbald's *Nature and Art* – *Caleb Williams* greatly exceeds its declared intent by combining political didacticism with a psychologically complex exploration of its unreliable first-person narrator. The grounds supplied by Godwin to gauge that unreliability – allusions to earlier works, conflict between individual and familial identity, the ambivalent truth value of various textual forms – are standard to eighteenth-century fiction. Here, however, they are directed to plumbing the protagonists' interiority in ways that anticipate the nineteenth-century doppelganger fictions of Mary Shelley (*Frankenstein*), James Hogg (*Memoirs and Confessions of a Justified Sinner*), and Robert Louis Stevenson (*The Strange Case of Dr. Jekyll and Mr. Hyde*).

In the opening paragraph of *Caleb Williams*, the narrator presents his motive for writing as self-exculpation: his life "has for several years been a theatre of calamity" not of his making. The "story" that he will unfold through "the penning of these memoirs," he promises, "will at least appear to have that consistency, which is seldom attendant but upon truth" (3). The hint of artfulness carried by the theatrical metaphor, coupled with the equivocal resonances of a story that rests its claims to truth on a show of consistency, suggest that we should regard Caleb's vindication with skepticism. Over the course of the novel, his reliance on sentimental motifs deepens our sense that his commitment to matters of fact may be compromised by a habit of patterning his experience on inherited literary models. He thus defines his persecutor, Ferdinando Falkland, in recognizably Burkean terms as a chivalric figure with an unwavering aristocratic attachment to family name and reputation; Falkland's countertype is Tyrrel, the brutal country squire whose public humiliation of Falkland and subsequent murder have haunted Falkland's life, despite his being acquitted of the crime (two other victims of Tyrrel's malice, a neighboring farmer, Hawkins, and his son, were subsequently tried and, on circumstantial evidence, executed for the murder). When the orphaned Caleb some years later joins the household as Falkland's private secretary, curiosity, the "spring of action which, perhaps more than any other, characterised the whole train of my life" (4), leads him to press the family steward, Collins, for details of the scandal. That Caleb's Biblical namesake is a spy tinges his inquisitiveness with unsavory connotations, hinting perhaps at a primal desire to overpower the father surrogate by possessing his secrets (an interpretation strengthened by Caleb's subsequently casting himself as denied son each time he moves to a new location). Once he confronts Falkland and extracts the admission that he murdered Tyrrel and allowed the innocent Hawkinses to hang, Caleb discovers that the truth, far from leaving him powerful or autonomous, binds him in perpetuity to the stereotypically sentimental role of victim to his oppressive master.

The alienating and irreversible effects of forbidden knowledge are subsequently addressed through two models of dangerous overreaching. The first and more traditional refers to Adam and Eve's Biblical violation: the tasting of the prohibited fruit that led to their exile from Paradise. The second and entirely modern version represents the fall into knowledge in proto-Wordsworthian terms: the painful but inevitable lapse from a state of childhood wholeness into adult disengagement that all individuals undergo. Caleb, one might argue, resists this maturation by trying to escape from Falkland – the embodiment of lonely solipsism – in an inverted quest that sees him fleeing from the very knowledge he once sought. But each of the disguises he assumes to elude Falkland's "eye of omniscience" (305), as Eric Rothstein points out, in fact attracts attention by marking him as a suspicious outcast: a beggar (economic), Irishman (political), Jew (religious), disabled (physical). The memoir's intertextual references confirm that despite Caleb's protestations to the contrary, he is emotionally bound to his persecutor by ties he neither can nor will dissolve. To elicit sympathy from his readers, he casts himself as an innocent casualty by echoing (without acknowledging his indebtedness) scenes and phrases from *Clarissa* and *Sir Charles Grandison*. But the differences between mid-century and later representations of sensibility prove to be telling. In Richardson's novels, like other fictions in the same vein including *The Man of Feeling* and *Evelina*, the exploration of individual consciousness finally gives way to the reassertion of collective values. Each of the earlier works therefore ends – through tragic means or comic – by suggesting that adaptability to changing circumstances is essential to survival. Those unable to relinquish past ideals for present realities – Harley and Clarissa – die; those who compromise – Belford, Harriet Byron, Evelina – live (and marry). Godwin's novel, by contrast, refuses such accommodations and, in doing so, realizes its opening promise to render the "domestic and unrecorded despotism, by which man becomes the destroyer of man" (1).

The mutuality of this destruction is crucial to Godwin's comprehensive indictment of "things as they are" and he prepares carefully for the final leveling of Caleb and Falkland. Over the course of the novel, the latter's agent, Gines, shadows Caleb, blocking his repeated attempts to build ties with surrogate families and in the process tightening Falkland's remote but absolute control over every aspect of his life. When his final despairing choice to emigrate is foiled, Caleb decides that he will seize the initiative and use the only means at his disposal – the secret that will blast Falkland's reputation – to destroy his adversary. In Richardson's sentimental narrative, Clarissa famously prevented a repetition of Lovelace's assaults by threatening to stab herself with a pen-knife (a scene reprised in Tobias Smollett's 1753 *Ferdinand Count Fathom*). Caleb protests that "Falkland has invented against me every species of foul accusation," and declares that he will now have his revenge: "With this engine, this little pen I defeat all his machinations; I stab him in the very point he was most solicitous to defend!" (315). In redirecting Clarissa's self-destructive gesture outward, Caleb seems to confirm the late-century faith in the power of print to combat injustice. But the novel's Postscript brilliantly adjusts this broad truth to fit Godwin's anarchistic distrust of institutions, particularly the law, and to question the protagonist's apparent heroics.

Caleb travels from Harwich to the town closest to Falkland's residence, visits the chief magistrate there, and signs a deposition charging his former employer with murder. In the final courtroom encounter between the two antagonists, Falkland unexpectedly declares himself "conquered" by Caleb's "greatness and elevation" of mind and then "threw himself into [his] arms" (324). When Falkland dies three days later, Caleb does not respond by noting the passing of the old chivalric mode and the triumph of individual identity. Instead, he describes himself as a murderer and recasts the narrative as Falkland's:

> I began these memoirs [he writes in the final paragraph] with the idea of vindicating my character. I have now no character that I wish to vindicate: but I will finish them that thy story may be fully understood; and that, if those errors of thy life be known which thou so ardently desiredst to conceal, the world may at least not hear and repeat a half-told and mangled tale.   (326)

Equivocal to the last, Caleb now construes the triple murders as "errors" and represents his own overturning of Falkland's desire to "conceal" them as something of a public service. Such rationalizing allows him at once to disclaim the vanity of seeking his own vindication while also securing it and to mark a lasting triumph over (and indissoluble textual connection to) his former oppressor. The ending, in short, validates *both* psychological and political interpretations: the strange coupling of the central figures demonstrates how "man becomes the destroyer of man" within a culture whose hierarchies sanction oppression.

Caleb Williams is unusual in refusing to use family structures to explore the relation between old and new orders. Robert Bage's *Hermsprong; Or Man As*

He Is Not (1796) more typically makes domestic politics the vehicle for a larger argument about the corruptions of old-style patriarchalism. Representing the family as a social microcosm allows Bage to suggest its internal and incremental reform as an alternative to the wholesale rejection of the status quo demanded by Godwin's anarchism. To advance its mildly progressive agenda, *Hermsprong* contrasts the aged libertine Lord Grondale (associated through his penchant for litigation and his toady Rev. Blick with orthodox principles of law, property, and religion) with the eponymous hero, a man whose egalitarian beliefs originate in his youth among the "Aborigines of America."[7] Throughout the novel, negative characters are identified by their contempt for figures associated with the French revolutionary cause: gossips deride "Mrs. Wolstonecraft" for advocating women's education, while Dr. Blick preaches a sermon against Thomas Paine's *Rights of Man*. The narrator, Gregory Glen, is, in turn, an iconoclast, set by birth and disposition to resist prevailing attitudes. A bastard and hence "son of nobody" (171), he is marked as a consummate outsider by the biographical details he initially provides.

Gregory, however, abandons first- for third-person narrative with the introduction in the tenth chapter of Hermsprong as the rescuer of Lord Grondale's daughter, Caroline Campinet. The shift in point of view anticipates the novel's slow turn away from the sponsoring of radical change toward a new attention, through the medium of the courtship plot, to cross-generational and gender issues, all of them ultimately settled by a conventional marriage ending. Hermsprong buys a house in the neighborhood of Grondale Castle and falls in love with Caroline; the counterpoint to their companionate relationship is the lascivious Lord Grondale's attempted seduction of Maria Fluart (the Anna Howe/Charlotte Grandison to Caroline's Clarissa/Harriet Byron). Here, as in Richardson, secondary female characters are licensed to satirize male behavior, leaving the heroine to exemplify traditional compliant femininity. Maria, more than her nominal lover's intellectual match, parries with him to win concessions for her close friend, Caroline. But Lord Grondale eventually loses patience with her stratagems, banishes her from the Castle, and orders Caroline to marry the odious Sir Philip Chestrum. A plan hatched by Maria foils the arranged marriage; the enraged Grondale renounces his daughter and then uses Hermsprong's appearance among the rioting Cornish miners (an event that dates the action of the novel to 1795) as a pretext for his arrest as a French spy.

Typically, radical fiction – *Caleb Williams*, *Victim of Prejudice*, *Nature and Art* – uses trial scenes to arraign abuses of power by the privileged. Here, however, while Grondale and Blick are individually held to account, juridical process itself is upheld. The justices, convinced by an eye-witness that Hermsprong pacified the Cornish miners with private charity and a speech proving that "there is no possible *equality* of *property* which can last a *day*" (314), return to the bench after their deliberations and instead of sentencing him ask for more biographical information. At this point, he reveals that he is the son of Grondale's older brother and thus rightful heir of the family estates he intends to reclaim from his usurping uncle. Caroline, forced to choose between loyalty to her disgraced father and the man she loves, writes to Lord Grondale and asks to "return to your house, and to my duty" (320). After an elaborate sequence of additional twists – Grondale has a debilitating stroke, repents, and before he dies signals his blessing of his daughter's following her heart – Hermsprong is formally acknowledged as Sir Charles Campinet and marries Caroline.

The novel's co-ordination of courtship and inheritance plots (in the tradition of *Tom Jones* and *Humphry Clinker*) undermines the pattern the novel initially forecast when it made the hero's ties to the American and French Revolutions predictive of a future restructuring of English society. To emphasize the regressive qualities intrinsic to this conclusion, Bage sets it against a number of eighteenth-century fictional conventions relating to familial and social structures. A long-standing device for representing an emergent bourgeoisie, for instance, was the eventual success of disempowered second sons (or illegitimate ones, as in *Tom Jones*) relative to elder siblings whose inheritance of family estates tied them through primogeniture to the old order. The reversion of the Grondale lands to Hermsprong, only son of a first-born son, goes against the grain of this standard trope. Bage further emphasizes his departure from fictional norms by carefully specifying the terms of the inheritance.[8] In the novel's final paragraph, Gregory Glen comments that the marriage of Caroline and Hermsprong, now Sir Charles Campinet, "will prove unfortunate only to the gentlemen of the law; for Sir Charles having no body to go to law with but himself, is under the necessity of not going to law at all; which will be so obliging as to give him a full title to his property, by what the gentlemen of the science call a remitter" (339). The reference here to the common law principle that assigns priority to an earlier claim over a later one when both are valid reminds the reader that Hermsprong is doubly entitled to the estate. Like Sir Charles Grandison, he inherits on the death of his father; yet as Tom Jones eventually will with the Western estate, he also comes into his possession through marriage to Grondale's heir, Caroline. The disclosure of their relationship as cousins means that their wedding, like the inheritance, straddles the divide between traditional and modern: it is not only a dynastic and a companionate marriage, it is also a celebration of given and chosen family, in both instances sanctioned by the daughter's earlier and important choice of "duty" over the individual passion that is itself finally rewarded.

Gregory Glen's ironic tone somewhat mutes the novel's retreat from radical identities, a retreat particularly evident in the naturalizing of primogeniture, the practice that secured the power of the aristocracy and gentry by passing undivided estates from father to eldest son. The last chapter's tongue-in-cheek address to the "dear ladies" (339) further deflects attention from the weakening of political commentary. Glen's mock compliance with the romance demands of the "thousand of my fair readers" (338) has as its counterpoint an equally gendered camaraderie with Hermsprong. The friendship between the two originates in mutual respect for a "manly freedom of thinking and speaking" (97), a manliness distinct not only from the effeminizing consumption of novels, but also more generally from the taint of professional authorship. Like Caleb Williams, Gregory Glen was briefly involved in the print trade. Godwin's Caleb, masquerading as "a deserted, solitary lad of Jewish extraction" (258), uses Mrs. Marney as go-between to place Addisonian essays and plagiarized translations of criminal biographies with a magazine publisher; before he settled in the Grondale neighborhood, Glen also spent time in London, but retreated back to the country after he failed to secure a publisher for "some pieces of poetry which I thought sublime" (69). Both protagonists authenticate their subsequent "memoirs" of masculine sociability relative to these antecedent, derivative works by proclaiming their textual and personal distance from the London print marketplace.

It is tempting to see the frustrated early authorial careers of Caleb Williams and Gregory Glen as versions of Godwin and Bage's own concern with the transformative potential of their writings in a crowded literary field. Beyond this possible autobiographical connection, lies an indisputable and pervasive anxiety about the relation between writer and audience. While ubiquitous in the 1790s, the anxiety is differently voiced, however, in the women-authored fictions of both radicals (Mary Hays, Charlotte Smith, and Elizabeth Inchbald) and loyalists (Elizabeth Hamilton and Jane West). Unlike their male peers, they tend not to patronize novel readers as "dear ladies," nor do they make male friendship an ideal figure for social interaction. Instead, they focus on the connections between under- or ill-educated women and their oppression by institutionalized sexual, behavioral, and political double standards (Hays, Inchbald, Smith) and on the dangers of unsupervised reading, particularly of sentimental fiction, that leaves women prey to usurping villains (Hamilton and West). As the discussion following suggests, this shared interest in pedagogical issues transcends the contrary political orientations of radical and loyalist writing by women.

Elizabeth Inchbald's *Nature and Art* (1796), Charlotte Smith's *Young Philosopher* (1798), and Mary Hays's *Victim of Prejudice* (1799) have a number of features in common. All are overtly didactic, the *Young Philosopher* and *Victim of Prejudice* flagging their instructive intent through prefatorial addresses, *Nature and Art* through its fable-like tone and structure. But each also sets limits on the persuasive powers of fiction. When Smith promises "to expose the ill consequences of detraction," the "sad effects of parental resentment," and the dangers of a "too acute sensibility, too hastily indulged," she notes that these justifications are included as a sop to "those who are of opinion that some moral is necessary to a Novel."[9] Hays protects herself against the possibility that "dullness or malignity should again wrest" a false meaning from her work by insisting that when she criticizes the "too-great stress laid on the *reputation* for chastity in *woman*," she means "no disrespect … to this most important branch of temperance."[10] Inchbald makes explicit Smith's and Hays's sense of the uncertainties of reception when she distinguishes between those "of superior rank" who may "throw aside this little history," and the

> unprejudiced reader, whose liberal observations are not confined
> to stations, but who consider all mankind alike deserving your
> investigation; who believe that there exist in some, knowledge without
> the advantage of instruction; refinement of sentiment independent of
> elegant society; honourable pride of heart without dignity of blood;
> and genius destitute of art to render it conspicuous – *You* will, perhaps,
> venture to read on.[11]

The shared assumption that authorial good intentions have little force against hostile misreadings is internally echoed in the presentation of the heroines' education. Rebecca Rhymer, the clergyman's daughter and eventual wife of the male paragon in *Nature and Art*, Medora and Laura Glenmorris, the model mother and daughter in *The Young Philosopher*, and Mary Raymond in *The Victim of Prejudice* are all literate and thoughtful. But their cultivated personalities do not protect them from worldly assault and misconstruction. *The Victim of Prejudice* most fully develops the irony that education heightens women's awareness of their subjugation without offering them any practical means to resist it. Despite her egalitarian upbringing, the heroine Mary falls casualty to a system that countenances sexual violence against women and then punishes them for their supposed lapse from virtue.

The three novels expose the limiting effects of social convention on individual lives by literalizing the question Maria asks in Mary Wollstonecraft's posthumously published and incomplete *The Wrongs of Woman*, "Was not the world a vast prison, and women born slaves?" (79). In *Wrongs of Woman* and in *The Young Philosopher*, wives are locked away in private madhouses (Smith's wife at the behest of a wicked mother rather than husband). *Nature and Art* and *The Victim of Prejudice* emphasize the collusion of institutions in the oppression of women by contrasting the public and performative aspects of law with private and affective maternity in the novels' central trial scenes. In *Nature and Art*, the naïve Hannah Primrose, betrayed by the calculating William Norwynne, is driven from her birthplace with her illegitimate child. Sixteen years later, "fortune's frowns" (132) having reduced her from agricultural laborer to London prostitute and thief, she is brought before her former seducer, now Lord Chief Justice. For him, the court is theater and cultivating "the approbation of the auditors" (137), he speaks to the accused with an artful tenderness that Hannah, still faithful to her early love, believes sincere. As he stands to deliver sentence, she cries out,

> 'Oh! not from *you!*'
>   The piercing shriek which accompanied these words, prevented their being heard by part of the audience; and those who heard them, thought little of their meaning, more, than that they expressed her fear of dying.
>   Serene and dignified, as if no such exclamation had been uttered, William delivered the fatal speech, ending with – 'Dead, dead, dead.' (138)

Inchbald intensifies the dramatic irony of the encounter – Hannah remains unrecognized throughout her court appearance – by having William subsequently happen upon a broadsheet of her "last dying words, speech and confession" and a petition she has prepared in which she begs that if he "cannot pardon me, be merciful to the child I leave behind" (141). Hoping to redress the wrongs done to Hannah by offering help to their son, he goes in search of him only to discover that he died of sorrow two days after his mother's execution.

As so often in 1790s fiction, scenes of reading model the experience of the "real" audience: here, William Norwynne's conversion by Hannah's heartfelt story directs our responses (although the narrowness of his concern for his son and for his own sense of guilt is tacitly distinguished from our more inclusive condemnation of the father and empathy for both mother *and* child). At the same time, the emblematic title, *Nature and Art*, alerts us to themes beyond the seduction narrative. The generational plot, with its contrasts between the lives of the two brothers and their two sons, makes repetition-with-variation the novel's organizing principle: William senior and junior, respectively Bishop and Chief Justice, illustrate the correspondence between worldly success and domestic misery, the two Henrys, the reverse pattern of poverty, virtue, and true contentment. The rubrics are rather mechanically applied to support a number of radical themes: the evils of colonialism (Henry raises his son in

Sierra Leone and sympathizes with the native resistance there to exploitation), the separation of law from justice, the sexual and social double standards that allow behaviors rigorously punished in the poor to be condoned in the wealthy, the contrast of society and government (the latter supported by allusions to Rousseau). The conclusion, however, is oddly regressive in its political stance. The younger Henry returns to England after a nineteen-year quest to rescue his father from imprisonment in Sierra Leone; together, they witness the funeral of the elder William, then decide not to visit William the younger, since "each felt himself happy in being a harmless wanderer on the face of the earth, rather than living in splendour, while the wants, the revilings of the hungry and the naked, were crying to heaven for vengeance" (149). The younger Henry then marries his now-aged beloved, Rebecca, and father, son, and daughter-in-law "found themselves the thankful inhabitants of a small house or hut, placed on the borders of the sea" (153). The novel ends with a conversation in which the two men respond to Rebecca's tentative questions about the afflictions of the poor by praising the dignity of labor and sharply criticizing those who "murmur against th[e] government." There is no evidence that we are intended to interpret as ironic this arch-conservative claim that the disadvantaged are fortunate in having "nothing to lose" (154). There is also no sense that the trio can assure the continuity of their hard-won insights, either biologically through children who might carry their contentment into the future, or, given their situation on the "borders" of society, through serving as positive social examples to others.

The second-generation failures of maternity documented in *Nature and Art* – both Hannah's (as the effective cause of her son's death) and Rebecca's (as temporary surrogate mother to Hannah's infant and then, once married, physically beyond child-bearing years) – have a parallel in the representation of male power as both absolute and unregenerative. In this context, the absence of heirs equally binds the two very different sons to the perpetuation of "things as they are." The marriages of both the vicious William and the virtuous Henry hinge on the actions of their fathers, cementing the control of the older over the younger generation: William Senior ignores the "curse of barrenness" (75) that afflicts his patron's family when he arranges the younger William's marriage to their dependent niece because of her "great connections" (88). The junior Henry's wedding is postponed until he finds his father in Africa. Male bonds between father and son, we might infer, help to maintain the status quo and, as the closing conversation indicates, dissenting female opinion is soon quashed.

In *The Victim of Prejudice* and *The Young Philosopher*, maternal themes are also germane to the novels' larger social critiques, although differences in their generational plots lead them to respectively more and less bleak conclusions. *Evelina* and *Simple Story* provide an interesting point of comparison here. Like Smith and Hays's works, Burney and Inchbald's make the mother's plot pre-dictive: Arthur Villars resists his ward's departure for Lady Howard's, fearful that her "entrance into the world" will end, as Caroline Evelyn's did, in prema-ture death; Mr. Sandford, Matilda's mentor, expresses similar anxieties about her dangerous physical resemblance to the dead Lady Elmwood. Both of these novels, however, turn the potential tragedy of maternal inheritance to comic ends when they reconcile daughters with their fathers and then orientate this generational concord toward the future with the heroines' eminently suitable marriages (in the process converting idiosyncratic relationships with men into entirely orthodox marital ones). In *The Victim of Prejudice*, the compact between daughter and mentor reappears, but the power of the dead mother over her child is registered not in the private and consolatory terms of senti-mental fiction, but in the public and punitively social ones of radical polemic.

The Victim of Prejudice is the first-person retrospective narrative, written from prison, of Mary Raymond. The story she tells connects her victimiza-tion to a number of factors, none of them under her control. An intelligent and beautiful orphan, she is raised by the virtuous Mr. Raymond, latterly with the brothers William and Edmund Pelham, "heirs to a gentleman of an ancient family and ample fortune" (7) who has arranged their private edu-cation to ensure that the "family honour" will be "preserved uncontamin-ated" (8). The novel's subsequent treatment of reputation – both familial and personal – relates suggestively to Michael McKeon's argument that over the course of the eighteenth century the formerly dominant concept of "honour as virtue" becomes detached from its origins in an elite masculine culture and newly identified with female chastity through a process that ends with women being represented "not just as the conduit but as the repository of an honour that has been alienated from a corrupt male aristocracy."[12] In *The Victim of Prejudice*, punitive versions of both the older and more recent models of honor retain their power to subjugate: the Pelhams and the libertine villain Sir Peter Osborne confirm the persistence of the aristocratic view, while the linked fates of Mary and her mother suggest a new-order, bourgeois intolerance of lapses (chosen or forced) from female chastity. To underscore the ubiquity of this oppression of women and to define it as the product of social attitudes rather than a "natural" subordination, Hays adjusts the terms of the customary mother–daughter plot. Mary Raymond becomes aware of her mother's history only in adulthood when her guardian, justifiably afraid that Mr. Pelham will oppose his son William's love for her, gives her the memoir her mother wrote in prison just before she was executed for murder. Mary's responses to this embedded first-person narrative (recorded as she reads it) reflexively direct our own interpretation of *The Victim of Prejudice* by encouraging empathy with the heroine's attempts to preserve her chastity in the face of male assaults.

Determined to learn from the memoir, Mary decides that renouncing William will protect her from her mother's fate (shunned by family and society after the birth of her illegitimate daughter, the mother, like Hannah in *Nature and Art*, began a downward trajectory that ended in prostitution and murder). But despite Mary's noble intentions, she is left defenseless after a series of catastrophes: her protector Mr. Raymond dies and she is separated from her friends the Nevilles; she is raped by Osborne; William betrays her by contracting a dynastic marriage; and Mr. Pelham (like Falkland in *Caleb Williams*) so successfully maligns her that she is unable to find employment and is imprisoned for debt. As she asks, with a rhetorical excess that is unfortunately typical of the novel, "what credit has the simple asseverations of the sufferer … to look for against the poison of detraction, the influence of wealth and power, the bigotry of prejudice, the virulence of envy, the spleen and the corruption engendered in the human mind by barbarous institutions and pernicious habits?" (163). The retrospective account ends with a return to the novel's opening moment of her imprisonment; this is followed, after a two-year gap, with a further brief summary of succeeding events that, as in *Caleb Williams*, provides a coda to the main narrative, here by illustrating through the history of Mrs. Neville the ways in which sensibility makes victims of women who feel too deeply.

Like *Nature and Art* and *The Victim of Prejudice*, Charlotte Smith's *The Young Philosopher* uses a mother–daughter plot to denounce sexual orthodoxies, but casts a wider thematic net than Inchbald and Hays by adapting the structures of given and chosen families and of nationalism and cosmopolitanism to its social critique. The novel's central contrast between the English Delmonts and the American Glenmorrises domesticates eighteenth-century travel and colonial fiction, most obviously through the courtship of the national representatives George Delmont and Medora Glenmorris, but also through narrative devices familiar from earlier accounts of imagined and real voyages. The opening, for instance, centers on a moment familiar from Sarah Scott's *Millenium Hall*: a group of characters, having lost their way, happens upon a mystifyingly unconventional estate. Here, however, the dynamics of the encounter between the bewildered reactionary interlopers and the radical George Delmont of Upwood are graphed in overtly political terms and given satiric edge by having Mrs. Crewkherne, Delmont's reactionary aunt, supply the visitors with the family history. Entirely unsympathetic to George's innovations, she blames his mother for schooling him at home until he was eleven, encouraging him to work out "a set of opinions of his own, which he never was flogged out of, as he ought to have been, at Eton" (16). The implication that maternal tutelage in these formative years was crucial to his development – a variation on Philip Ariès's argument that links the eighteenth-century "invention of childhood" with the consolidation of the nuclear family – is strengthened by the contrast with his elder brother Adolphus, educated outside the home and now a thoroughly dissolute libertine.

Smith subsequently uses Mrs. Crewkherne's horror at the rumored marriage of George to Medora Glenmorris to add layers of legal, religious, and national parochialism to her backward-looking politics:

> "Nothing [says Mrs. Nixon], can be more just, dear Mrs. Crewkherne, than all you say. To be sure, such a thing [as this marriage] would be not only very affecting indeed to Mr. Delmont's family, but, as one may say, a sort of national concern for nothing can be worse than for great families to demean themselves by low alliances, and especially with folks not properly born according to the laws of England – and then an American too! – a race that for my part seems to me not to belong to Christian society somehow, and who, I understand, are no better than atheists; for I am told there are no clergy in America, as our's are, established by law, to oblige and compel people to think right; but that all runs wild, and there are no tithes, nor ways of maintaining that holy order, as we have, but every body prays their own way."   (41)

As so often in radical novels of the 1790s, genre has evaluative functions, with satire, as here, flagging the corrupt and reactionary, and sensibility, the marker of the innocent and progressive (as we will see below, loyalist writers partly as a result of hostility to Rousseau reverse this pattern).

Using minor characters to introduce and develop connections between significant narrative themes is a hallmark of Smith's fiction. Mrs. Crewkherne's vocal conservatism incites George to express not only his preference for chosen and affective relationships over given and dynastic ones, but also his skepticism about the relation between familial and national loyalty. These views in turn link the novel to wider period controversies. When Medora's mother, Laura, asks him whether he feels obliged to comply with his wealthy aunt's views on marriage, his answer – "where submission is voluntary, it should be given only to those such as have better sense of judgment, than a man is himself conscious of possessing" (66) – would be understood by contemporary readers as both a personal and political statement. They would recognize that his resistance to Mrs. Crewkherne is couched in the terms radicals used to argue for the rights of citizens to question and, when necessary, replace autocratic rulers. A seemingly innocuous conversation about domestic matters, in other words, has broader applications that the 1790s revolution debate cued

novel audiences to grasp. In this context, Delmont's defense of individual judg-
ment challenges the "philosophic analogy" between government and family
Edmund Burke made central to his *Reflections on the Revolution in France*.
Through "the choice of inheritance," Burke argued,

> we have given to our frame of polity the image of a relation in blood,
> binding up the constitution of our country with our dearest domestic
> ties; adopting our fundamental laws into the bosom of our family
> affections; keeping inseparable, and cherishing with all the warmth of all
> their combined and mutually reflected charities, our state, our hearths,
> our sepulchres, and our altars.   (120)

Thomas Paine's *Rights of Man* takes direct aim at this notion of a permanent
"entailed inheritance" when it asserts that "[e]very age and generation must be
as free to act for itself, *in all cases* as the ages and generations which preceded
it. The vanity and presumption of governing beyond the grave, is the most
ridiculous and insolent of all tyrannies. Man has no property in man; neither
has any generation a property in the generations which are to follow" (63–4).
Subsequent novelists, most memorably perhaps Jane Austen in *Sense and
Sensibility*, *Pride and Prejudice*, and *Persuasion*, covertly allude to this political
understanding of entailment when they devise plots involving tied estates.

The first volume of *The Young Philosopher* explores these issues of governance, inheritance, obligation, and individual choice through the present-
moment courtship of George and Medora. Volume II looks back a generation
through Laura Glenmorris's account of her maltreatment by two representatives of aristocratic privilege: her own wicked mother, Lady Mary (of whom
Laura declares in true radical vein, "I never had a mother, for she who bore
me seemed to have thrown me off in my infancy as an impediment to her
ambition"[122]) and her husband's extended family of Catholic Highland
Jacobites, who imprison Laura after Glenmorris is kidnapped and then seize
his estate for themselves. When the couple is finally reunited, his reports on
his time in America offer another critical perspective on English policy; the
Americans, he tells her, "had one great and predominant feature in their character which I loved and honoured – they were determined to be *free*, and
were now making the noblest exertions to resist what they deemed oppression" (148). The third and fourth volumes detail the near-financial ruin of the
Delmonts and Glenmorrises and the kidnapping and secret confinement of
Laura in an insane asylum (at the behest of her mother) and of Medora by an
avaricious suitor who locks her away in a remote Gothic mansion in Yorkshire.
After her rescue, Medora comments that while there, she "recollected [her]
mother's singular story, and particularly the time she was a prisoner, a sick and

suffering prisoner, in the Abbey of Kilbrodie. Her courage, her trust in heaven, did not fail her, said I, in that trying hour, and wherefore should I allow mine to sink under circumstances of less danger?" (314). The power of narrative to sustain individuals at moments of crisis is a recurring motif in 1790s fiction.

The working out in this novel of the predictive influence of the mother's plot (seen also in *Evelina, Victim of Prejudice, Simple Story*) and of the father's (in *Nature and Art*) ends happily for the younger protagonist, less so for the older one. Both women escape their oppressors, but Laura never fully recovers her intellects. Her husband, newly arrived from America, convinces Delmont, once he is married to Medora, to return there with them and discover for himself "that wherever a thinking man enjoys the most uninterrupted domestic felicity, and sees his species the most content, *that* is his country" (352). The domestic realm, detached from its more usual conservative identification in period fiction with British national sentiment, is associated here with cosmopolitan exile. Relocating her progressive characters to America allows Smith to sidestep the corrupting power of institutions that continues to shadow the protagonists in the endings of *Victim of Prejudice* and *Nature and Art*. Even if Smith is slightly tongue-in-cheek in representing the "almost perfect felicity" Medora enjoys with her "almost faultless" (354) husband, this ending diverges sharply from the social exclusion that is the lot of Hays's Mary Raymond and Inchbald's Henry Norwynne family.

The discussion of these three novels has revealed a number of shared features: all include mother/daughter plots played out across two generations in order to reinforce the representation of women's experiences as inextricable from male influence; all focus on instances of female oppression, privately through sexual threat and publicly through imprisonment and trial scenes; all discount the possibility that education alone can alleviate the enforced subordination that, as Wollstonecraft says in *Maria*, leaves women "bastilled" (155) for life. At a more abstract level, these thematic and structural repetitions reinforce the novels' political subtexts. Without concerted resistance to "things as they are," each work suggests, the status quo – with its support of the privileged and undercutting of those already marginalized by sex, class, or nation – will continue unabated. For liberal and radical writers, then, narrative iterations are a favored means of dramatizing the thwarting of individuals by a monolithic and unjust society (Godwin's doctrine of perfectibility develops the related principle that in the *absence* of such constraints all barriers to personal happiness would disappear, including human mortality).

Conservative novelists, responding directly to this characteristic radical trope, re-orient the principle of repetition in order to make the political appear meagerly personal. In their works, repetition directs the reader's attention not to extrinsic socio-economic conditions, but to the intrinsic narcissism, derivativeness, and anti-social bias of English "Jacobins" as both personalities and authors. The anti-Jacobins highlight the supposed self-interestedness of their adversaries by developing the satiric potential of repetition in a number of ways. One of these builds on the precedent of the *roman à clef* described earlier in this chapter in relation to Delarivier Manley's *New Atalantis* (1709) and continued by Tobias Smollett in *Peregrine Pickle* (1751) with his satiric sketches of a number of contemporaries who had thwarted him personally and professionally, including Henry Fielding, Chesterfield, and the actor and theater impresario, David Garrick. Late-century loyalist fiction also mixes invented with real-life characters, identifying its targets through distinguishing physical traits and parodies of published works as well as sexual scandals (the latter usually focused on women, including Mary Hays and, after Godwin published the *Memoirs* (1798) of his recently deceased wife, of Mary Wollstonecraft). William Godwin appears as Subtile in Isaac D'Israeli's *Vaurien: Or, Sketches of the Times: Exhibiting Views of the Philosophies, Religions, Politics, Literature, and Manners of the Age* (1797) and Myope in Elizabeth Hamilton's *Memoirs of Modern Philosophers* (1800); Joseph Priestley as Dr. Alogos in George Walker's *The Vagabond* (1799); Mary Wollstonecraft as Lady Mary Manhunt in Robert Bisset's *Douglas; Or, The Highlander* (1800); Mary Hays as Bridgetina Botherim in Hamilton's *Memoirs of Modern Philosophers* (1800), the latter portrait a negative rendering of Hays's self-justifying account of her relationships with William Frend and Godwin in *Memoirs of Emma Courtney* (1796) and cruelly personal in its description of Hays's person.

In addition to individual caricatures, conservative fictions also embed fragments of radical plots (both Bisset's *Douglas* and Mrs. Bullock's *Dorothea; Or A Ray of the New Light* (1801) make use of Holcroft's *Anna St. Ives*) and settings (Walker's *The Vagabond* travesties *The Young Philosopher*'s celebration of America as republican ideal). But their most overt and damaging form of repetition appears in the verbatim quoting by fictional acolytes of their favored radical authors, most often William Godwin, Mary Wollstonecraft, and Thomas Paine. Robert Bisset names the latter two in his attack on the rote thinking of revolutionary writers and the credulity of lazy readers in his anti-Jacobin novel, *Douglas; Or, The Highlander*:

> Superficial women think, as superficial men do, not from REASON, but from *authority* … [I]dle thinkers prefer subsisting on the charity of others mens [sic] thoughts to the labour of procuring independent food for their minds. The minor authoresses are, I believe, thinkers on the authority of Mrs. Wolstonecraft, as many of the minor moral writers are thinkers on the authority of Thomas Paine.[13]

The charge that radical thinkers – a tag mocked by the ringing of changes on the word in the quoted passage – reflexively submit to the authority of texts cuts deeply into the revolutionaries' claims to inspire independent judgment.

As his references to Wollstonecraft and Paine imply, Bisset is concerned not only with the activities of writing and reading, but also with the makeup of audiences, especially the women addressed by "authoresses" and the broad popular constituency that Paine attracted. Anxiety about the unsupervised reception and interpretation of radical works was widespread, with the more accessible genres – broadsheets, pamphlets, novels – a source of particular alarm. To defend "genuine Religion, Morality, and Liberty," loyalists determine to fight fire with fire, and convinced that "a *Novel* may gain attention, when arguments of the soundest sense and most perfect eloquence, shall fail to arrest the feet of the *Trifler*, from the specious paths of the new Philosophy," they transfer wholesale into *their* fictions material from radical ones.[14] George Walker's *The Vagabond* (1799), Elizabeth Hamilton's *Memoirs of Modern Philosophers* (1800) and Charles Lucas's *Infernal Quixote* (1801) thus have their gullible characters quote memorized blocks of text from Godwin, Hume, Paine, and Wollstonecraft. To emphasize the lack of contemplative distance between the acolytes' superficial reading and its mechanical recapitulation, the authors annotate these passages and then use the footnotes to engage their real readers in a virtual dialogue through close analysis of the cited material. The strategy of interruption makes the different physical experience of radical and anti-Jacobin fiction thematically significant. The headlong rush through a novel like *Victim of Prejudice*, encouraged by empathy with the first-person narrator, is replaced in loyalist fiction by the staccato rhythm created by the narrator's intrusive commentary and the criss-crossing from lateral to vertical text that reference to footnotes makes necessary. Hamilton's novel, however, differs from male-authored loyalist ones when it extends the customary exploration of education and reading to make the argument that women, both married and unmarried, contribute significantly to the maintenance of social order.

Memoirs of Modern Philosophers counterpoints the courtship experiences of three women: the well-born Julia Delmond who, beloved by the virtuous Churchill, is infatuated with and finally falls prey to the Jacobin villain Vallaton, the vulgar Bridgetina Botherim, a déclassé version of Emma Courtney in Mary Hays's 1796 novel, who pursues the resisting Henry Sydney to London, and Harriet Orwell whose reciprocated affection for Henry Sydney remains unvoiced while both discharge social duties at odds with their personal feelings. The resolution of these relationships – respectively through death, retreat, and fulfillment – corresponds thematically to the women's practices as romance, gullible, and sensible readers, practices that are in turn referred to the distinct custodial roles that members of the older generation adopt toward their charges. Hamilton interweaves these motifs of courtship, inheritance, sensibility, and education with a further contrast between the local (England and Scotland) and the foreign (France and Africa) to reinforce the triumph of the domestic over the political and the national over the cosmopolitan. Julia Delmond represents the most complex embodiment of these themes because she is successively advocate, victim, and opponent of radical doctrine (a reprise of the heroine of Jane West's *A Tale of the Times*, published a year earlier). Raised by a father besotted in his youth with seventeenth-century French romances (whose own father scoffed at religion as "a very proper thing for the common people … [but] quite beneath the notice of a gentleman" [78–9]), Julia is granted "free command of all the books which either the private collections of [her father's] friends or the circulating library could furnish" (85). As in *Adeline Mowbray*, where the daughter is similarly treated as her parent's companion rather than as a dependant, there is a competing formative influence: in Opie's novel, the grandmother, Mrs. Woodford, who compensates for Editha Mowbray's derelictions of duty, and in Hamilton's, the foster-parents with whom Julia is left when her father's regiment is posted abroad.

This hybrid education produces divided heroines, innately moral, but so susceptible to the blandishments of theory that they fatally breach the social conventions their parents have taught them to regard as beneath their attention. Opie's less overtly doctrinaire novel represents Adeline's extramarital relationship with Glenmurray with some sympathy, but Julia's seducer Vallaton satanically exploits her romance habit of seeing the world through the distorting lens of radical fiction. In an echo of Inchbald's *Nature and Art* and Hays's *Victim of Prejudice*, Vallaton is the presumed child of an executed prostitute, but stripped here of the earlier works' sentimental representation of maternal love (and hence reminiscent of Smollett's 1753 variant in the mother of the anti-hero of *Ferdinand Count Fathom*). Rescued from the streets and taken into the household of "a good lady, who was a great reader of novels" (53), he connives his way from underservant, to hairdresser, author, and finally leader of a Jacobin cell in London.

The reading and upbringing of Bridgetina Botherim and Harriet Orwell establish them as contrasting foils to Julia Delmond. Bridgetina dismisses her doting mother's praise of her familiarity with the holdings of the local circulating library. Why, she retorts, would she "take the trouble of going through all the dry stuff … history and travel, sermons and matters of fact? I hope I have a better taste! You know very well I never read any thing but novels and metaphysics" (38). When Bridgetina runs away to London, a distracted Mrs.

Botherim reveals to Dr. Orwell that she, like Captain Delmond, referred to her own circumstances in educating her daughter:

> Seeing my late dear Mr. Botherim [a clergyman] consider me as nobody, because I was not book-read, I thought I would take care to prevent my daughter's meeting with such disrespect from her husband; and so I encouraged her in doing nothing but reading from morning until night. Proud was I when they told me she was a philosopher; for few women, you know, are philosophers; and so I thought she must be wiser than all her sex, and that all the men of sense would be so fond of her!   (225–6)

Dr. Orwell's child, Harriet, though now motherless (perhaps a fortunate circumstance given the negative influence of Mrs. Delmont and Botherim) is a social not singular, critical not credulous, genteel not vulgar, detached not passionate, reader. Early in the novel, we see her from the perspective of Henry Sydney as he enters the room where she sits, "at her work with her aunt and sister, listening to Hume's History of England, as it was read to them by a little orphan girl she had herself instructed." Hamilton directs our interpretation of the scene by invoking the disbelief of "some notable housewife" that any real-life woman "'should get time to listen to books,'" and then asking this imagined figure to cast up the hours daily wasted in the mismanagement of servants; if she would "consider the amount," she would recognize Harriet's activities not as the "nonsense these *men authors* speak" but as a fair estimate of the "time sufficient for the cultivation of her understanding, and the fulfilment of every social as well as every domestic duty" (73).

Harriet Orwell, like Clarissa, portions her day to fit both personal and familial responsibilities. Unlike Richardson's heroine, however, she is supported in her virtue by her maiden aunt, Mrs. Goodwin. Mrs. Goodwin's death-bed speech – a favored moment in period novels for concentrated piety – warns Harriet that "the path of passion is often mistaken for the road of virtue" (187). But she also holds out the promise that the single state is entirely consistent with the "conscious dignity of the being who endeavours to fulfil the duties of humanity, and to make progressive improvement in knowledge and in virtue" (191). That Henry Sydney also has a positive, unmarried female mentor, Mrs. Fielding, helps to align him with Harriet and against Julia and Bridgetina, with their flawed nuclear families. Mrs. Fielding, a model of the philanthropic spinster, advances the marriage of the principals, having first tested her protégé Henry by withholding financial support and Harriet by questioning why the young woman rejected a wealthy suitor in favor of the impoverished Henry. Harriet's answer – "all my habits have been those of active industry, and all my hopes of happiness have been taught to rest in the bosom of domestic peace"

(351) – convinces Mrs. Fielding that the lovers are both personally compatible and socially responsible and she provides the fortune that makes their wedding possible.

Just before the couple marries, the three heroines reconvene at Mrs. Fielding's Asylum for "destitute females," a private charity whose costs are offset by the "honest industry" (301) of the more than 1,000 women who have taken shelter there since its founding (this, presumably, a strike at Wollstonecraft and Hays's representation in *Wrongs of Woman* and *Victim of Prejudice* of prostitution as the inevitable lot of the poor). A pregnant and remorseful Julia, who has taken shelter at the Asylum, provides a summary history of her fall from the moment she began listening "with avidity to the reveries of the new theorists, whose doctrines promised emancipation from the tyranny of prejudice, and seemed to offer the rights of equality to the hitherto degraded part of the human race" (372), through her seduction by Vallaton and abandonment of her parents, to a failed suicide attempt (another of the details of Mary Wollstonecraft's life made notorious when Godwin published his *Memoirs of the Author of the Vindication of the Rights of Woman*). The counsel Harriet and Mrs. Fielding offer her – Bridgetina, by this point cured of her radicalism and reconciled to her mother is a silent auditor – reflects the increasing prominence assigned to women's domestic and exemplary roles in the 1790s. Mid-century fiction, by contrast, appears more variable in its responses to sexual lapses and less inclined to make them emblematic of larger forms of social disorder. While Clarissa's and Julia's histories are clearly linked, Henry Fielding's *Tom Jones* assumes a relatively casual attitude to premarital sex, evident not only in Tom's encounters with a range of women across the social spectrum from Molly Seagrim to Lady Bellaston, but also in his rebuking Nightingale for false modesty when he at first refuses to marry Nancy Miller after seducing her. When *Memoirs of Modern Philosophers* stages detailed conversations about the possible steps Julia might take to recover the course of virtue, by contrast, sexual frailty is made an issue of communal significance. Harriet urges her friend to "avoid too keen a recollection of past events" (368), while Mrs. Fielding advocates a private birth followed by retirement to Ireland, insisting that a renewed commitment to a socially productive life morally justifies the concealment of her history. Julia, however, proves that she has fully and appropriately internalized her guilt by rejecting the possibility of worldly happiness and then (like Clarissa) dying. As in *Adeline Mowbray*, this ending satisfies both religious and social imperatives, representing "the Almighty as a GOD of hope and consolation" (371), while at the same time insisting on expiatory punishment for the unchaste.

The summary account of the remaining Jacobin enthusiasts predictably details the unraveling of their plots: Bridgetina returns to her mother; Citizen

Myope's plan to emigrate with his fellow radicals to join the Hottentots ("an exalted race of mortals … who so far from having their minds cramped in the fetters of superstition, and their energies restrained by the galling yoke of law, do not so much as believe in a Supreme Being, and have neither any code of laws, nor any form of government" [161]), is abandoned; Vallaton, betrayed to the French authorities by his mistress, the Amazonian Emmeline, is guillotined. The last paragraph underscores the loyalist repudiation of radical fiction by sandwiching a quote from Mary Hays's *Emma Courtney* (1796) about "*this corrupt wilderness of human society*" between two direct citations from James Thomson's *Seasons* and Edward Young's *Night Thoughts*, poems upholding the providential order that in Hamilton's novel triumphs over the "dark and gloomy dogmas of modern philosophy" (389). The prominence assigned to these quoted passages confirms the thoroughgoing implication of *Memoirs of Modern Philosophers* in the revolution debate. As the next chapter will detail, an alternative, less overtly sectarian model for representing political experience had emerged over the course of the eighteenth century, a model whose triumph in the early nineteenth century challenged the partisan novels of the 1790s and ensured their subsequent treatment as historical curiosities, perhaps even literary dead ends.

Chapter 8

Historical fiction and generational distance

The main and running titles of Walter Scott's 1814 novel offer a convenient starting point for speculating about differences between eighteenth- and nineteenth-century historically minded fiction. *Waverley* – like Henry Fielding's *Tom Jones* (1749), Laurence Sterne's *Tristram Shandy* (1765–7), and (with some irony) Tobias Smollett's *Humphry Clinker* (1771) – signals the exemplary status of its hero. The running title, *Or, 'Tis Sixty Years Since* foregrounds the mediatory temporal distance that earlier writers, including Jane Barker and Daniel Defoe, make critical to their representation of historical events and that, as this chapter will detail, Fielding, Smollett, and Sterne also utilize. Only with the nineteenth-century novel, however, as the synoptic *Waverley; Or, 'Tis Sixty Years Since* suggests, is the integration of historical change and individual maturity made central to the understanding of what is lost and gained both publicly and personally with the passage of time. In *Waverley*'s final chapter, "A Postscript, which should have been a Preface," Scott juxtaposes the "complete … political and economical" alteration of Scotland after the collapse of the second Jacobite rebellion in 1745 and the nearly "vanished" cultural memory of those of the generations before his "who still cherished a lingering, though hopeless attachment to the house of Stuart."[1] Scott's balancing here of the empirical and the elegiac, the political and the sentimental, presumes a stable vantage point that enables critical appraisal and idealization of the past. In *Tom Jones, Humphry Clinker*, and *Tristram Shandy*, the mid-century novels that begin self-consciously to manipulate the relationship between completed and ongoing historical experience, that stability remains elusive. As this chapter will argue, in these novels threatened identities – individual, social, and national – are instead the focus of attention. Their resolutions correspondingly depend less on the naturalizing of changes in consciousness pursued in *Waverley*, and more on the sanctioning of institutions by authorial fiat. By the 1790s, as the concluding examination of Charlotte Smith's *Old Manor House* (1793) and George Walker's *The Vagabond* (1799) will suggest, such narrative manipulations in the face of revolutionary unrest have a distinctly tendentious air. The internalizing of historical processes by Scott's heroes seems, from this perspective, a response to the impasse reached when late eighteenth-century fictions look to external factors to reconcile singularity and sociability with support for existing hierarchies.

In advance of this more detailed discussion, one further extrapolation from the eponymous titles may help to indicate the differences between eighteenth- and early nineteenth-century historical fictions. Waverley is a proper name, but it is also a personality trait – the "wavering and unsettled habit of mind" aggravated in Scott's hero by "the vague and unsatisfactory course of reading which he had pursued" (31) at his uncle's house. The habits of reverie that make his immersion in the Jacobite cause possible, however, are susceptible (in the case of the hero and Scott) to the discipline of retrospection. Separated from his compatriots, Waverley is removed from direct action as the Hanoverian army routs the Stuart forces. Forced to remain in hiding, "in many a winter walk by the shores of Ulswater … [he] acquired a more complex mastery of a spirit tamed by adversity, than his former experience had given him" and ultimately "felt himself entitled to say firmly, though perhaps with a sigh, that the romance of his life was ended, and that its real history had now commenced" (283). His "real history," as the dark heroine Flora Mac-Ivor had predicted, will be shaped not by "high and perilous enterprise" but by the "quiet circle of domestic happiness" (250), symbol of both Waverley's and Britain's achievement, post-1745, of progress through compromise and accommodation.

While Waverley's name and plot herald a solution to the problem of political intractability and absolutism, those of Tom Jones and Humphry Clinker offer a bleaker assessment of the possibilities for incremental improvement. As illegitimate sons without inherited identities, their assigned and hence unmoored names stand in for wider failures of generational continuity. Sterne's *Tristram Shandy* reveals related concerns. Tristram, in a variation on Fielding and Smollett's motif of imperfect connection, is the name that the servant Susannah, the "leaky vessel" who cannot "carry Trismegistus in [her] head, the length of the gallery" (229), blurts out to the curate waiting to christen the child. To his father, Walter Shandy, who believes that "there was a strange kind of magick bias, which good or bad names, as he called them, irresistibly impress'd upon our characters and conduct" (43), "Tristram" – Susannah's garbling of the more auspicious "Trismegistus" – is synonymous with "*Nicompoop*" (47) and does his son an "injury" that could "never be undone – nay he doubted even whether an act of parliament could reach it" (46). Unentitled, alienated from their fathers, made marginal by accidents of birth (or, in the case of the crashing sash-window that circumcises Tristram, of early childhood), Tom Jones, Humphry Clinker, and Tristram Shandy seem set to embody a mid-century crisis of confidence. In their very different ways, however, all three ultimately testify to their authors' abilities to call upon the power of design to prevail over accident and of tradition to absorb vanguard energies.

In *Tom Jones* as in *Joseph Andrews*, Henry Fielding formalizes a literary commitment to classical tradition through semi-ironic references to his novel as a "Heroic, Historical, Prosaic Poem" (138) and an example of "prosai-comi-epic Writing" (187). The epic affiliations that underpin what Coleridge deemed "one of the three most perfect plots ever planned" testify to the continued authority of neo-Augustan aesthetics: *Tom Jones*'s eighteen Books fall into three groups of six chapters, marking out a beginning (the cause of action is provided and the hero, Tom, is set against his adversary, Blifil), a middle (the journey toward London charted through detailed topographical references), and an end (resolution and return to the country after a testing period in London).² Direct addresses to the reader in the first chapter of each Book reinforce these divisions and help to prepare for the subsequent tonal variations between intimate conversation and detached narration. Over the course of the novel, the omniscient, obtrusive narrator gradually sheds the deference he assumed in the first of these introductory lectures when he likened his role as author to that of the keeper of a "public Ordinary" who provides a "Bill of Fare" in order that his customers "may either stay and regale with what is provided for them, or may depart to some other Ordinary better accommodated to their Taste" (35).

Once we have made the choice to travel with him through the "long journey" (812) of the novel, he flexes his power, at times withholding crucial information and then taunting us for not anticipating outcomes that invariably confirm the discrepancy between his inclusive vision and our very partial one. Fielding's objective, it becomes clear, is to develop a parallel between narratorial and divine omniscience, using the microcosmic working out of the plot to echo the macrocosmic operations of Providence. In both instances, submission to authority is critical to understanding the principles that regulate and give meaning to what should be the mutually defining spheres of secular and religious experience. As Tom Jones's conversion moment illustrates, however, the process of enlightenment is not a matter of rote compliance with abstract rules. Toward the end of the novel, after Partridge blurts out that his master has "been a-bed with [his] own Mother," a horrified Tom quickly represses his initial lament that "Fortune will never have done with me, 'till she hath driven me to Distraction" and acknowledges his personal culpability: "But why do I blame Fortune? I am myself the Cause of all my Misery. All the dreadful Mischiefs which have befallen me, are the Consequences only of my own Folly and Vice" (814). This individual testimony – in conversion narratives the customary prelude to redemption – alters the novel's course. From this point forward, the apparently random impulses of Fortune give way to a novelistic enactment of Alexander Pope's vision of immanent design:

> All Nature is but Art, unknown to thee;
> All Chance, Direction, which thou canst not see;
> All Discord, Harmony, not understood;
> All partial Evil, universal Good:
> And, spite of Pride, in erring Reason's spite,
> One truth is clear, 'Whatever IS, is RIGHT.'
>
>   (I.289–94)

Pope anticipates this ending of *Essay on Man*'s first Book with an opening invitation to his addressee, Bolingbroke, to consider both poem and world as "A mighty maze! but not without a plan" (I.6). In *Tom Jones*, as well, the journey has powerful resonances that reinforce the novel's didacticism.

The journey as metaphor is particularly useful for Fielding since it can function straightforwardly as a figure for advancement or, when used ironically, signal failure to progress; has both elite classical associations and low-cultural picaresque ones; and enables contact between socially distinct groups removed from domestic certainties and therefore more susceptible to the pressure of public events. In formal terms, the structure provides Fielding with opportunities for displaying the artistry of the plot, as with the scene in the inn at Upton where the principals leave the road to congregate in separate groups, discover crucial information about particular individuals, and change direction, all without actually coming into direct contact with others. As the plot unfolds, journeys help readers to discriminate primary from secondary characters: only the former make complete circuits from the country to the city and back to the country; the latter either remain in the same place or take shorter trips. The arc of the protagonists' travels – from leave-taking to return – aligns them with the perfect figure of the circle (a hint perhaps that Tom and Sophia forecast their eventual status as icons of order when they reconfigure what for both begin as linear journeys). More palpably, the movement of characters through landscapes and urban settings familiar to Fielding's readers testifies to his interest in exploring the wider and at times political contexts of individual action. In this sense, travel becomes a vehicle for what anthropologists call "thick description," the setting of human behavior within material and national culture, here through references to (and occasionally puffing of) specific places, businesses, and products.

Comparison with *Pamela* suggests the sharp differences between Richardson's and Fielding's spatial sensibility: when Richardson's heroine is sent from the Bedfordshire to the Lincolnshire estate (and then back), the pattern of exile and return is related to the motif of "virtue rewarded" that allows Pamela to re-write the standard seduction narrative. Topographical details are deliberately repressed in the outward passage – when Pamela asks, "pray, Mr. Robert, there is a Town before us, What do you call it?" (103), there is no answer provided – and on the return journey, a more literal obscurity also reigns: "We could not reach further than this little poor Place, and sad Ale-house rather than Inn; for it began to be dark, and Robin did not make so much haste as he might have done" (247). In *Tom Jones*, by contrast, the locatedness evoked by travel provides a testing ground for considering the position of individuals in time, individuals both invented and historical. Place and time, the hallmarks of realist fiction, here assume reciprocally questioning functions that in the political argument Fielding sets in motion ultimately endorse Hanoverian compromise over Stuart absolutism. Even before Tom is ejected from Paradise Hall and embarks on the travels that bring him into contact with the 1745 Jacobite uprising, Fielding invites scrutiny of the relation between history as event and history as record. Initially, this is framed through comic treatment of the discrepancy between private reality and public document. Later, on the road, a more somber consideration of historical representation emerges through references to Monmouth's 1685 rebellion and the 1715 and 1745 rebellions.

Book II questions the plausibility of official records in its closing passage, a reproduction of the epitaph carved on the tombstone of Captain John Blifil, Bridget's despised husband, by order of Mr. Allworthy. In common with "Men of true Wisdom and Goodness [who] are contented to take Persons and Things as they are, without complaining of their Imperfections, or attempting to amend them" (99), Allworthy had remained blissfully unaware of the couple's fractious relationship. In introducing the inscription, the more critical narrator injects a decidedly ironic note when he comments that, "the Epitaph was written by a Man of as great Genius as Integrity, and one who perfectly knew the Captain" (101). Each of the attributes it celebrates ("a dutiful son, a tender Husband, an affectionate Father, a most kind Brother") is discounted by what we know of Captain Blifil, with the culminating point in the catalog of misrepresentations the assertion that his "inconsolable Widow hath erected this Stone" as a "Monument of his Virtues, and his Affection" (106). The direct address immediately following in Book III chapter one, builds on the factitious nature of print (or sculpted text) by scoffing at the unedited flow of information in newspapers and periodicals, the "daily and weekly Historians of the Age, in reading which, great Numbers of Persons consume a considerable Part of their Time" (108). Toward the end of the novel, "History" and "Play" (822) are added to the list of literary kinds whose depictions of experience are tailored to fit the demands of the given genre. After Nightingale's defense of Tom has staggered Allworthy's belief in his guilt, the narrator steps in and comments:

> we will stop here to account for the visible Alteration in Mr. Allworthy's Mind, and the Abatement of his Anger to Jones. Revolutions of this Kind, it is true, do frequently occur in Histories and dramatic Writers, for no other Reason than because the History or Play draws to a Conclusion, and are justified by Authority of Authors, yet though we insist upon as much Authority as any Author whatever, we shall use this Power very sparingly, and never but when we are driven to it by Necessity.   (822)

Over the course of *Tom Jones*, Fielding's contrasts of prestigious and vulgar forms at once underscore and subvert genre hierarchies, in part to claim standing for the novel as a mode of writing that is no less bound by conventions of representation than others. In foregrounding this literary consciousness, Fielding shatters the illusion of transparency that Richardson's epistolary "writing to the moment" had cultivated. He also prepares his readers to respond in comparably skeptical terms to the arguments advanced by opponents and supporters of the 1715 and 1745 Jacobite rebellions. A quizzical response to texts that trumpet their own probity thus becomes the foundation for advocating habitual close scrutiny of both verbal and print representations of public events, past and present.

The domestic residue of the 1715 attempt by James Stuart, the Old Pretender, to assert his claim to the throne appears in *Tom Jones* in the ongoing skirmishes between Squire Western and his sister, Di Western, respectively Jacobite and Hanoverian, Tory and Whig, Country and Court supporter. Fielding brilliantly parodies their fierce partisanship, while also integrating it within a romance plot that confirms the gap between avowed belief and actual practice. For despite their loudly proclaimed political opposition, Squire Western and his sister close ranks on the subject of dynastic marriage (although each has a very different view of the interests to be satisfied in the disposal of their daughter and niece, Sophia Western). United in their opposition to Sophia's choice, Tom Jones, since he has neither property nor legitimate name, and initially supportive of his rival, Blifil, they ultimately fall out over the third prospect, Lord Fellamar. To Squire Western, he is a "confounded Son of a Whore of a Lord, who … shall never have a Daughter of mine by my Consent. They have beggared the nation, but they shall never beggar me. My Land shall never be sent over to *Hannover*" (781). To Di Western, the proponent of Whiggish monied interests and social aspiration, he offers "'one of the best Matches in England; a Match which besides its Advantage in Fortune, would do Honour to almost any Family, and hath indeed in Title, the Advantage of ours'" (789). As so often in eighteenth-century novels, marriage provides a focus for generational conflict, with the older asserting its prerogative to decide the future of the younger.

Squire and Di Western's combat also indicates how directly inheritance and authority relate to issues of public governance. Strictly speaking, the Stuarts had more powerful claims to the throne than the Hanoverians who displaced them once the post-1688 settlements instituted a parliamentary balance of powers and ensured a Protestant succession. *Tom Jones* works to resolve these generational and political conflicts through a model of compromise that manages to acknowledge both perspectives, while also subordinating them to the prospect of a future based on concord, rather than dissent. The closing harmony that comes with the revelation of Tom's identity as a member of the Allworthy family, his marriage to Sophia Western, their retirement to a country estate, and the birth there of "two fine Children, a Boy and a Girl" (874) is, significantly, not a product of patrilineal inheritance: there is no last-minute revelation of a secret marriage between Bridget and Mr. Summer (Tom's birth father). Despite his legal status as bastard, Tom is allowed fully to enjoy with Sophia the ideals of continuity and order through companionate marriage and the affective family: "next to pleasing [Sophia], one of [Tom's] highest satisfactions is to contribute to the Happiness of the old Man," Western, who "resigned his Family-Seat, and the greater Part of his Estate to his Son-in-Law"; "Allworthy was likewise greatly liberal to Jones on the Marriage and hath omitted no Instance of showing his Affection to him and his Lady, who love him as a Father" (874). Overcoming an earlier history of antipathy and prejudice, the three groups settle into amicable coexistence.

Fielding prepares us for the triumphant amalgamation of given and chosen families through two important "concentration narratives" – narratives that epitomize, in near-allegorical terms, larger patterns of meaning – the encounter first, with the Man of the Hill and second, with the "*Egyptian* Majesty" (590) or Gypsy king. Concentration narratives invite interpretation, most often in contrastive or comparative terms, and as such relate intrinsically to this novel's preference for symmetrical pairings (Thwackum and Square, Squire Western and Di Western, Blifil and Tom). The central figures of the episodes embody alternative views of family and society: the Man of the Hill, a near-parody of alienation and autonomy, the Gypsy of tightly bound community. Their structural significance appears in their location in the novel's middle section, one before, the other after the gathering at the central point of Upton. Tom encounters the Man of the Hill when, momentarily deflected from his intention to enlist with the government forces to combat the Jacobites, he and his new companion

Partridge leave Gloucester and journey toward Upton. After they have left the Inn at Upton, with Tom in a state of despair at Sophia's discovery of his infidelity with Mrs. Waters, the two travelers stumble upon the gypsy wedding celebration. The two episodes, in short, underscore the pivotal importance of Upton as the moment at which a possible, but finally unrealized, public plot of direct engagement with history yields to the private plot of courtship and conciliation on which the remainder of the novel focuses. After the encounter with the gypsies, that courtship plot not only becomes dominant, but also assumes a more conventional direction through a reversal of course in which Sophia's initial pursuit of Tom turns into his pursuit of her. Read in light of the concerns of this study's first and second sections on singularity and sociability, we might also see the experiences with the Man of the Hill and the gypsy festival as demonstrating both the attractions and perils of autonomy and community.

The reclusive Man of the Hill feels obligated to tell his life story – one of ill behavior, prison, and repentance – after Tom rescues him from attack by thieves. The elegant economy of his narrative contrasts with Partridge's frequent and pointless interjections, a distinction that reinforces the class differences between the two tale-tellers in ways that Gothic authors in particular would develop to characterize garrulous servants. Here, Partridge's expressive limits also serve reflexively to emphasize the skill of the intrusive narrator, who like the Man of the Hill (though with a more comprehensive temporal grasp) reminds the reader of the political crises of the four historical events – 1685, 1688, 1715, and 1745 – addressed in this interpolated account. Books I–VI, Martin Battestin speculates, were written before Charles Edward Stuart's July 1745 landing in Scotland, and the packed allusions to the Jacobite uprising in Books VII–XII thus reflect the pressing topicality of questions relating to legitimacy, rebellion, and inheritance both as aspects of the plot and of the novel's historical moment. The Man of the Hill episode suggests that Fielding – like Tobias Smollett and Walter Scott – engages the political implications of the present crisis by invoking a distant event that has maintained an iconic currency in the nation's collective memory and a vestigial presence in aged survivors, like the now eighty-eight-year-old Man of the Hill. The defining incident of *his* life was his participation in the failed 1685 Whig–Protestant uprising led by the Duke of Monmouth against the Catholic James II. On the run after the battle of Sedgemoor, the Man of the Hill is betrayed to the King's forces, fortuitously escapes, and "at length," he recounts, "arrived at this Place, where the Solitude and Wildness of the Country invited me to fix my Abode … [and where he] remained concealed, till the News of the glorious Revolution [in 1688] put an End to all my Apprehensions of Danger" (421). He emerges from hiding at that point to negotiate an annuity with his brother, whose "Behaviour in this last Instance, as in all others, was selfish and ungenerous" and then "took my Leave of him, as well as of my other Acquaintances; and from that Day to this my History is little more than a Blank" (421).

His history, in fact, is so blank that he is unaware of the "two Rebellions in favour of the Son of King James, one of which is now actually raging in the very Heart of the Kingdom" (419), that is, he knows nothing of either the 1715 or the 1745 Jacobite uprisings led by the Old and New Pretenders. When informed of the resurgence of the Stuart claims, he expresses horror at the discovery that "Human Nature" could arrive at "that Pitch of Madness" (420). For the worldlier Tom, the recurrence of internecine conflict appears no less extraordinary. It is, he says, one of

> 'the most wonderful Things I ever read of in History, that so soon after this convincing Experience, which brought our Nation to join so unanimously in expelling King James, for the Preservation of our Religion and our Liberties, there should be a Party among us mad enough to desire the Placing his Family again on the Throne.'   (418)

In grappling with history, this concentration narrative incorporates contrary paradigms: on the one hand, the Man of the Hill's linear model in which conflict simply ends – he assumed that the 1688 Revolution had definitively resolved Stuart claims – and, on the other, something closer to the Latin original of revolution, a "turning" in which historical process is imagined as ongoing. The appearance of the 1745 uprising as backdrop to *Tom Jones*, coupled with the references to the events of 1685 (the Monmouth rebellion), 1688 (the Glorious Revolution), and 1715 (the first Jacobite rebellion), strongly favors the latter representation. The comparative and contrastive sensibility invoked through this sequence is repeated at the level of plot in the many points of contact between the Man of the Hill's and Tom's experiences: both have brothers who take financial advantage of them; both learn to distinguish Fortune from Providence; both undergo reconciliation scenes while in prison (with actual or surrogate fathers). But ultimately it is their contrary embodiments of solipsism and sociability that demarcate them, with the ethical distinctions between the two states much favoring the latter.

The Man of the Hill revels in the "absolute Solitude" (424) of his existence:

> As I have no Estate, I am plagued with no Tenants or Stewards; my Annuity is paid me pretty regularly … Visits I admit none; and the old Woman who keeps my House knows, that her Place entirely depends upon her saving me all the Trouble of buying the Things that I want, keeping off all Sollicitation or Business from me, and holding her Tongue whenever I am within hearing.   (424)

His misanthropy refuses all forms of social exchange, from the most mundane details of everyday life, through conversation, to protection of the vulnerable (he simply watches, for instance, as Tom exerts himself to save Mrs. Waters from Ensign Northerton, just as he had earlier rescued the Man himself). His virtue, in other words, is negatively defined as little more than the absence of vice, a passivity Fielding devalues relative to Allworthy's Shaftesburian benevolence and Tom's active commitment to improvement: "[t]hough I have been a great, I am not a hardened Sinner"; he tells Allworthy at the end of the novel, "'I thank Heaven I have had Time to reflect on my past Life, where, though I cannot charge myself with any gross Villainy, yet I can discern Follies and Vices more than enough to repent and to be ashamed of'" (854). With Tom's marriage to Sophia, private virtue becomes comprehensively social. Unlike the Man of the Hill, Tom exists fully in time: he makes peace with the past by forgiving his enemies (including his half-brother); through the present management of his estate he serves as positive example to his neighbors; and through his children he reactivates the inheritance motif and looks forward with confidence to the future.

The novel's final celebratory paragraph envisions a communal ideal radiating out from (and returning to) the couple's companionate relationship:

> They preserve the purest and tenderest Affection for each other, an
> Affection daily encreased and confirmed by mutual Endearments,
> and mutual Esteem. Nor is their Conduct towards their Relations
> and Friends, less amiable than towards one another. And such is their
> Condescension, their Indulgence, and their Beneficence to those below
> them, that there is not a Neighbour, a Tenant or a Servant who doth
> not most gratefully bless the Day when Mr. *Jones* was married to his
> *Sophia*.   (874–5)

Like the image of the "small pebble [that] stirs the peaceful lake" in Pope's *Essay on Man*, the figure of marriage acquires here a focalizing energy:

> The centre mov'd, a circle strait succeeds,
> Another still, and still another spreads,
> Friend, parent, neighbour, first it will embrace,
> His country next, and next all human race,
> Wide and more wide, th'o'erflowings of the mind
> Take ev'ry creature in, of ev'ry kind;
> Earth smiles around, with boundless bounty blest,
> And Heav'n beholds its image in his breast
> (IV.365–72).

To prepare us to understand marriage as a form of concord achieved and sustained through compromise (and hence applicable to other institutional and social structures), Fielding contrasts it with alternative models of community, including the "Company of *Egyptians*, or as they are vulgarly called, *Gypsies*" (587) that Tom and Partridge encounter just after they leave Upton.

The symmetrical pairing of the gypsy episode with the Man of the Hill depends on similarities (they are threshold experiences to which Partridge responds with superstitious fear, Tom with a pragmatic eye to their need for shelter) and differences (the Man epitomizes isolation, the gypsy encampment, conviviality and kinship). As part of the novel's historical subtext, both also link issues relating to family, justice, betrayal, and government to the Stuart cause. After Tom responds with enthusiasm to the Gypsy King's summary punishment of a band member who sought to profit from his wife's flirtatiousness, the narrator steps in to address the reader directly on the subject of "arbitrary Power" (591). While the Man of the Hill's resistance to King James's trampling on "the Liberties and the Rights of his People" (419) was manifested in his personal involvement with the Monmouth rebellion, the narrator here assumes the more detached perspective of the political theorist by using this episode as a test case to evaluate the relative worth of "absolute Monarchy" compared to a "limited Form of Government" (591). He understands the appeal of the Gypsy King's rigorous verdict and cites precedents from classical reigns in which the "Dominion of a single Master" seemed at first sight to produce a comparable "Degree of Perfection." But the overwhelming evidence of both "History" and "Religion," he concludes, is that only those who wish "to do Harm" seek "absolute Power" (592). Governments wisely rein in such autocratic impulses through constitutional settlements (such as those that support Hanoverian monarchs and reject Stuart claims).

The episode with the Gypsy King is followed (as was the Man of the Hill) by a scene focused on liberation: in the earlier one of Mrs. Waters from her assailant, here of the highwayman who, having pled the pressure of "five hungry Children, and a Wife lying in of a sixth" (599) as an excuse for his desperate attempt to rob the travelers, is rewarded with a charitable "couple of Guineas" (599). Both encounters immediately demonstrate Tom's instinctive generosity and, in the longer term, highlight the plot's coherence, since the two beneficiaries of his kindness subsequently help restore him to Allworthy's good graces. From this point forward, with the setting in London, the novel focuses on Tom's amatory adventures and his submerged but finally triumphant love for and successful courtship of Sophia. With their return to the country, the co-ordination of private and public plots is complete. As the Hanoverian monarchy is to the nation, the conclusion implies, so the estate owner is to his landed property.

The journey structure is as central to Tobias Smollett's *The Expedition of Humphry Clinker* as it is to *Tom Jones*. Brief comparison of *Tom Jones*, *Humphry*

Clinker, and *Waverley*, however, reveals their authors' distinctive development of the literal and metaphorical potential of journeying. While each work makes travel the prelude to individual conversion experiences, Fielding defines his hero's reformation in large part as an adjustment to given circumstances rather than a consequence of inward turmoil. Allworthy's moral summary thus notes Tom's culpability in acting without regard to others' perceptions of him: "You now see, Tom, to what Dangers Imprudence alone may subject Virtue (for Virtue, I am now convinced, you love in a great Degree). Prudence is indeed the Duty which we owe to ourselves" (854). Tom has learned the importance of discretion and forethought, but in keeping with early eighteenth-century assumptions about human nature, this knowledge is achieved not through pensive self-analysis, but through the combined agency of Providence and his own innate and unalterable virtue (just as Blifil's evil is ultimately exposed and punished).

In *Humphry Clinker* and *Waverley*, by contrast, the authors counterpoint inward and outer journeys to heighten awareness of the simultaneously personal, social, and political transformations Matthew Bramble and Edward Waverley undergo as a result of their travels. *Humphry Clinker*'s medial position between the mid-century *Tom Jones* and the early nineteenth-century *Waverley* can, in turn, be gauged through the different relation to history assumed by each protagonist. On the one hand, Tom Jones's engagements with Stuart attempts to re-write revolution confirm the legitimacy of established authorities and the overarching value of hierarchical structures; on the other, *Waverley*'s immersion in, and final repudiation of, the Jacobite cause represents historical experience as more contingently shaped by idiosyncrasies of time and place. Smollett, unlike Fielding, closely observes his protagonist's inner responses to the changes he witnesses over the course of his travels and directly ties these to Matthew Bramble's gradual shedding of the misanthropy that initially defines him. But unlike Scott, Smollett relies on classical economic and cultural paradigms to interpret the corrosive social effects of contemporary luxury and to advance, as alternative to a public narrative of national decline, a model of withdrawal to private estates where civic humanist principles can flourish apart from a degrading urban consumerism. In broad terms, then, this trio of novels suggests a growing interest in relating self-knowledge to the variables of historical experience, an interest stabilized in the early nineteenth century, as Linda Colley argues, through the consolidation of "Britons" as a corporate identity whose imperial, political, and cultural dominance originates in the 1707 Acts of Union that joined England and Scotland. Smollett's and Scott's novels highlight the social consequences of this legislative change in assigning metaphoric importance to their protagonists' literal border crossings between England and Wales, Scotland and England, the Lowlands and the Highlands, with each traversal signaling the extension of individual and collective knowledge.

As its title suggests, however, *The Expedition of Humphry Clinker* differs from both *Tom Jones* and *Waverley* in the role it assigns the eponymous "hero" in effecting the conciliation of inwardness and sociability, private and historical experience. Like Tom Jones and Edward Waverley, Humphry Clinker is driven by circumstances beyond his control. But unlike them, he is not a hero in the customary mode. Appearing for the first time well into the Bramble family's journey, he has a peripheral status relative to the privileged male correspondents, Matthew Bramble and his nephew Jery Melford, most strikingly evidenced in his complete exemption from the exchange of letters that makes up the novel. In genre terms, Humphry Clinker as character is affiliated with the picaresque tradition on which Smollett had earlier drawn in *Roderick Random* (1748), *Peregrine Pickle* (1751), and *Ferdinand Count Fathom* (1753) with their roguish anti-heroes, narratives focused on the open road, and satiric probings of low life. But he is at the same time crucial to the novel's investigation of the sentimental motifs of failed paternity and obstructed inheritance, familiar from Henry Fielding, Samuel Richardson, and Laurence Sterne. Humphry is in fact at once tangential and pivotal: a "flat" character who epitomizes the increasingly outmoded values of unquestioning obedience and loyalty (as both servant and son), he is also fully implicated in the succession of changes that leads the initially divided travelers to discover common purpose and family feeling. His semi-ironic elevation to titular prominence highlights a further oddity of this novel. Joseph Andrews, Tom Jones, Sir Charles Grandison, and Tristram Shandy are all young major characters; the real protagonist in *Humphry Clinker* is not the youthful eponymous hero but, by default, Matthew Bramble, the director of the family expedition and irascible member of an older generation. A valetudinarian, he travels from his estate in Wales to Bath, London, and then north to Scotland, accompanied by his sister Tabitha, her maid Win Jenkins, and his wards, his nephew, Jery Melford and niece, Lydia.

The diversity and number of correspondents allow multiple perspectives on places and events to be juxtaposed, with each view shaped by the leading characteristics of the letter writer. At the beginning of the novel, and particularly in their polarized reactions to city life, there seems little compatibility between the various accounts. Bramble's letter to Dr. Lewis registers his disgust with "the general tide of luxury, which hath overspread the nation," while Jery affects a sophisticated pleasure in the same spectacle: "chaos," he writes to his college friend, Sir Watkin Phillips, "is to me a source of infinite amusement."[3] These discordant responses to Bath, their first extended resting place after they leave Wales, are weighted to give evaluative priority to Matthew's orthodox commitment to hierarchical principles. As a spa town habituated by nouveau riche who come seasonally to take the healing waters, Bath confirms all that Matthew finds grievously wrong with present-day mores, particularly the relish for mobility (through both literal travel and figurative social climbing) and its licensing of body over mind, mixing over distinction, and social emulation over habitual deference. In the face of his uncle's despair at the eclipse of traditional structures, Jery advances a variant on the liberal Scottish Enlightenment argument for the long-term ameliorative effects of a culture of politeness: "those plebeians who discovered such eagerness to imitate the dress and equipage of their superiors," he asserts, "would likewise, in time, adopt their maxims and their manners, be polished by their conversation, and refined by their example" (50). While Jery follows the conventions of the eighteenth-century novel's generational plot in his progressive orientation toward the future, Matthew's coffee-house encounter with the now-decrepit friends of his youth emblematizes the broken links between past and present. Now reduced to near objects – one "bent into a horizontal position, like a mounted telescope," another "the bust of a man, set upright in a wheel machine, which the waiter moved from place to place" – they provoke in him a poignant sense that the "renovation of youth" he hoped to discover through travel has turned into something more nearly resembling the "resuscitation of the dead" (55–6).

Bramble's sensations of melancholy and misanthropy in Bath are aggravated by his experience of London. Metaphorically rendered as "an overgrown monster; which, like a dropsical head, will in time leave the body and extremities without nourishment and support" (87), the city sums up all that he loathes about the tilt of contemporary culture toward autonomy, competitiveness, and materialism. The astonishing growth of London over the course of the century – estimated at 630,000 in 1715, its population was c. 740,000 by 1760, more than 1 million at the time of the first reliable modern census in 1801, and 1.4 million by 1815 – was a result of internal and international migration (particularly after the end of the Seven Years War in 1763 and the American War in 1783), rising fertility, and declining infant mortality. As the figure of the monstrously distended head suggests, this growth presented a systemic threat to rural hierarchies, a point made vivid by the novel's comparison of tainted urban food and drink with their rustic alternatives. The morbid accumulation of fluids in the "dropsical head" thus relates closely to Bramble's ongoing contrast of country water, the "virgin lymph, pure and crystalline as it gushes from the rock" (118) and its adulterated city version, drawn in London either from

> the maukish contents of an open aqueduct, exposed to all manner of
> defilement ... [or] from the river Thames, impregnated with all the filth
> of London and Westminster – Human excrement is the least offensive

> part of the concrete, which is composed of all the drugs, minerals, and poisons, used in mechanics and manufacture, enriched with all the putrefying carcases of beasts and men; and mixed with the scourings of all the wash-tubs, kennels, and common sewers, within the bills of mortality. (120)

The Swiftian inversion that turns the Thames into a sink of toxic effluent – human, animal, and industrial – aligns Smollett with the neo-classical tradition of translating pastoral images – water, song, social harmony – into urban equivalents. As in Swift's "Description of a City Shower," the city appears a negative mirror of the country even as its debased pastoralism invites the reader to infer the existence of an alternative vision. Matthew's rage accordingly dissipates once the chaos of London is left behind and the group travels north and then crosses into what he calls the Scottish Arcadia. There he finds not only a way of life distinct from the consumerism of Bath and London, but also more generative bonds between past and present. Appropriately, his reanimated connection to history emerges through his encounters with the legacy of the 1745 Jacobite uprising. London and Bath have already been condemned for their heedless rush to the future (as Bramble writes, "London is literally new to me; new in its streets, houses and even in its situation" [86]). The Stuart cause raises the opposite, but finally equally untenable, mistake of fealty to a superseded past. Smollett uses these distinct temporal orientations to map Bramble's compromise position as one that, while alert to new national imperatives and old loyalties, is nevertheless intent on preserving traditional mores.

As we have seen, Fielding set *Tom Jones* in the midst of the '45, while also referring through the Man of the Hill episode to the Monmouth rebellion and, in the Man of the Hill's conversation with Tom and Partridge, to the first Jacobite uprising of 1715. Smollett, writing in 1771, is similarly a half-generation from the 1745 rebellion and like Fielding, therefore, describes an event whose contours are not yet fully settled. Scott's running title "*'Tis Sixty Years Since*" foregrounds the doubling of this time span in *Waverley*, introducing the distance of a complete generation and with it expanded possibilities for elegiac evocation. Smollett's treatment of the aftermath of the '45 makes clear that his interests lie less with the powers of individual and collective memory and more with the pragmatics of agricultural improvement, seen here as the means by which an alienated populace might be integrated within a renewed Britain. Bramble thus represents the Scots who were freed from the "*patriarchal*" (255) structures of the clan system by the post-1760 Highland Clearances as a potentially "diligent and alert" (253) work force, distinguished from the London mob by instinctive habits of deference. To break down their surviving loyalties to the Chieftains who "[threw] the whole Kingdom of Great Britain into confusion" in the "last rebellion" (254) and to prevent depopulation through emigration, he advocates the founding of fisheries and linen manufactures. These "commercial schemes" (256) are positioned as mediatory through contrast with, on the one hand, the unrestricted consumerism of urban centers, and on the other, Obadiah Lismahago's reactionary assertions that the Union has proven disastrous to Scotland not least in its encouraging of a "commerce [that] would, sooner or later, prove the ruin of every nation, where it flourishes to any extent" (204). The counterview articulated by Bramble identifies a positive commerce as one that develops natural resources to produce what contemporary writers called "necessaries" (as opposed to one that responds to imaginary desires with "luxuries"). Modern historians have detailed what Smollett here elides: the politically expedient wish to relocate to coastal areas a recalcitrant native population dispossessed of their lands as a result of the Highland Clearances and through the discipline of labor to transform them from "Gaels" to "Britons."

Lieutenant Lismahgo, who joins the group just before they cross into Scotland, serves as Bramble's interlocutor in these explorations of political and economic themes. Their conversations make apparent the simultaneous turn, on the part of the novel and its key character, from body to mind, from hypochondria to health, from Juvenalian rage against urban decay to projects for agricultural and commercial improvement. This expanded scope – in both personal and conceptual range – is also evident in the narrative's pausing at the northernmost part of the journey to give voice to wider topical issues including husbandry, Scottish Enlightenment history and sociology, and, through the subplots of Lismahago and Martin the penitent highwayman, colonialism and imperialism. An *authorial* self-consciousness about the ideological patterns developed in the Scotland and Border sections of the novel had earlier been introduced through the device of the frame narrative: *Humphry Clinker* opens with an exchange of letters between the Reverend Jonathan Dustwich and the bookseller Henry Davis on the subject of the writing and publishing of the Bramble family correspondence. Dustwich's Latin tags and hair-splitting legalism indirectly advance the question of his right to dispose of the correspondence (thus launching, as an aspect of the material form of the novel itself, the subsequent themes of property, possession, and the circulation of goods), while Henry Davis's answer to him reveals that the publishing industry is infected by the transactional mentality Bramble's letters condemn. Davis invites Dustwich to send him the manuscript, but rejects Dustwich's proposed financial terms with a breezy dismissal of merit as irrelevant to his decision to publish:

Writing is all a lottery – I have been a loser by the works of the greatest
men of the age – I could mention particulars and name names; but don't
chuse it – The taste of the town is so changeable. Then there have been
so many letters upon travels lately published – What between Smollett's,
Sharp's, Derrick's, Thickness's, Baltimore's and Baretti's, together with
Shandy's Sentimental Travels, the public seems to be cloyed with that
kind of entertainment – Nevertheless, I will, if you please, run the
risque of printing and publishing, and you shall have half the profits
of the impression – You need not take the trouble to bring up your
sermons on my account – No body reads sermons but Methodists and
Dissenters. (2–3)

Parson Adams in *Joseph Andrews* and *Waverley*'s Jacobite tutor, Pembroke,
found their homiletic writings similarly spurned, but Smollett's inclusion of
his own *Travels through France and Italy* (1766) in the list of works jaded audiences now reject adds to the commentary a self-deprecating in-joke.

Humphry Clinker's opening representation of the proliferation of books as
mirroring a print culture driven by fashion and hostile to evaluative distinctions between authors and hacks (or works of inherent value and those running on the tides of modishness) meshes with contemporary changes in the
publishing industry. The specific issue raised by Dustwich's letter – who owns
the Bramble family correspondence? – was, as we have seen, currently being
more largely considered by the courts in the contexts of copyright. The London
booksellers' fight to retain perpetual copyright for their cartel was resolved by
the Lords' 1774 ruling on *Donaldson* v. *Beckett*, a decision that created the conditions for the emergence of what William St. Clair calls the "reading nation."
The more philosophical question of privacy raised by the publication of family
documents was soon, in turn, to erupt into controversy when William Mason
based his 1775 *Memoir of the Life and Writings of Mr. Gray* on Thomas Gray's
confidential correspondence.

The contrasts defining this frame narrative – private and public, buying and
selling, contemplative and voracious reading – are elaborated in the distinct
styles and content of the correspondence in the novel proper. The benevolence,
inclusiveness, and masculine authority of the polished, if often intemperate,
letters Matthew Bramble sends to Dr. Lewis diverge sharply from the petty,
materialistic, and semi-literate litany of instructions Tabitha Bramble hurls at
Mrs. Gwyllim, housekeeper at Brambleton-hall (their "lowness" summed up,
typically given Smollett's penchant for scatology, in Tabitha's ongoing obsession
with the bowels of her dog Chowder who has been "terribly constuprated ever
since we left huom" [6]). The prose of the younger set of siblings reflects, while
also refining (as might be expected given the novelistic conventions associated

with generational patterns), this gendered opposition between impartiality and interestedness. Jery and Lydia are both immature, but the brother's standard or King's English, unlike his sister's derivative sentimental phrasing, forecasts his greater potential for individual development. Older women, in fact, are negatively identified throughout with a larger feminization of culture that the novel presents as a source of national decline through its emphasis on body over mind in Bath and London, on passion over reason in Methodism, and on consumerism over conservation in the visit to the Baynard estate. The latter occupies an important pivotal position in the structure of *Humphry Clinker* in its symbolizing of Britain's potential for rehabilitation if feminine misrule could once again be made subject to masculine order.

The Bramble family, with Lismahago now in tow, stops at the Baynard estate after re-entering England on their leisurely return home to Wales. At this juncture, the historically specific analysis of post-1745 conditions in Scotland gives way to a representation of broader social changes, filtered here, as in the Bath letters, through Bramble's memory of an idyllic past. As the party approaches "the place where [the long-time friends] had spent so many happy days together," he is disconcerted by his inability to recognize "any one of those objects, which had been so deeply impressed upon my remembrance":

> The tall oaks that shaded the avenue, had been cut down, and the iron gates at the end of it removed, together with the high wall that surrounded the court yard … Now the old front is covered with a screen of modern architecture; so that all without is Grecian, and all within Gothic – As for the garden, which was well stocked with the best fruit which England could produce, there is not now the least vestige remaining of trees, walls, or hedges – Nothing appears but a naked circus of loose sand, with a dry bason and a leaden triton in the middle.   (285)

The source of these catastrophic changes is Baynard's wife, low-born heir to an East India fortune, whom he wed in an attempt to free himself of debts incurred through youthful extravagances, including a contested election. Smollett's attention to the contexts surrounding this status-inconsistent marriage illustrates his habit of packing each narrative encounter with as much social baggage as possible: here, Harriet Baynard's cunning manipulation of her tender-hearted husband, her pursuit of fashion at the cost of traditional country-house hospitality, her undermining of the estate's former self-sufficiency by mimicking "every article of taste and connoisseurship" (292) she observed on the Grand Tour, even her production of a "shambling, blear-eyed" (290) son, indict cross-class unions as unnatural.

The literal and figurative associations of the estate with stability, continuity, and hierarchy meant that it had long served in eighteenth-century literature as positive counter to upstart pretension. Mrs. Baynard's near-bankrupting of her husband's inheritance thus looks back to Alexander Pope's satire of nouveau riche aspiration in *Epistle to Burlington* and forward to Austen's more inwardly defined treatment of landscape "improvement" as a moral barometer in *Mansfield Park*. But as comparison with another 1770s novel, *Evelina*, suggests, the redemptive masculinity *Humphry Clinker* advances as the antidote to contemporary social ills additionally depends on an aggressive misogyny. In Burney's novel, influential older women – Lady Howard, Mrs. Mirvan, Mme. Duval, Mrs. Selwyn – are enabling figures who advance the heroine's integration of individual, familial, and social identity while also strengthening her bonds to both surrogate (Villars) and actual (Lord Belmont) fathers. In *Humphry Clinker*, however, the humiliation of older women appears an indispensable first step to the recovery of masculine purpose. In a dark recapitulation of the favored eighteenth-century heroines' plots, the death of Baynard's wife releases him from "unmanly acquiescence [to her] absurd tyranny" (293), while Tabitha's marriage to Lismahago is similarly necessary to the future peace of her erstwhile quasi-partner, Bramble.

Bramble's return to the Baynard estate to witness Harriet's death is followed by his vigorous measures to expunge her influence and restore the manor to its former productivity. He curbs expenses, sells off the wife's effects, sends the son to boarding school, oversees the redirection of the diverted "rivulet into its old channel" (343), and turns the pleasure-ground back to cornfield and pasture. Matthew's conversion from misanthropic defeatist to benevolent activist in the interval between his first and second visits to the Baynard estate has been effected by his encounter with an old friend, Charles Dennison, who provides shelter to the Bramble family after a coaching accident. As with Mr. Wilson in *Joseph Andrews* and the heroes of *Amelia* and *Tom Jones*, Dennison has been rehabilitated through a plot of second chances centered on a loving marriage and retreat from the corruptions of London. In search of rural "health of body, peace of mind, and the private satisfaction of domestic quiet" (322), the Dennisons restore to self-sufficiency the ruined estate he inherits, using the methods that Matthew later brings into play at Baynard's. Mrs. Dennison is the older generational equivalent of the anodyne Lydia. While both are exempted from the misogynist slurs that attach to the novel's other women, their narrative function is limited to aiding the return of errant men (Charles and subsequently his wandering son, George) to civic humanist ideals. Mrs. Dennison's role as consort is, in fact, more perfectly fulfilled by their neighbor, Jack Wilson, Charles's "constant companion, counsellor, and commissary" since their retirement to the country twenty-two years previously. As Charles encomiastically details, they "walked, and rode, and hunted, and fished together," made "experiments in agriculture, according to the directions of Lyle, Tull, Hart, [and] Duhamel" (327), and in the process forged a male comradeship that the novel advances as essential to social regeneration.

The importance of the Dennison estate, however, extends well beyond its contrastive relation to the Baynard household. The episode as a whole operates as a concentration narrative, gathering together and recalibrating the novel's dominant themes to enable its comic resolution. It begins with an accident, the overturning of the family coach, which is followed, in quick succession, by Humphry's rescue of Matthew from drowning (a redemptive use of water imagery that anticipates the novel's approaching conclusion), the hospitable offer of shelter at a neighboring house, the discovery that its owner is an old university friend of Bramble's, the revelation that Humphry is Matthew's illegitimate son, and that Dennison's son, George, traveling like Humphry under an assumed not family name, is Lydia's beloved, who had disguised himself as a strolling player to avoid an arranged marriage, but is now revealed to be a member of the landed gentry. Many of these elements are familiar from Henry Fielding's and Smollett's earlier novels: the dramatic recognition scenes, the affirmation of inheritance, the juxtaposition of contingency and Providence, and most allusively, the restoration of identity through the revelation of misplaced tokens of identification or of purloined letters (realist variations, perhaps, on Joseph Andrews's romance figure of the strawberry birth mark). As in the previous works, this clustering signals a narrative shift from quotidian particulars to overarching design.

The contexts that explain Bramble's ignorance of his son's existence also indirectly confirm the novel's ongoing emphasis on the relation between masculine identity and real property (and its complementary identification of women with uncertainty and threatened entitlement). While a student at Oxford, Matthew explains, he had temporarily assumed his mother's name in order to inherit her property, but when he came of age, he sold her lands in order to clear his paternal estate and resumed his real name, "so that I am now Matthew Bramble of Brambleton-hall in Monmouthshire." Humphry's mother, Dorothy Twyford, a barmaid at an English pub, wrote to tell him of the child's birth, but "in consequence of [Matthew's] changing his name and going abroad at that very time," mother and child were "left to want and misery." Maternal inheritance, whether in the privileged form that Matthew experiences or the more fraught versions suggested by Evelina's feminized variation on *her* mother's surname, by Tom Jones's hidden relationship to Bridget Allworthy, or by

Humphry's re-naming by the man to whom he is apprenticed generates confusion and social dislocation.

The distresses visited on children in these novels as a consequence of their mothers' passions (redoubled in *Evelina* since Caroline Evelyn marries Belmont to escape *her* mother's rule) are also, of course, traceable to paternal failures, either deliberate or unintentional. The absent or inadequate father – a motif in novels from Richardson's *Pamela* and *Clarissa*, Fielding's *Joseph Andrews*, *Tom Jones*, and *Amelia*, Burney's *Evelina*, Smollett's *Humphry Clinker*, and Scott's *Waverley* to Austen's *Persuasion* – is both a provocation to the plot's unfolding, since it justifies the mobility of the younger generation, and a central element in its resolution. *Humphry Clinker*'s conclusion, with its triple marriages, double restorations of sons to fathers, and multiple recoveries of estates, literal and metaphorical, represents a late, nearly hyperbolic working out of the eighteenth-century association between patriarchy and social order. Its extravagant excess may, perhaps, be taken as a sign of the weakening cultural power of the orthodoxies Smollett celebrates as ideal (while also preserving an element of skepticism – in the uncertainty of Jery's future, in Bramble's single state, and in Humphry's and Lismahago's limits as spouses – about the real-life feasibility of such ideals). Yet even if Smollett appears to be at once more assertive and less confident than Fielding, the tonal changes in *Humphry Clinker* do not foreshadow a more general novelistic retreat from the social conservatism the two authors share. As Scott's *Waverley* confirms, contemporary fiction continued to modify the inheritance trope in ways that made landed property the favored image of personal, social, and national stability.

There are, of course, significant exceptions to this positive reading of the estate, among them Jane Austen's *Persuasion*. Anne Elliot's independence of mind and Wentworth's growing recognition of its pre-eminent value are set against Sir Walter Elliot's blinkered assumption that he should be accorded all the privileges of rank without exercising any of the traditional social responsibilities of the well-born. Sir Walter, in fact, embodies the leading traits many eighteenth-century novels assigned to women, in *Persuasion* (with brilliant irony) made emblematic of the landed gentry's sense of entitlement to a cultural power they no longer deserve to wield: he is physically vain, happy to grovel before the better-born, and so fiscally irresponsible that he is forced to rent out his estate and move his family to lodgings in Bath. As in other Austen novels, such failures of imagination and empathy are summed up in habits and kinds of reading, here given structural prominence by their appearance in the novel's opening paragraph:

> Sir Walter Elliot, of Kellynch-hall, in Somersetshire, was a man who, for his own amusement, never took up any book but the Baronetage; there

> he found occupation for an idle hour, and consolation in a distressed
> one; … there if every other leaf were powerless, he could read his own
> history with an interest which never failed … [on] the page at which the
> favourite volume always opened.   (3)

Sir Walter's dynastic and self-absorbed private "history" is diminished through
contrast with its public complement, the realm of national and global affairs
actively engaged by Wentworth in the interval between his rejection by Anne
and present return to the Kellynch neighborhood, eight years later. The couple's
recovery of a once-thwarted love is anticipated by each taking on the defining
traits of the other in terms that reverse traditional gender constructs. Anne,
reprising Wentworth's peripatetic naval life, visits all of the novel's locales (and
is the only character to do so); he, conversely, adopts the feminine stance of
passive auditor and then covert letter writer during Anne's climactic conversation with Harville about the nature and representation of women. As in
the second-chance plots of *Pamela* and *Amelia*, the male protagonist must
eventually, as Wentworth ruefully notes, "learn to brook being happier than
I deserve" (269). But unlike the earlier novels, there is no culminating retreat
to the country in *Persuasion*, and hence no tacit subordination of female virtue to the institutional primacy of men that retirement to the estate habitually
imaged in period fiction. Instead, the possibility held out by the novel that
Wentworth may reach Anne's high standards of thought and behavior is positively resolved in their shared inwardness (and, more particularly, admission
of past errors) and in the novel's ascribing "worth" to those who demonstrate a
comparable mix of individuality, social purpose, and future-mindedness.

Significantly, *Persuasion* does not position Anne and Wentworth as har-
bingers of a new middling order set to defeat existing structures of power.
Although the next heir to the entailed Kellnych-hall, the meretricious but corrupt Mr. Walter Elliot, is even less palatable than the current placeholder, his
ascendancy is assured. In extricating Anne and Wentworth from the landed
gentry and identifying them with the entrepreneurial energies of naval life,
Austen diverges from the traditional Toryism of Scott's *Waverley*. The new
direction in nineteenth-century fiction that both novels presage, however,
owes less to their different representations of class, and more to their decisive
turn toward inwardness and its mediation of historical, social, and cultural
knowledge.

Re-orientations of the novel, of course, are neither abrupt in nature nor
purely literary in origin. To contextualize the nineteenth-century preference
for filtering experience through individual consciousnesses, we need to look
back to the transformative social, political, and literary effects of the revolutionary and Napoleonic wars. In two works from this era, Charlotte Smith's

Old Manor House (1793) and George Walker's *The Vagabond* (1799), we see variations on the way in which Fielding and Smollett explored problems associated with epochal change by artfully managing the distance between historical event and its narrative evocation. But while *Tom Jones* and *Humphry Clinker* invoke the conflicts of a previous generation (the Monmouth rebellion, the 1715 and 1745 Jacobite uprisings) to gain a purchase on the restorative compromises both authors wish to advocate, Smith and Walker reverse their predecessors' temporal direction. They transpose the still unfolding and highly polarized revolutionary controversy of the 1790s on to two *earlier* and comparably destabilizing events, setting their fictions at the time of the American conflict (*Old Manor House*) and the Gordon Riots (*The Vagabond*) to critique present-day politics. Like Fielding and Smollett, in other words, they exploit the gap between completed and ongoing historical experience. But unlike them, they rely on the reader's ability to grasp the past depicted in their novels as a refraction of exactly contemporary circumstances and, once having inferred the parallels, to regard real-life events in newly perceptive ways.

The Old Manor House and *The Vagabond* also confirm the intensifying factionalism and polemical tone of 1790s writing. At the beginning of the decade, Charlotte Smith, like Robert Bage and Elizabeth Inchbald, occupies a broadly progressive middle ground sympathetic to the ideals of the more radical William Godwin, Thomas Holcroft, Mary Wollstonecraft, and Mary Hays. But by 1793, with the execution of Louis XVI and Marie Antoinette, the beginning of the Reign of Terror under Robespierre, Britain's declaration of war on France (a conflict that would last twenty-two years), and the increasingly repressive governmental measures taken to limit radical proselytising, public sympathies shifted. The widespread dimming of domestic support for revolutionary ideals was matched by a surge in scare-mongering loyalist novels, among them Jane West's *A Tale of the Times* (1799), Elizabeth Hamilton's *Memoirs of Modern Philosophers* (1800), and Charles Lucas's *The Infernal Quixote. A Tale of the Day* (1801). As author of both the liberal *Theodore Cyphon* (1796) and the reactionary *The Vagabond* (1799), George Walker embodies the decade's larger pattern of political and literary apostasy. But as the discussion that follows will argue, the numbing predictability of anti-Jacobin fiction, coupled with its parasitical dependence on radical conspiracy, had an unexpected contrarian effect.

By the second decade of the nineteenth century, overtly partisan historical novels, and most especially those that touched on anti-Jacobin themes, had fallen out of fashion (a reflection also, perhaps, of the concurrent separation of "imaginative" writing from other forms of literature). The opening address in Frances Burney's last novel *The Wanderer* (1814) thus returns to now-outmoded themes in laying out its setting in the French Revolution, "a period which," the author maintains, since it is "completely past, can excite no rival sentiments, nor awaken any party spirit; yet of which the stupendous iniquity and cruelty, though already historical, have left traces, that, handed down, even but traditionally, will be sought with curiosity, though reverted to with horrour, from generation to generation."[4] The promise to transcend "party spirit" by investigating an "already historical" decade did not attract readers to the degree that the publishers, presuming on Burney's earlier popularity, had anticipated. The sluggish sales of the novel may reflect its dogged reworking of elements inherited from Richardson, Radcliffe, Mackenzie, Hamilton, Hays, and Reeve. More abstractly, *The Wanderer* seems uninflected by the genre negotiations that, after the impasse reached in 1790s loyalist fiction, yield the distinctive vision of Austen's last novel and Scott's first one. Comparison of the treatment of history in *The Old Manor House* and *The Vagabond* suggests how late-century novels reflect both the strengths and limitations of their precursors.

In *The Old Manor House*, Smith engages obliquely with the events of the revolutionary decade by choosing a 1770s setting and addressing through it her sense that the 1790s have been shaped by comparable forces of political dissent and governmental oppression. Grace Rayland, the last surviving of three maiden sisters who together maintained their father's retrograde commitment to the Royalist cause in the English Civil War, grooms her distant relation Orlando Somerive to be her legatee, without, however, making any formal provisions to assure his future. Here, as in the novel's later treatment of General Tracy and his nephew Warwick, we have intimations of the suspended existence of heirs in nineteenth-century novels like George Eliot's *Middlemarch* and Charles Dickens's *Bleak House*. Orlando finds himself in a position marked by all the difficulties of a second son without any of the advantages of that status: forced to dance court on an aged temperamental woman and resented by his elder brother Philip, whose miscreant behavior makes Orlando the principal support of a family left to survive on the mother's small jointure after the mid-novel death of his father. Orlando is at the same time excluded, by Mrs. Rayland's opinion of trade as undignified and the lassitude this encourages in him, from the potentially liberating course of forging an independent identity through travel or a profession.

Smith uses the relationship between Mrs. Rayland and Orlando to explore the reciprocally degrading effects of an aristocratic culture that binds the weak to the tyrannical through patronage and primogeniture. The reach of that system is demonstrated through an ancillary range of characters, some of whom act, as Mrs. Rayland does, on the prerogatives of birth (including Sir John Belgrave, whose name echoes the libertines of Richardson's *Sir Charles Grandison* and

Burney's *Evelina*, and the aged General Tracy who plots to seduce Orlando's sister), others of whom feed on the carcass of privilege (including the larcenous servants who use Ryland Hall as a storehouse for smuggled goods). While Gothic novels depict aristocratic power as destructive but exotically foreign through castles like Radcliffe's Udolpho, the titular Old Manor House where Mrs. Rayland holds court represents an indigenous and hence more threatening form of individual, familial, and national tyranny. Through allusions to Gothic (as literary mode and architectural remnant of medievalism), colonial and travel narratives, and particularly to the American revolutionary wars, Smith expands the initial focus on Mrs. Rayland's authoritarianism to encompass global contexts. The latter provide an opportunity to link the American and French revolutionary struggles for independence and to argue that both bear directly on England's domestic and diplomatic policy.

The impulse behind this focus on international affairs is cosmopolitan in origin. Volume III opens with a summary factual review of the events of 1776, followed by the curiously parallel responses to them by General Tracy, who hopes to see the "insolent colonists" forced to "submit" to the superior British force, and Orlando's mother, who

> having heard only one side of the question, and having no time or inclination to investigate political matters ... now believed that the Americans were a set of rebellious exiles, who refused on false pretences 'the tribute to Caesar,' which she had been taught by scriptural authority ought to be paid. Thus considering them, she rejoiced in their defeat, and was insensible of their misery; though, had not the new profession of Orlando [as soldier] called forth her fears for him, she would probably never have thought upon the subject at all – a subject with which, at that time, men not in parliament and their families supposed they had nothing to do. They saw not the impossibility of enforcing in another country the very imposts to which, unrepresented, they would not themselves have submitted. Elate with national pride, they had learned by the successes of the previous war to look with contempt on the inhabitants of every other part of the globe; and even on their colonists; men of their own country – little imagining that from their spirited resistance
> 'The child would rue that was unborn
> The taxing of that day.'[5]

The abrupt turn from Mrs. Somerive's views to the narrator's commentary presses home the difference between the assumed present moment and that of the novel's setting. Thomas Paine's *Rights of Man* had argued in 1791–2 that "once dispelled," ignorance "is impossible to re-establish ... It is not originally a thing of itself, but it is only the absence of knowledge; and though man may be *kept* ignorant, he cannot be *made* ignorant" (140). The wider knowledge stimulated by the 1790s revolution controversy is brought into play here to convey the unprecedented political awareness of Smith's reading audience and to suggest its potential to spur change in government policy. As the references to "men at that time" and to the "previous [Seven Years] war" suggest, the narrator here calls attention to a chronological gap in terms reminiscent of the distance Fielding invoked with his allusions to the 1715 Jacobite rebellion and Smollett to the 1745 one, although with the contrary intent to express sympathy for the rebels, and to urge change, not compromise.

Her obtrusive attempts to activate and direct public opinion by foregrounding government policy also distinguish Smith's novels from Austen's, a telling deviation given their other shared features. The latter range from a common focus on the effects on women of property laws relating to primogeniture to the more particular echoes of *The Old Manor House* in Austen's "estate" novel, *Mansfield Park*. Both *The Old Manor House* and *Mansfield Park* refer to colonial exploitation (in Sir Thomas Bertram's case, through Antigua plantations), have elder sons whose profligacy compromises the family economy, and daughters whose financially advantageous marriages their fathers dimly recognize as inappropriate but fail to stop. In *Mansfield Park*, Sir Thomas quickly "discern[s] some part of the truth – that Mr. Rushworth was an inferior young man, as ignorant in business as in books, with opinions in general unfixed, and without seeming much aware of it himself" and resolves to "speak seriously" to Maria Bertram about her fiancé.[6] When she rebuffs him and declares herself determined to marry, the narrator remarks that "Sir Thomas was satisfied; too glad to be satisfied perhaps to urge the matter quite so far as his judgment might have dictated to others" (234). Behind Maria's decisiveness and Sir Thomas's capitulation lies a complex family history (defined by her willful selfishness, his authoritarian distance from his children, their mother's passivity, and their aunt Norris's meddling) that works to disperse responsibility for her subsequent abandoning of her husband for Henry Crawford. Fanny, removed from Mansfield to her nuclear family's Portsmouth house after she has refused Crawford's proposal (a marriage both Sir Thomas and Edmund Bertram urge her to accept), learns of Maria's elopement from a newspaper scandal column passed to her by her father. Austen's careful integration here of individual personality, familial dynamics, ephemeral print forms, social commentary, and plot development is entirely characteristic. In *The Old Manor House*, Mr. Somerive experiences sensations close to Sir Thomas's when he "at once rejoiced in having his daughter so well established, and yet feared that to the dazzling advantages of rank and fortune she might sacrifice her happiness"

(283). And Orlando, like Edmund, also reneges on his filial responsibilities. But set next to *Mansfield Park*, the projected marriage of Isabella to the ancient General Tracy appears more mechanical than organic in conveying Smith's analogies between sexual and national exploitation.

As the nearly completed dynastic marriage of General Tracy and Isabella Somerive suggests, the critique of *ancien régime* attitudes is also advanced in *The Old Manor House* by a skeptical treatment of the traditional courtship plot. This appears in its most complex form in Orlando's pursuit of Monimia, poor relation to Mrs. Rayland's housekeeper, the iron-willed Mrs. Lennard. In developing this relationship, Smith places increasing stress on the negative connotations of romance as both literary form and behavioral code. Orlando's pursuit of a secret love he knows would be abhorrent to Mrs. Rayland is narcissistic in its inattention to the social consequences of a private passion he directs (especially given the threat it poses to Monimia's continued place in the household). In this sentimentalized variation of libertine entitlement, Monimia appears to him as

> this gem, which he alone had found ... set where nature certainly intended it to have been placed – it was to him, not only its discovery, but its lustre was owing – he saw it sparkle with genuine beauty, and illuminate his future days; and he repressed every thought which seemed to intimate the uncertainty of all he thus fondly anticipated, and even of life itself. (309)

The care he takes to buff this gem by educating her to his taste is reminiscent of the real-life efforts of Thomas Day, who adopted two young foundlings with the intention eventually of making the better-behaved his wife (Day applies the same Rousseauian pedagogy in his children's novel, *The History of Sandford and Merton*). When Orlando's regiment is ordered to America, however, Monimia is left entirely unprotected.

At this point, Smith suspends the romance plot and focuses instead on England's prosecution of what she represents as an unjust civil war with the American colonies. To authenticate her own ostensibly fictional representation as reliable, she contrasts it with the suspect practices of traditional narrative history. Earlier in the novel, a satirical version of the latter had been identified with Miss Hollybourn, who "knew all manner of history – could tell the dates of the most execrable actions of the most execrable of human beings – and never had occasion to consult, so happy was her memory, Trusler's Chronology" (186). Orlando's thoughts on patriotism as he crosses the Atlantic to begin his active military service are qualified by their association with a similar, but much darker, mode of chauvinistic reading:

> If, for a moment, his good sense arose in despite of this prejudice
> ["to love glory"], and induced him to enquire if it was not from a
> mistaken point of honour, from the wickedness of governments, or
> the sanguinary ambition or revenge of monarchs, that so much misery
> was owing as wars of every description must necessarily occasion; he
> quieted these doubts by recurring to history – our Henries and our
> Edwards, heroes whose names children are taught to lisp with delight,
> as they are bid to execrate the cruel Uncle [Richard III] and the bloody
> Queen Mary; and he tried to believe that what these English Kings had
> so gloriously done, was in their descendants equally glorious, because
> it went to support the honour of the British name. – Then Alexander,
> Caesar, and all the crowned murderers of antiquity – they were heroes
> too whom his school studies had taught him to admire, and whom his
> maturer reflection had not yet enabled him to see divested of the meteor
> glare which surrounded them.   (348)

First-hand experience of "the horrors and devastations of war" (356) combined with his friendship with the Iroquois scout, Wolf-hunter, completes his
political education in historical misrepresentation, the limits of heroism, and
the hollowness of patriotic fervor. Having survived Saratoga, turning point of
the American War of Independence, he is returning to England when the ship
is taken by the French and he is landed in Brittany. His impressions on disem-
barking there – "France contrasted with his banishment in America, seemed
to him to be part of his country, and in every French-man he saw, not a *natural*
enemy, but a brother" (389) – invite readers to consider the parallels between
Britain's oppressive response to the American Revolution in the 1770s and its
current martial foreign policy. In 1793, this is an incendiary comment, made
more conspicuous by Smith's momentary lapse from the fiction of historical
distance she observed when describing the American theater of war.

As with Lismahago's return to Scotland after his sojourn in America or
Edward Waverley's to Tully-Veolan after the Jacobite forces are routed, Orlando's
homecoming is shadowed by spectral forms from the past. In *Humphry Clinker*,
when Lismahago discovers his ancestral estate has been converted to a manufactory, he horsewhips his nephew who assumes that the avenging figure is
"the ghost" (273) of Lismahago's father; when Waverley comes back to Tully-
Veolan, Davie Gellatly initially believes he sees "his ghaist" (298), and after he
recognizes him takes him to the similarly altered Baron Bradwardine, now a
"tall boney gaunt figure in the remnants of a faded uniform" (299). Orlando,
too, experiences the nearly complete loss of all that he expected to find familiar and present: Monimia is gone, her whereabouts unknown, Mrs. Rayland is
dead, her estate willed to Mrs. Lennard and the Bishop, and Rayland-hall has

been left to fall into ruins. His father's house has changed hands, sold by his elder brother Philip, who now lies dying in London after a life of debauchery.

The impoverished Orlando eventually locates Monimia and learns of her suffering during his absence. He also with much effort extracts from Mrs. Lennard (now Roker) the hiding place of Mrs. Rayland's actual legal will, and re-enters the shuttered Rayland-hall with a constable to retrieve it. In the moment that he crosses the threshold, we are told, he could not

> help fancying, that the scene resembled one of those so often met with in old romances and fairy tales, where the hero is by some supernatural means directed to a golden key which opens an invisible drawer, where a hand or an head is found swimming in blood, which it is his business to restore to the inchanted owner.   (527)

The events that follow the legitimating of the recovered will, while not defined by such Gothic excesses, do involve a disconcertingly abrupt reversion to the formulaic terms of the "old romances and fairy tales" from which the novel had previously distanced itself. Orlando becomes heir to nearly all the "real and personal" wealth of Mrs. Rayland on condition that he perpetuates the patrilineal customs of her forebears while also advancing their status aspirations: he must purchase a baronetcy, assume the name and arms of the Rayland family, and entail the estate to his male heirs. He and Monimia restore both Rayland-hall and West Wolverton (where they install his mother and sisters). Even the disinheritance of Warwick by General Tracy is undone and the patrimony of *his* two sons with Orlando's sister, Isabella, is assured.

As we have seen in numbers of novels, among them *Tom Jones* and *Humphry Clinker*, some combination of recovered estates and identities, happy marriages, and births of male heirs conventionally mark the endings of novels committed to affirming conservative values. But these motifs, sanctioned in Fielding and Smollett by providential agency, are incompatible with all that precedes Orlando's entry into the "inchanted" Old Manor House to search for the "golden key" that will reverse his fortunes. Up to the point of his return from America, human cruelty and greed motivate the concealment of the legal will; Mrs. Roker's equally unsavory desire for revenge prompts, in turn, her subsequent decision to reveal its existence. But in the rosy glow of the novel's ending, the order of the estate works to render that larger world – of individual passion, colonial tyranny, and resistance to the principles of liberty – tangential. Austen's strategy for rationalizing "happy endings" – from *Northanger Abbey* to *Persuasion*, the foregrounding of literary artifice in her final paragraphs hedge with irony their variations on distributive justice – is not invoked in Smith's conclusion. As a result, the closing scenes veer away from the novel's critique of "things as they are" and align themselves with the retrograde impulses that shape anti-Jacobin fictions, among them George Walker's *The Vagabond*, a work whose loyalist excesses position it as in all other ways politically contrary to *The Old Manor House*.

The Vagabond is self-consciously a pastiche of eighteenth-century literature in its original sense of subsuming fictional, philosophical, historical, aesthetic, and political writing. At its center is a graphic description of the 1780 Gordon Riots in London, an event that stands in for the national chaos England would experience if radical principles were realized. Like Smith, then, Walker uses the vantage point of a past conflict that continued to exercise a powerful hold on the collective memory (Austen, too, makes the Gordon Riots a touchstone of civil unrest in *Northanger Abbey*) in order to comment on present circumstances and forecast future developments. The transparent relation between the ostensible setting of *The Vagabond* in 1780 and its late 1790s contexts is underscored by the contemporaneity of the novel's allusions. As in Delarivier Manley's early eighteenth-century key-novels and Smollett's mid-century ones, *The Vagabond* has a constellation of minor characters with real-life equivalents ("Citizen Ego" is John Thelwall, "Dr. Alogos" is Joseph Priestley, "Stupeo" is William Godwin). The first-person protagonist, Frederick Fenton, an uncritical supporter of Jacobinism, is the vehicle for the translation of Godwinian principles (and Humean skepticism) into disastrous action.

Each episode in *The Vagabond* demonstrates the radicals' hostility to the principles of social hierarchy and gender distinction that Walker makes foundational to national concord. His adaptation of Godwin's assertion that "that life ought to be preferred which will be most conducive to the general good" (illustrated in the *Enquiry concerning Political Justice* by a hypothetical fire from which, it is argued, Fénelon rather than his valet should be saved) is thus carefully modified to render Jacobin heartlessness from a sentimental vantage point: Frederick stands by and watches a burning house consume Amelia, whom he has seduced and abandoned, while he considers whether the father or his pregnant daughter should be rescued (and in the process refuses to release the ladder that would allow them to escape the fire). This female victim of seduction is linked to later, more culpable "fallen" women, including Mary (initially betrayed by arguments Frederick borrows from Hume, this Wollstonecraft figure is responsible for the deaths of her husband and two children). Against them is set Alogos's niece and authorial surrogate, the heroine Laura, who defends gender hierarchies on the grounds that "those men who preach up promiscuous intercourse of sex do it merely to cover up their own depraved desires, and avoid the stigma of the world by rendering it common" (155). In the moral universe of this novel, law and custom are essential to the suppression of inherent wickedness.

When Frederick flees to America, radical utopianism and the soft primitivism on which it was often based in the period (as in *Henry Willoughby*, discussed above in Chapter 5) comes under attack. In *The Vagabond*, the noble Wolf-hunter of Smith's *The Old Manor House* is replaced by nameless masses of Native North Americans who practice slavery, incest, polygamy, and eugenics. The travelers initially claim that Native barbarity must be owing to contact with European settlers, and only finally begin to question the possibility of an idyllic state of anarchy after their encounter with a malfunctioning republic, clearly intended to forecast Britain's dystopian future should its property laws be abandoned. While Dr. Alogos and Frederick are ultimately converted to the reality of divine omniscience, Stupeo resists the repeated natural, social, and political evidence of religious truth and is dealt an appropriate fate after another "tribe of Indians" takes them prisoner and, completing the novel's pattern of fire imagery, burns him at the stake, "the termination of that enlightened great man, who, while he lived, endeavoured to kindle the world, and set society in a flame, but expired himself in the midst of a blaze" (241). Frederick and Alogos are rescued by Vernon, who, having left England for America after the seduction of his beloved Amelia, discovers the kidnapped Laura, and then goes with her in search of her uncle. His appearance is taken as evidence of the workings of "eternal Providence" (242) and the novel quickly moves toward a highly conventional resolution in keeping with this by now assertively anti-modern principle of novelistic structure. Vernon and Laura marry and the group returns to Great Britain, celebrated in Alogos's closing speech as uniquely blessed by God.

The grafting of a providential ending on to a plot that conjoins sectarian politics and stereotypical courtship, inheritance, and familial motifs highlights the outmoded nature of each of the novel's constituent elements. The pre-eminent value assigned to Laura as exemplar of England's "fair daughters" who know that "modesty and maternal feelings are the chief ornaments of a celestial mind" (244) casts her as a latter-day Sophia, a woman who like *Tom Jones's* heroine serves as a beacon of wisdom and virtue to the novel's errant men. But as a late-century writer, Walker can no longer tap into the mid-century confidence that fiction mirrors a providentially ordained and all-encompassing hierarchy. In relying on narratorial praise to distinguish Laura, Walker pursues a line contrary to Austen who gives us access to the heroine's intelligent conversation and her interior life. By the same token, the partisanship of *The*

Vagabond might be seen to press Fielding's and Smollett's engagement with Jacobite politics to a terminal point of explicitness. The more organic and evolutionary representation of historical experience in nineteenth-century fiction will rely on filtering extrinsic event through the consciousness of the individual: Waverley, Sidney Carton, Henry Esmond, Romola.

Afterword: the history of the eighteenth-century novel

The early nineteenth-century publication of two important collections, Anna Laetitia Barbauld's fifty volume *The British Novelists* (1810) and Walter Scott's ten volume *Ballantyne's Novelist's Library* (1821–4) signaled the enhanced status and commercial viability of novels in the post-revolutionary age. While both collections built on James Harrison's successful weekly installments of reprinted fiction in *The Novelist's Magazine* (1779–88), they had a cultural prestige Harrison's lacked. That authority owed much to the introductory essays Barbauld and Scott included, essays that satisfied a growing period taste for literary criticism, with its mandate to order, catalog, and appraise. But the presuppositions embodied in the two collections were not equally influential. The rapid eclipse of Barbauld's progressive narrative by Scott's more conservative one had significant implications for later representations of the eighteenth-century novel. Understanding the principles that shaped their observations and the choices they made of authors and texts helps to explain why Scott's account prevailed well into the twentieth century.

As exercises in evaluation, Barbauld's prefatory "On the Origin and Progress of Novel Writing" and Scott's individual biographies contributed to the formation of a novelistic canon, a grouping of fictions designed to exemplify and endorse the new genre's standing. Or, perhaps, given the afterlives of their collections, the authors should more properly be said to have projected *two* canons, directed by distinctive principles of selection and commentary. Barbauld's *The British Novelists* assigned first place to Richardson, gave priority to epistolary and domestic fiction, and emphasized the contributions of women writers. Walter Scott, by contrast, was narrower in his range of preferred texts and very nearly exclusionary in terms of gender. The endurance of his catalog of noteworthy authors can be measured by its closeness to Ian Watt's triumvirate of Defoe, Richardson, and Fielding (with nods to Smollett, Sterne, and Burney as partial exceptions to Watt's judgment that there was little of "intrinsic merit" [290] after 1750). Scott's mapping of early fiction – in part an expression of a desire to present his own novel writing as a suitably gentlemanly occupation – proved easily adaptable, unlike Barbauld's, to the conservative institutional priorities of the rapidly expanding numbers of schools and universities in the nineteenth century and beyond.

In relation both to its literary standards and projected audience, Barbauld's *The British Novelists*, by contrast, was less cohesive and more reflective of the combativeness of late-century writing. Barbauld's accommodation of experimentalism, diversity, and political engagement in her choices speaks to her liberal view of the novel as "a species of books which every body reads."[1] The genre's appeal to a broad, not privileged, constituency, as the final sentence of her introductory essay suggests, grows out of a shared appetite for change and a tolerance of dissent on the part of its readers: "It was said by Fletcher of Saltoun, 'Let me make the ballads of a nation, and I care not who makes the laws.' Might it not be said with as much propriety, Let me make the novels of a country, and let who will make the systems?" (416–7). The eclecticism implicit in Barbauld's choices, with their recognition that modern social systems are distinguished less by conformity than by contradiction, has been explored throughout this study by considering the relationship between secrecy and sociability, singularity and compliance, solitude and family, cosmopolitanism and nation-building.

Notes

Introduction

1 Samuel Johnson, *Rambler,* 4, 31 March 1750, in *The Works of Samuel Johnson, Volume. III,* ed. W. J. Bate and Albrecht B. Strauss (New Haven and London: Yale University Press, 1969), 21, 19, 21.

2 Ian Watt, *The Rise of the Novel. Studies in Defoe, Richardson and Fielding* (Berkeley and Los Angeles: University of California Press, 1957), 32. Subsequent references are by page number in the text.

3 *Essay on Man Epistle* I.237, 267 in *The Poems of Alexander Pope,* ed. John Butt (London: Methuen, 1963). Subsequent references to Pope's poetry are from this edition and appear in the text.

4 Frances Burney, *Evelina, Or, A Young Lady's Entrance into the World. In a Series of Letters* (1778), ed. Susan Kubica Howard (Peterborough, ON: Broadview Press, 2000), 279. Subsequent references are by page number in the text.

5 Charles Taylor, *The Sources of the Self. The Making of the Modern Identity* (Cambridge, MA: Harvard University Press, 1989), 234.

6 Elizabeth Hamilton, *Memoirs of Modern Philosophers* (1800), ed. Claire Grogan (Peterborough, ON: Broadview Press, 2000), 227. Subsequent references are by page number in the text.

1 The power of singularity

1 Daniel Defoe, *The Life, Adventures, and Pyracies of the Famous Captain Singleton* (1720), ed. P. N. Furbank (London: Pickering & Chatto, 2008), 19–20. Subsequent references are by page number in the text.

2 Daniel Defoe, *The Fortunes and Misfortunes of the Famous Moll Flanders* (1721), ed. Liz Bellamy (London: Pickering & Chatto, 2009), 28. Subsequent references are by page number in the text.

3 Daniel Defoe, *The History and Remarkable Life of the Truly Honourable Col. Jacque* (1723), ed. Maurice Hindle (London: Pickering & Chatto, 2009), 33. Subsequent references are by page number in the text.

4 Daniel Defoe, *The Life and Strange Surprizing Adventures of Robinson Crusoe* (1719), ed. W. R. Owens (London: Pickering & Chatto, 2008), 60. Subsequent references are by page number in the text.

5 Aphra Behn, *The Fair Jilt* (1688), in *The Works of Aphra Behn, Volume III*, ed. Janet Todd (Columbus: Ohio State University Press, 1995), 42.

6 Daniel Defoe, *The Fortunate Mistress* (1724), ed. P. N. Furbank (London: Pickering & Chatto, 2009), 80. Subsequent references are by page number in the text (where it is cited by its customary title, *Roxana*).

2   The virtue of singularity

1 Dror Wahrman, *The Making of the Modern Self: Identity and Culture in Eighteenth-Century England* (New Haven and London: Yale University Press, 2004), 198.

2 Mary Davys, *The Reform'd Coquet; A Novel* (1724) (London: 1724), 5. Subsequent references are by page number in the text.

3 Thomas Keymer and Peter Sabor, *Pamela in the Marketplace. Literary Controversy and Print Culture in Eighteenth-Century Britain and Ireland* (Cambridge University Press, 2005), 1.

4 Samuel Richardson, *Pamela; Or, Virtue Rewarded* (1740), ed. Thomas Keymer and Alice Wakely (Oxford University Press, 2001), 11. Subsequent references are by page number in the text.

5 Michael McKeon, "Historicizing Patriarchy: The Emergence of Gender Difference in England, 1660–1760," in *Eighteenth-Century Studies* 28 (1995), 295–322.

6 E. P. Thompson, "Patrician Society, Plebeian Culture," *Journal of Social History* 7 (1974), 389, 388.

7 Samuel Richardson, *Clarissa or The History of a Young Lady* (1747–8), ed. Angus Ross (Harmondsworth: Penguin Books, 1985), 39. Subsequent references are by page number in the text.

8 Ruth Perry, *Novel Relations. The Transformation of Kinship in English Literature and Culture 1648–1818* (Cambridge University Press, 2004), 7.

9 Henry Fielding, *The History of the Adventures of Joseph Andrews and of his Friend Mr. Abraham Andrews* (1742) and *An Apology for the Life of Mrs. Shamela Andrews* (1741), ed Douglas Brooks-Davies (Oxford University Press, 1970), 15. Subsequent references are by page number in the text.

10 The title of Bernard Mandeville's 1714 work, *The Fable of the Bees: Or, Private Vices, Public Benefits*, foregrounds this relationship.

11 Alexander Pope, *Windsor-Forest* ll. 15–16.

12 Henry Fielding, *Amelia* (1751), ed. Martin Battestin (Oxford University Press, 1983), 25, 24. Subsequent references are by page number in the text.

3   The punishment of singularity

1 Jane Austen, *Sense and Sensibility* (1811), ed. Edward Copeland (Cambridge University Press, 2006), 228–9. Subsequent references are by page number in the text.

2 Charlotte Lennox, *The Female Quixote Or The Adventures of Arabella* (1752), ed. Margaret Dalziel; introduction Margaret Anne Doody (Oxford University Press, 1989), 5, 6. Subsequent references are by page number in the text.

3 Sarah Fielding, *The History of Ophelia* (1760), ed. Peter Sabor (Peterborough, ON: Broadview Press, 2004), 75. Subsequent references are by page number in the text.

4 Frances Sheridan, *Memoirs of Miss Sidney Bidulph* (1761), ed. Patricia Köster and Jean Coates Cleary (Oxford University Press, 1995), 19–20. Subsequent references are by page number in the text.

5 Tony Tanner, "Introduction," to Jane Austen, *Sense and Sensibility* (1811), ed. Tony Tanner (Harmondsworth: Penguin Books, 1969).

6 Tobias Smollett, *The Adventures of Roderick Random* (1748), ed. Paul-Gabriel Boucé (Oxford University Press, 1979), 119. Subsequent references are by page number in the text.

7 Laurence Sterne, *The Life and Opinions of Tristram Shandy, Gentleman* (1765–7), ed. Ian Campbell Ross (Oxford University Press, 1983, 2000), 6. Subsequent references are by page number in the text.

8 Sarah Fielding, *The Adventures of David Simple* (1744) and *Volume the Last* (1753), ed. Peter Sabor (Lexington: University Press of Kentucky, 1998), 247. Subsequent references are by page number in the text.

9 Laurence Sterne, *A Sentimental Journey through France and Italy* (1768) and *Continuation of the Bramine's Journal*, ed. Melvyn New and W. G. Day (Indianapolis, IN: Hackett Publishing, 2006), 3. Subsequent references are by page number in the text.

10 Henry Mackenzie, *The Man of Feeling* (1771), ed. Brian Vickers (London: Oxford University Press, 1967), 17. Subsequent references are by page number in the text.

11 Henry Brooke, *The Fool of Quality: Or, The History of Henry Earl of Moreland* (1766–70) (London: 1770), II.169.

12 William Godwin, *Fleetwood: Or, The New Man of Feeling* (1805), ed. Gary Handwerk and A. A. Markley (Peterborough, ON: Broadview Press, 2001), 63. Subsequent references are by page number in the text.

4   The reformation of family

1 Samuel Richardson, *The History of Sir Charles Grandison* (1753–4), ed. Jocelyn Harris (London: Oxford University Press, 1972), I.133. Subsequent references are by page number in the text.

2 John Cleland, *Memoirs of a Woman of Pleasure* (1748–9), ed. Peter Sabor (Oxford University Press, 1985), 93, 88.

3 Thomas Holcroft, *Anna St. Ives* (1792), ed. Peter Faulkner (London: Oxford University Press, 1970), 37. Subsequent references are by page number in the text.

4 Oliver Goldsmith, *The Vicar of Wakefield. A Tale supposed to be Written by Himself* (1766), ed. Arthur Friedman (Oxford University Press, 1981), 13. Subsequent references are by page number in the text.

5 Eliza Haywood, *The History of Miss Betsy Thoughtless* (1751), ed. Beth Fowkes Tobin (Oxford University Press, 1997), 179. Subsequent references are by page number in the text.

6 Eliza Haywood, *Love in Excess, or The Fatal Enquiry* (1719–20), ed. David Oakleaf (Peterborough, ON: Broadview Press, 2000), 58.

7 Jane Austen, *Emma* (1815), ed. Richard Cronin and Dorothy McMillan (Cambridge University Press, 2005), 21. Subsequent references are by page number in the text.

8 Jane Austen, *Persuasion* (1817), ed. Janet Todd and Antje Blank (Cambridge University Press, 2006), 175. Subsequent references are by page number in the text.

9 Frances Burney, *Camilla or A Picture of Youth* (1796), ed. Edward A. Bloom and Lillian D. Bloom (Oxford University Press, 1983), 484.

10 George Walker, *Theodore Cyphon; Or The Benevolent Jew: A Novel* (1796) (London: 1796), v–viii. Subsequent references are by page number in the text.

11 Eliza Fenwick, *Secresy; Or, The Ruin on the Rock* (1795), ed. Isobel Grundy (Peterborough, ON: Broadview Press, 1998), 129. Subsequent references are by page number in the text.

12 Cited in "Introduction" to Jane Austen, *Emma*, xxx.

5   Alternative communities

1 Sarah Scott, *A Description of Millenium Hall* (1762), ed. Gary Kelly (Peterborough, ON: Broadview Press, 1995), 111. Subsequent references are by page number in the text.

2 Sarah Scott, *The History of Sir George Ellison* (1766), ed. Betty Rizzo (Lexington: University Press of Kentucky, 1996), 22. Subsequent references are by page number in the text.

3 C. B. Macpherson, *The Political Theory of Possessive Individualism. Hobbes to Locke* (Oxford University Press, 1962), 3.

4 *The Genuine Memoirs of the Celebrated Maria Brown* (1766) (London: 1766), II.33. Subsequent references are by page number in the text.

5 Clara Reeve, *The School for Widows* (1791) (Dublin: 1791), I.49. Subsequent references are by page number in the text.

6 Clara Reeve, *Plans of Education; With Remarks on the Systems of Other Writers in a Series of Letters between Mrs. Darnford and her Friends* (1792) (London: 1792), 30. Subsequent references are by page number in the text.

7 Robert Paltock, *The Life and Adventures of Peter Wilkins* (1751), ed. Christopher Bentley (London: Oxford University Press, 1973), 103.

8 *Berkeley Hall: Or, The Pupil of Experience* (1796) (London: 1796), I.234. Subsequent references are by page number in the text.

9 Frances Brooke, *The History of Emily Montague* (1769), ed. Mary Jane Edwards (Ottawa: Carleton University Press, 1991), 24.

10 *The Female American; Or, The Adventures of Unca Eliza Winkfield* (1767), ed. Michelle Burnham (Peterborough, ON: Broadview Press, 2001), 35. Subsequent references are by page number in the text.

11 Aphra Behn, *Oroonoko: Or, The Royal Slave. A True History* (1688), in *The Works of Aphra Behn, Volume III,* ed. Janet Todd (Columbus: Ohio State University Press, 1995), 88. Subsequent references are by page number in the text.

12 Elizabeth Hamilton, *Translations of the Letters of a Hindoo Rajah* (1796), ed. Pamela Perkins and Shannon Russell (Peterborough, ON: Broadview Press, 1998), 56, 70. Subsequent references are by page number in the text.

13 Phebe Gibbes, *Hartly House, Calcutta* (1789), ed. Michael J. Franklin (New Delhi: Oxford University Press, 2007), 76, 105.

14 George Cumberland, *The Captive of the Castle of Sennaar An African Tale* (1798) and *The Reformed* (c. 1800), ed. G. E. Bentley, Jr. (Montreal and Kingston: McGill–Queen's University Press, 1991), 13. Subsequent references are by page number in the text.

15 Thomas Paine, *Rights of Man* (1791–2), ed. Henry Collins (Harmondsworth: Penguin Books, 1969), 181. Subsequent references are by page number in the text.

16 William Godwin, *Things As They Are; Or, The Adventures of Caleb Williams* (1794), ed. David McCracken (London: Oxford University Press, 1970), 1. Subsequent references are by page number in the text.

17 T. J. Mathias "The Pursuits of Literature" (1794–7), in *Works of the Author of The Pursuits of Literature* (Dublin: 1799), 43–4.

18 Ann Radcliffe, *The Mysteries of Udolpho* (1794), ed. Bonamy Dobrée (Oxford University Press, 1980), 227. Subsequent references are by page number in the text.

19 Matthew Lewis, *The Monk* (1796), ed. Howard Anderson (Oxford University Press, 1973), 356, 357–8. Subsequent references are by page number in the text.

20 Ann Radcliffe, *The Italian, Or, The Confessional of the Black Penitents A Romance* (1797), ed. Frederick Garber (London: Oxford University Press, 1968), 94. Subsequent references are by page number in the text.

21 Edmund Burke, *A Philosophical Enquiry into the Origin of our Ideas on the Sublime and Beautiful* (1757) (Menston: Scolar Press, 1970), 95.

22 Edmund Burke, *Reflections on the Revolution in France* (1790), ed. Conor Cruise O'Brien (Harmondsworth: Penguin Books, 1969), 120, 119–20. Subsequent references are by page number in the text.

23 Mary Wollstonecraft, *Mary* (1788) and *The Wrongs of Woman: Or Maria. A Fragment* (1798), ed. Gary Kelly (Oxford University Press, 1976), 79. Subsequent references are by page number in the text.

6 The sociability of books

1 Elizabeth Inchbald, *A Simple Story* (1791), ed. J. M. S. Tompkins and Jane Spencer (Oxford University Press, 1988), 7. Subsequent references are by page number in the text.

2 William Beckford, *Modern Novel Writing or, The Elegant Enthusiast; and Interesting Emotions of Arabella Bloomville. A Rhapsodical Romance Interspersed with Poetry* (1796) (London: 1796), II.79–80. Subsequent references are by page number in the text.

3 Jane Austen, "Love and Freindship," ed. Juliet McMaster (Edmonton, Ala.: Juvenilia Press, 1995), 2.

4 Eaton Stannard Barrett, *The Heroine Or Adventures of a Fair Romance Reader* (1814) (London: 1814), III.299. Subsequent references are by page number in the text.

5 Jane Austen, *Northanger Abbey* (1817), ed. Barbara M. Benedict and Deirdre Le Faye (Cambridge University Press, 2006), 48. Subsequent references are by page number in the text.

7   History, novel, and polemic

1 Jane Barker, *Love Intrigues: Or, The History of the Amours of Bosvil and Galesia* (1713), in *The Galesia Trilogy and Selected Manuscript Poems of Jane Barker*, ed. Carol Shiner Wilson (New York: Oxford University Press, 1997), 7.

2 Kathryn King, *Jane Barker, Exile. A Literary Career 1675–1725* (Oxford: Clarendon Press, 2000), 6.

3 Delarivier Manley, *The Adventures of Rivella* (1714), ed. Katherine Zelinsky (Peterborough, ON: Broadview Press, 1999), 44.

4 Daniel Defoe, *A Journal of the Plague Year* (1722), ed. John Mullan (London: Pickering & Chatto, 2009), 99. Subsequent references are by page number in the text.

5 Quoted in William St. Clair, *The Reading Nation in the Romantic Period* (Cambridge University Press, 2004), 109.

6 William Hazlitt and Thomas Holcroft, *Memoirs of the Late Thomas Holcroft; Written by Himself; and Continued to the Time of his Death, from his Diary, Notes and Other Papers* (1816) (London: Longman, Brown, Green, and Longmans, 1852), 149.

7 Robert Bage, *Hermsprong; Or, Man As He Is Not* (1796), ed. Pamela Perkins (Peterborough, ON: Broadview Press, 2002), 139. Subsequent references are by page number in the text.

8 April London, *Women and Property in the Eighteenth-Century English Novel* (Cambridge University Press, 1999), 152–3.

9 Charlotte Smith, *The Young Philosopher* (1798), ed. Elizabeth Kraft (Lexington: University of Kentucky Press, 1999), 6. Subsequent references are by page number in the text.

10 Mary Hays, *The Victim of Prejudice* (1799), ed. Eleanor Ty (Peterborough, ON: Broadview Press, 1998), 1. Subsequent references are by page number in the text.

11 Elizabeth Inchbald, *Nature and Art* (1796), ed. Shawn Lisa Maurer (Peterborough, ON: Broadview Press, 2005), 138–9. Subsequent references are by page number in the text.

12 Michael McKeon, *The Origins of the English Novel, 1600–1740* (Baltimore: Johns Hopkins University Press, 1987), 158.
13 Robert Bisset, *Douglas; Or, The Highlander* (1800) (London: 1800), III.305. Subsequent references are by page number in the text.
14 George Walker, *The Vagabond* (1799), ed. W. M. Verhoeven (Peterborough, ON: Broadview Press, 2004), 53. Subsequent references are by page number in the text.

8 Historical fiction and generational distance

1 Walter Scott, *Waverley; Or, 'Tis Sixty Years Since* (1814), ed. Claire Lamont (Oxford University Press, 1986), 340. Subsequent references are by page number in the text.
2 Thomas Keymer, "Introduction," *The History of Tom Jones, A Foundling* (1749), ed. Thomas Keymer and Alice Wakely (London: Penguin Books, 2005), xiv.
3 Tobias Smollett, *The Expedition of Humphry Clinker* (1771), ed. Lewis M. Knapp and Paul-Gabriel Boucé (Oxford University Press, 1984), 37, 49. Subsequent references are by page number in the text.
4 Frances Burney, *The Wanderer; Or, Female Difficulties* (1814), ed. Margaret Anne Doody, Robert L. Mack, and Peter Sabor (Oxford University Press, 1991), 6.
5 Charlotte Smith, *The Old Manor House* (1793), ed. Anne Henry Ehrenpreis and Judith Phillips Stanton (Oxford University Press, 1989), 246. Subsequent references are by page number in the text.
6 Jane Austen, *Mansfield Park* (1816), ed. John Wiltshire (Cambridge University Press, 2005), 233, 234. Subsequent references are by page number in the text.

Afterword: the history of the eighteenth-century novel

1 Anna Laetitia Barbauld, "On the Origin and Progress of Novel-Writing," in *Anna Letitia Barbauld: Selected Poetry and Prose*, ed. William McCarthy and Elizabeth Kraft (Peterborough, ON: Broadview Press, 2002), 416. Subsequent references are by page number in the text.

Guide to further reading

Primary sources

Adventures of an Air Balloon (1780). London: 1780.

Adventures of a Bank-Note (1770–1). London: 1770–1.

The Adventures of a Black Coat (1762). London: 1762.

Berkeley Hall: Or, The Pupil of Experience (1796). London: 1796.

The Female American; Or, The Adventures of Unca Eliza Winkfield (1767), ed. Michelle Burnham. Peterborough, ON: Broadview Press, 2001.

The Genuine Memoirs of the Celebrated Maria Brown (1766). London: 1766.

Henry Willoughby. A Novel (1798). London: 1798.

Austen, Jane. *Emma* (1815), ed. Richard Cronin and Dorothy McMillan. Cambridge University Press, 2005.

    Mansfield Park (1816), ed. John Wiltshire. Cambridge University Press, 2005.

    Northanger Abbey (1817), ed. Barbara M. Benedict and Deirdre Le Faye. Cambridge University Press, 2006.

    Persuasion (1817), ed. Janet Todd and Antje Blank. Cambridge University Press, 2006.

    Pride and Prejudice (1813), ed. Pat Rogers. Cambridge University Press, 2006.

    Sense and Sensibility (1811), ed. Edward Copeland. Cambridge University Press, 2006.

    Sense and Sensibility (1811), ed. Tony Tanner. Harmondsworth: Penguin Books, 1969.

Bage, Robert. *Hermsprong; Or, Man As He Is Not* (1796), ed. Pamela Perkins. Peterborough, ON: Broadview Press, 2002.

Barbauld, Anna Laetitia. "On the Origin and Progress of Novel-Writing," in *Anna Letitia Barbauld: Selected Poetry and Prose*, ed. William McCarthy and Elizabeth Kraft. Peterborough, ON: Broadview Press, 2002.

Barker, Jane. *The Galesia Trilogy and Selected Manuscript Poems of Jane Barker* (1713–26), ed. Carol Shiner Wilson. New York: Oxford University Press, 1997.

    The Lining of the Patch-Work Screen; Design'd for the Farther Entertainment of the Ladies (1726), in *The Galesia Trilogy and Selected Manuscript Poems of Jane Barker*, ed. Carol Shiner Wilson. New York: Oxford University Press, 1997.

Love Intrigues: Or, The History of the Amours of Bosvil and Galesia (1713), in *The Galesia Trilogy and Selected Manuscript Poems of Jane Barker,* ed. Carol Shiner Wilson. New York: Oxford University Press, 1997.

A Patch-Work Screen for the Ladies; Or Love and Virtue Recommended (1723), in *The Galesia Trilogy and Selected Manuscript Poems of Jane Barker,* ed. Carol Shiner Wilson. New York: Oxford University Press, 1997.

Barrett, Eaton Stannard. *The Heroine Or Adventures of a Fair Romance Reader* (1814). London: 1814.

Beckford, William. *Modern Novel Writing or, The Elegant Enthusiast; and Interesting Emotions of Arabella Bloomville. A Rhapsodical Romance Interspersed with Poetry* (1796). London: 1796.

Vathek (1786), in *Three Gothic Novels,* ed. Peter Fairclough. Harmondsworth: Penguin Books, 1968.

Behn, Aphra. *The Fair Jilt* (1688), in *The Works of Aphra Behn, Volume III,* ed. Janet Todd. Columbus: Ohio State University Press, 1995.

Oroonoko (1688), in *The Works of Aphra Behn, Volume III,* ed. Janet Todd. Columbus: Ohio State University Press, 1995.

Bisset, Robert. *Douglas; Or, The Highlander* (1800). London: 1800.

Brooke, Frances. *The History of Emily Montague* (1769), ed. Mary Jane Edwards. Ottawa: Carleton University Press, 1991.

Brooke, Henry. *The Fool of Quality: Or, The History of Henry Earl of Moreland* (1766–70). London: 1770.

Bullock, Mrs. *Dorothea; Or, A Ray of the New Light* (1801). London: 1801.

Burke, Edmund. *A Philosophical Inquiry into the Origin of our Ideas on the Sublime and the Beautiful* (1757). Menston: Scolar Press, 1970.

Reflections on the Revolution in France (1790), ed. Conor Cruise O'Brien. Harmondsworth: Penguin Books, 1969.

Burney, Frances. *Camilla or A Picture of Youth* (1796), ed. Edward A. Bloom and Lillian D. Bloom. Oxford University Press, 1983.

Cecilia, Or Memoirs of an Heiress (1782), ed. Peter Sabor and Margaret Anne Doody. Oxford University Press, 1988.

Evelina, Or, A Young Lady's Entrance into the World. In a Series of Letters (1778), ed. Susan Kubica Howard. Peterborough, ON: Broadview Press, 2000.

The Wanderer; Or, Female Difficulties (1814), ed. Margaret Anne Doody, Robert L. Mack, and Peter Sabor. Oxford University Press, 1991.

Chesterfield, Lord. *Letters to his Son and Others* (1774), intro. R. K. Root. London: Everyman's Library, 1984.

Cleland, John. *Memoirs of a Woman of Pleasure* (1748–9), ed. Peter Sabor. Oxford University Press, 1985.

Coventry, Francis. *The History of Pompey the Little; Or, The Life and Adventures of a Lap-Dog* (1751), ed. Nicholas Hudson. Peterborough, ON: Broadview Press, 2008.

Cumberland, George. *The Captive of the Castle of Sennaar An African Tale* (1798) and *The Reformed* (c. 1800), ed. G. E. Bentley, Jr. Montreal and Kingston: McGill–Queen's University Press, 1991.

D'Israeli, Isaac. *Vaurien: Or, Sketches of the Times: Exhibiting Views of the Philosophies, Religions, Politics, Literature, and Manners of the Age* (1797). London: 1797.

Davys, Mary. *The Reform'd Coquet; A Novel* (1724). London: 1724.

Defoe, Daniel. *The Fortunate Mistress* (1724), ed. P. N. Furbank. London: Pickering & Chatto, 2009.

The Fortunes and Misfortunes of the Famous Moll Flanders (1721), ed. Liz Bellamy. London: Pickering & Chatto, 2009.

The History and Remarkable Life of the Truly Honourable Col. Jacque (1723), ed. Maurice Hindle. London: Pickering & Chatto, 2009.

A Journal of the Plague Year (1722), ed. John Mullan. London: Pickering & Chatto, 2009.

The Life, Adventures, and Pyracies of the Famous Captain Singleton (1720), ed. P. N. Furbank. London: Pickering & Chatto, 2008.

The Life and Strange Surprizing Adventures of Robinson Crusoe (1719), ed. W. R. Owens. London: Pickering & Chatto, 2008.

Dodd, William. *The Sisters; Or, The History of Lucy and Caroline Sanson, Entrusted to a False Friend* (1754). London: 1754.

Fenwick, Eliza. *Secresy; Or, The Ruin on the Rock* (1795), ed. Isobel Grundy. Peterborough, ON: Broadview Press, 1998.

Fielding, Henry. *Amelia* (1751), ed. Martin Battestin. Oxford University Press, 1983.

The History of Tom Jones, A Foundling (1749), ed. Thomas Keymer and Alice Wakely. London: Penguin Books, 2005.

The History of the Adventures of Joseph Andrews and of his Friend Mr. Abraham Andrews (1742) and *An Apology for the Life of Mrs. Shamela Andrews* (1741), ed. Douglas Brooks-Davies. Oxford University Press, 1970.

Fielding, Sarah. *The Adventures of David Simple* (1744) and *Volume the Last* (1753), ed. Peter Sabor. Lexington: University Press of Kentucky, 1998.

The History of Ophelia (1760), ed. Peter Sabor. Peterborough, ON: Broadview Press, 2004.

Gibbes, Phebe. *Hartly House, Calcutta* (1789), ed. Michael J. Franklin. New Delhi: Oxford University Press, 2007.

Godwin, William. *Enquiry concerning Political Justice* (1793), ed. Isaac Kramnick. Harmondsworth: Penguin Books, 1976.

Fleetwood: Or, The New Man of Feeling (1805), ed. Gary Handwerk and A. A. Markley. Peterborough, ON: Broadview Press, 2001.

Memoirs of the Author of the Vindication of the Rights of Woman (1798). London: 1798.

Things As They Are; Or, The Adventures of Caleb Williams (1794), ed. David McCracken. London: Oxford University Press, 1970.

Goldsmith, Oliver. *The Vicar of Wakefield. A Tale Supposed to be Written by Himself* (1766), ed. Arthur Friedman. Oxford University Press, 1981.

Hamilton, Elizabeth. *Memoirs of Modern Philosophers* (1800), ed. Claire Grogan. Peterborough, ON: Broadview Press, 2000.

Translations of the Letters of a Hindoo Rajah (1796), ed. Pamela Perkins and Shannon Russell. Peterborough, ON: Broadview Press, 1998.

Hays, Mary. *Memoirs of Emma Courtney* (1796), ed. Marilyn L. Brooks. Peterborough, ON: Broadview Press, 2000.

The Victim of Prejudice (1799), ed. Eleanor Ty. Peterborough, ON: Broadview Press, 1998.

Haywood, Eliza. *The History of Miss Betsy Thoughtless* (1751), ed. Beth Fowkes Tobin. Oxford University Press, 1997.

Love in Excess, or The Fatal Enquiry (1719–20), ed. David Oakleaf. Peterborough, ON: Broadview Press, 2000.

Hazlitt, William and Thomas Holcroft. *Memoirs of the Late Thomas Holcroft; Written by Himself; and Continued to the Time of his Death, from his Diary, Notes and Other Papers* (1816). London: Longman, Brown, Green, and Longmans, 1852.

Holcroft, Thomas. *Anna St. Ives* (1792), ed. Peter Faulkner. London: Oxford University Press, 1970.

Inchbald, Elizabeth. *Nature and Art* (1796), ed. Shawn Lisa Maurer. Peterborough, ON: Broadview Press, 2005.

A Simple Story (1791), ed. J. M. S. Tompkins and Jane Spencer. Oxford University Press, 1988.

Johnson, Samuel. *The Rambler* in *The Works of Samuel Johnson, Volume III*, ed. W. J. Bate and Albrecht B. Strauss. New Haven and London: Yale University Press, 1969.

Johnstone, Charles. *Chrysal: Or, The Adventures of a Guinea* (1760–5). London: 1760–5.

Lennox, Charlotte. *The Female Quixote Or The Adventures of Arabella* (1752), ed. Margaret Dalziel; introduction Margaret Anne Doody. Oxford University Press, 1989.

Lewis, Matthew Gregory. *The Monk* (1796), ed. Howard Anderson. Oxford University Press, 1973.

Mackenzie, Henry. *Julia de Roubigne* (1777). London: 1777.

The Man of Feeling (1771), ed. Brian Vickers. London: Oxford University Press, 1967.

Manley, Delarivier. *The Adventures of Rivella* (1714), ed. Katherine Zelinsky. Peterborough, ON: Broadview Press, 1999.

Secret Memoirs and Manners of Several Persons of Quality of Both Sexes. From The New Atalantis, an Island in the Mediterranean (1709). London: 1709.

Mathias, T. J. *Works of the Author of The Pursuits of Literature*. Dublin: 1799.

Opie, Amelia Alderson. *Adeline Mowbray* (1805), ed. Anne McWhir. Peterborough, ON: Broadview Press, 2010.

Paine, Thomas. *Rights of Man* (1791–2), ed. Henry Collins. Harmondsworth: Penguin Books, 1969.

Paltock, Robert. *The Life and Adventures of Peter Wilkins* (1751), ed. Christopher Bentley. London: Oxford University Press, 1973.

Pope, Alexander. *The Poems of Alexander Pope*, ed. John Butt. London: Methuen, 1963, rpt 1968.

Radcliffe, Ann. *The Italian, Or, The Confessional of the Black Penitents A Romance* (1797), ed. Frederick Garber. London: Oxford University Press, 1968.

The Mysteries of Udolpho (1794), ed. Bonamy Dobrée. Oxford University Press, 1980.

Reeve, Clara. *The Old English Baron* (published as *The Champion of Virtue* [1777]; reissued as *The Old English Baron* [1778]), ed. James Trainer. London: Oxford University Press, 1967.

Plans of Education; with Remarks on the Systems of Other Writers in a Series of Letters between Mrs. Darnford and her Friends (1792). London: 1792.

The Progress of Romance (1785). London: 1785.

The School for Widows (1791). Dublin: 1791.

Richardson, Samuel. *Clarissa or The History of a Young Lady* (1747–8), ed. Angus Ross. Harmondsworth: Penguin Books, 1985.

The History of Sir Charles Grandison (1753–4), ed. Jocelyn Harris. London: Oxford University Press, 1972.

Pamela; Or, Virtue Rewarded (1740), ed. Thomas Keymer and Alice Wakely. Oxford University Press, 2001.

Scott, Sarah. *A Description of Millenium Hall* (1762), ed. Gary Kelly. Peterborough, ON: Broadview Press, 1995.

The History of Sir George Ellison (1766), ed. Betty Rizzo. Lexington: University Press of Kentucky, 1996.

Scott, Walter. *Waverley; Or, 'Tis Sixty Years Since* (1814), ed. Claire Lamont. Oxford University Press, 1986.

Sheridan, Frances. *Memoirs of Miss Sidney Bidulph* (1761), ed. Patricia Köster and Jean Coates Cleary. Oxford University Press, 1995.

Smith, Adam. *The Theory of Moral Sentiments* (1759), ed. D. D. Raphael and A. L. Macfie. Oxford University Press, 1976.

Smith, Charlotte. *The Old Manor House* (1793), ed. Anne Henry Ehrenpreis and Judith Phillips Stanton. Oxford University Press, 1989.

The Young Philosopher (1798), ed. Elizabeth Kraft. Lexington: University Press of Kentucky, 1999.

Smollett, Tobias. *The Adventures of Ferdinand Count Fathom* (1753), ed. Damian Grant. Oxford University Press, 1971.

The Adventures of Peregrine Pickle (1751), ed. James L. Clifford and Paul-Gabriel Boucé. Oxford University Press, 1983.

The Adventures of Roderick Random (1748), ed. Paul-Gabriel Boucé. Oxford University Press, 1979.

The Expedition of Humphry Clinker (1771), ed. Lewis M. Knapp and Paul-Gabriel Boucé. Oxford University Press, 1984.

The Life and Adventures of Sir Launcelot Greaves (1760–1), ed. David Evans. Oxford University Press, 1973.

Sterne, Laurence. *The Life and Opinions of Tristram Shandy, Gentleman* (1765–7), ed. Ian Campbell Ross. Oxford University Press, 1983, 2000.

A Sentimental Journey through France and Italy (1768) and *Continuation of the Bramine's Journal*, ed. Melvyn New and W. G. Day. Indianapolis, IN: Hackett Publishing, 2006.

Walker, George. *Theodore Cyphon; Or The Benevolent Jew: A Novel* (1796).
     London: 1796.
     The Vagabond (1799), ed. W. M. Verhoeven. Peterborough, ON: Broadview
     Press, 2004.
Walpole, Horace. *Castle of Otranto,* in *Three Gothic Novels,* ed. Peter Fairclough.
     Harmondsworth: Penguin Books, 1968.
Wollstonecraft, Mary. *Mary* (1788) and *The Wrongs of Woman: Or Maria. A
     Fragment* (1798), ed. Gary Kelly. Oxford University Press, 1976.

Secondary sources

Altick, Richard D. *The English Common Reader: A Social History of the Mass
     Reading Public 1800–1900*. Chicago and London: University of Chicago
     Press, 1957.
Ariès, Philip. *Centuries of Childhood*. New York: Vintage Books, 1962.
Armstrong, Nancy. *Desire and Domestic Fiction: A Political History of the Novel*.
     New York: Oxford University Press, 1987.
Ballaster, Ros. *Seductive Forms: Women's Amatory Fiction from 1684 to 1740*.
     Oxford: Clarendon Press, 1992.
Battestin, Martin C. *The Providence of Wit*. Oxford: Clarendon Press, 1974.
Benedict, Barbara. *Curiosity: A Cultural History of Early Modern Inquiry*.
     University of Chicago Press, 2001.
Brown, Homer Obed. *Institutions of the English Novel from Defoe to Scott*.
     Philadelphia: University of Pennsylvania Press, 1997.
Colley, Linda. *Britons: Forging the Nation, 1707–1837*. New Haven: Yale
     University Press, 1992.
Davis, Lennard. *Factual Fictions. The Origins of the English Novel*. New York:
     Columbia University Press, 1983.
Doody, Margaret Anne. *The True Story of the Novel*. New Brunswick, NJ: Rutgers
     University Press, 1996.
Feather, John. *A History of British Publishing*. London and New York: Routledge,
     1988, reprinted with corrections, 1991.
Gallagher, Catherine. *Nobody's Story: The Vanishing Acts of Women Writers
     in the Marketplace, 1670–1820*. Berkeley: University of California Press,
     1994.
Gamer, Michael. "A Select Collection: Barbauld, Scott, and the Rise of the
     (Reprinted) Novel," in *Recognizing the Romantic Novel. New Histories
     of British Fiction, 1780–1830*, ed. Jillian Heydt-Stevenson and Charlotte
     Sussman. Liverpool University Press, 2008, 155–91.
Garside, Peter and Rainer Schöwerling (with the assistance of Christopher
     Skelton-Foord and Karin Wünsche). *The English Novel 1770–1829:
     A Bibliographical Survey of Prose Fiction Published in the British Isles
     Volume II: 1800–1829*. Oxford University Press, 2000.
Girouard, Mark. *Life in the English Country House. A Social and Architectural
     History*. New Haven and London: Yale University Press, 1978.

Hirschman, Albert O. *The Passions and the Interests*. Princeton University Press, 1976.

Hunter, J. Paul. *Before Novels. The Cultural Contexts of Eighteenth-Century English Fiction*. New York and London: W. W. Norton & Company, 1990.

Johnson, Claudia L. " 'Let me make the novels of a country': Barbauld's *The British Novelists* (1810/1820)," *Novel: A Forum on Fiction* **34** (2001), 163–79.

Keymer, Thomas. *Sterne, the Moderns, and the Novel*. Oxford University Press, 2003.

Keymer, Thomas and Peter Sabor. *Pamela in the Marketplace. Literary Controversy and Print Culture in Eighteenth-Century Britain and Ireland*. Cambridge University Press, 2005.

King, Kathryn. *Jane Barker, Exile, A Literary Career 1675–1725*. Oxford: Clarendon Press, 2000.

Kramnick, Isaac. *Republicanism and Bourgeois Radicalism. Political Ideology in Late Eighteenth-Century England and America*. Ithaca and London: Cornell University Press, 1990.

Langford, Paul. *A Polite and Commercial People. England 1727–1783*. Oxford University Press, 1993.

London, April. *Women and Property in the Eighteenth-Century English Novel*. Cambridge University Press, 1999.

Lynch, Deidre. *The Economy of Character: Novels, Market Culture, and the Business of Inner Meaning*. University of Chicago Press, 1998.

McIntosh, Carey. *The Evolution of English Prose 1700–1800 Style, Politeness, and Print Culture*. Cambridge University Press, 1998.

McKeon, Michael. "Historicizing Patriarchy: The Emergence of Gender Difference in England, 1660–1760," *Eighteenth-Century Studies* **28** (1995), 295–322.

   The Origins of the English Novel, 1600–1740. Baltimore and London: Johns Hopkins University Press, 1987.

   The Secret History of Domesticity: Public, Private and the Division of Knowledge. Baltimore and London: Johns Hopkins University Press, 2005.

Macpherson, C. B. *The Political Theory of Possessive Individualism. Hobbes to Locke*. Oxford University Press, 1962.

Miller, Nancy K. *The Heroine's Text: Readings in the French and English Novel, 1722–1782*. New York: Columbia University Press, 1980.

Perry, Ruth. *Novel Relations. The Transformation of Kinship in English Literature and Culture 1648–1818*. Cambridge University Press, 2004.

Raven, James and Antonia Forster (with the assistance of Stephen Bending). *The English Novel 1770–1829 A Bibliographical Survey of Prose Fiction Published in the British Isles Volume I: 1770–1799*. Oxford University Press, 2000.

Richetti, John. *The English Novel in History, 1700–1780*. London: Routledge, 1999.

    Popular Fiction before Richardson: Narrative Patterns, 1700–1739. Oxford: Clarendon Press, 1969; rpt. 1992.

Rivers, Isabel (ed). *Books and their Readers in Eighteenth-Century England*. Leicester University Press and St. Martin's Press, 1982.

Rizzo, Betty. *Companions without Vows. Relationships among Eighteenth-Century British Women*. Athens and London: University of Georgia Press, 1994.

Rothstein, Eric. *Systems of Order and Inquiry in Late Eighteenth-Century Fiction*. Berkeley and Los Angeles: University of California Press, 1975.

St. Clair, William. *The Reading Nation in the Romantic Period*. Cambridge University Press, 2004.

Said, Edward. *Orientalism*. New York: Vintage Books, 1978.

Spacks, Patricia Meyer. *Desire and Truth: Functions of Plot in Eighteenth-Century English Novels*. University of Chicago Press, 1990.

    Novel Beginnings: Experiments in Eighteenth-Century English Fiction. New Haven and London: Yale University Press, 2006.

Spencer, Jane. *The Rise of the Woman Novelist: From Aphra Behn to Jane Austen*. Oxford: Blackwell, 1986.

Tadmor, Naomi. *Family and Friends in Eighteenth-Century England: Household, Kinship and Patronage*. Cambridge University Press, 2001.

Taylor, Charles. *The Sources of the Self. The Making of the Modern Identity*. Cambridge, MA: Harvard University Press, 1989.

Thompson, E. P. "Patrician Society, Plebeian Culture," *Journal of Social History* 7 (1974), 382–405.

Todd, Janet. *The Sign of Angellica. Women, Writing, and Fiction, 1660–1800*. New York: Columbia University Press, 1989.

Tompkins, J. M. S. *The Popular Novel in England, 1770–1800*. London: Constable & Company, 1932.

Turner, Cheryl. *Living by the Pen: Women Writers of the Eighteenth Century*. London: Routledge, 1992.

Van Sant, Ann Jessie. *Eighteenth-Century Sensibility and the Novel: The Senses in Social Context*. Cambridge University Press, 1993.

Wahrman, Dror. *The Making of the Modern Self: Identity and Culture in Eighteenth-Century England*. New Haven and London: Yale University Press, 2004.

Warner, William B. *Licensing Entertainment. The Elevation of Novel Reading in Britain, 1684–1750*. Berkeley and Los Angeles: University of California Press, 1998.

Watson, Nicola J. *Revolution and the Form of the British Novel 1790–1825: Intercepted Letters, Interrupted Seductions*. Oxford: Clarendon Press, 1994.

Watt, Ian. *The Rise of the Novel. Studies in Defoe, Richardson and Fielding*. Berkeley and Los Angeles: University of California Press, 1957.

Index

Cambridge Introductions to…

AUTHORS

Margaret Atwood Heidi Macpherson

Jane Austen Janet Todd

Samuel Beckett Ronan McDonald

Walter Benjamin David Ferris

Chekhov James N. Loehlin

J. M. Coetzee Dominic Head

Samuel Taylor Coleridge John Worthen

Joseph Conrad John Peters

Jacques Derrida Leslie Hill

Charles Dickens Jon Mee

Emily Dickinson Wendy Martin

George Eliot Nancy Henry

T. S. Eliot John Xiros Cooper

William Faulkner Theresa M. Towner

F. Scott Fitzgerald Kirk Curnutt

Michel Foucault Lisa Downing

Robert Frost Robert Faggen

Gabriel Garcia Marquez Gerald Martin

Nathaniel Hawthorne Leland S. Person

Zora Neale Hurston Lovalerie King

James Joyce Eric Bulson

Thomas Mann Todd Kontje

Christopher Marlowe Tom Rutter

Herman Melville Kevin J. Hayes

Milton Stephen B. Dobranski

George Orwell John Rodden and John Rossi

Sylvia Plath Jo Gill

Edgar Allan Poe Benjamin F. Fisher

Ezra Pound Ira Nadel

Marcel Proust Adam Watt

Jean Rhys Elaine Savory

Edward Said Conor McCarthy

Shakespeare Emma Smith

Shakespeare's Comedies Penny Gay

Shakespeare's History Plays Warren Chernaik

Shakespeare's Poetry Michael Schoenfeldt

Shakespeare's Tragedies Janette Dillon

Harriet Beecher Stowe Sarah Robbins

Mark Twain Peter Messent

Edith Wharton Pamela Knights

Walt Whitman M. Jimmie Killingsworth

Virginia Woolf Jane Goldman

William Wordsworth Emma Mason

W. B. Yeats David Holdeman

TOPICS

American Literary Realism Phillip Barrish

The American Short Story Martin Scofield

Anglo-Saxon Literature Hugh Magennis

Comedy Eric Weitz

Creative Writing David Morley

Early English Theatre Janette Dillon

The Eighteenth-Century Novel April London

Eighteenth-Century Poetry John Sitter